Constructing Democracy

Sponsored by the Joint Committee on
Latin American Studies of the
Social Science Research Council and
the American Council of Learned Societies

CONSTRUCTING DEMOCRACY

Human Rights, Citizenship, and Society in Latin America

edited by

ELIZABETH JELIN

AND ERIC HERSHBERG

WestviewPress

A Division of HarperCollins*Publishers*

Copyright © 1996 by Westview Press, Inc., A Division of HarperCollins Publishers, Inc.

Published in 1996 in the United States of America by Westview Press, Inc., 5500 Central Avenue,
Boulder, Colorado 80301-2877, and in the United Kingdom by Westview Press, 12 Hid's Copse Road,
Cumnor Hill, Oxford OX2 9JJ

Library of Congress Cataloging-in-Publication Data
Constructing democracy : human rights, citizenship, and society in
    Latin America / edited by Elizabeth Jelin and Eric Hershberg.
        p.   cm.
Includes bibliographical references and index.
    ISBN 0-8133-2438-6. — ISBN 0-8133-2439-4 (pbk.)
    1. Human rights—Latin America.   2. Civil rights—Latin America.
    3. Citizenship—Latin America.   4. Democracy—Latin America.
    I. Jelin, Elizabeth, 1941– .   II. Hershberg, Eric.
JC599.L3C66   1996
323'.098—dc20   95-50932
                                                                         CIP

The paper used in this publication meets the requirements of the American National Standard for Permanence of Paper for Printed Library Materials Z39.48-1984.

10   9   8   7   6   5   4   3   2

Contents

Part 4 Structures of Discrimination: Individual and Collective Rights

Part 5 Conclusion

Acknowledgments

This book is the result of several years of work in the Joint Committee on Latin American Studies (JCLAS) of the Social Science Research Council (SSRC) and the American Council of Learned Societies. Beginning in 1989, a series of brainstorming discussions in the JCLAS underscored our sense that social scientific thinking about human rights–related issues in Latin America was at a crossroads and that the JCLAS might usefully stimulate interdisciplinary dialogue about the appropriate directions for the field. These in-depth and thoughtful discussions were crucial to giving the ensuing project focus, depth, and conceptual clarity. The support and guidance of the Committee made the entire venture possible.

A group of nearly twenty researchers and practitioners gathered following the 1991 meeting of the Latin American Studies Association in Washington, D.C., to exchange ideas about the proper dimensions of the field of human rights research during the remainder of the 1990s. Ideas generated during that meeting led the JCLAS to convene a conference in Buenos Aires at which initial versions of the chapters published in this volume were presented. The Buenos Aires meeting was made possible through the generous support provided to the JCLAS by the Ford Foundation. It is no exaggeration to say that without such support this project would not have come about.

We are grateful to our colleagues at the Centro de Estudios de Estado y Sociedad (CEDES) for hosting that seminar in October 1992. We are also indebted to the other participants of that meeting. Many of their ideas have been incorporated into the chapters of this book; indeed, their collective deliberations shaped our own thinking about the state of the field and the challenges that exist for the future. In particular, we appreciate the insights of Nancy Cardia, Margaret Crahan, Laura Gingold, Mario Lungo, Enrique Mayer, Juan Méndez, Emilio Mignone, Carina Perelli, Fernando Rojas, and Hilda Sábato.

Meanwhile, it has been a pleasure working with Barbara Ellington of Westview Press. From the outset, Barbara and her colleagues have provided encouragement as well as invaluable guidance concerning the structure and final revisions of the manuscript.

Finally, the project has benefited from the capable administrative support of several people on the staffs at the SSRC and CEDES, including Alexandra Cordero, Susana Espasa, Patricia Murillo, Liliana Petroni, and Jennifer Raskin.

Elizabeth Jelin
Eric Hershberg

About the Contributors

Carlos H. Acuña teaches comparative politics at the Universidad de Buenos Aires and is an associate researcher at the Centro de Estudios de Estado y Sociedad (CEDES) in Buenos Aires. In addition to dozens of scholarly articles on Argentine and Latin American politics, he is the author of *La burguesía industrial como actor político en la Argentina* and coeditor with William C. Smith and Eduardo A. Gamarra of *Latin American Political Economy in the Age of Neo-Liberal Reform: Theoretical and Comparative Perspectives* (1994) and *Democracy, Markets, and Structural Reform in Latin America* (1994).

Teresa P.R. Caldeira received her Ph.D. in anthropology from the University of California–Berkeley in 1992. She is currently a researcher at the Centro Brasileiro de Analise e Planejamento (CEBRAP) in São Paulo and a professor of anthropology at the Universidade de Campinas. She has written numerous scholarly articles and is the author of *City of Walls: Crime, Segregation and Citizenship in São Paulo* (forthcoming).

Manuel Antonio Garretón is senior researcher at the Facultad Latinoamericano de Ciencias Sociales (FLACSO) in Santiago, Chile. His most recent books include *Reconstruir la política: Transición y consolidación política en Chile* and *La Unidad Popular y el conflicto político en Chile* (1993). He is coeditor, with Marcelo Cavarozzi, of *Muerte y resurrección: Los partidos políticos en el autoritarismo y las transiciones en el Cono Sur* (1989) and, with Juan Corradi and Patricia Weiss Fagen, of *Fear at the Edge: State Terror and Resistance in Latin America* (1992).

Carlos Hasenbalg is director of the Centro de Estudos Afro-Asiaticos at the IUPERJ in Rio de Janeiro. He has published widely on issues of race and social stratification in Brazil, including *Descriminaçao e desigualdades raciais no Brasil* (1979).

Eric Hershberg is director of the Program on Latin America at the Social Science Research Council. He received his Ph.D. from the University of Wisconsin–Madison in 1989 and has written extensively on the political economy of democratization in Southern Europe and Latin America. He is the author of *Transición del autoritarismo y desaparición de la izquierda: Una reinterpretación del cambio político en España* (forthcoming).

Elizabeth Jelin is a researcher with CONICYT in Buenos Aires. She received her Ph.D. in sociology from the University of Texas–Austin and has taught in universities across Latin America and the United States. She is the author of dozens of articles and several books, including *Family, Household and Gender Relations in Latin America* (1991) and *Caring and Coping: Household, Communities and Public Services in the Making of Women's Daily Lives* (with Brenda Pereyra, 1990).

Fábio Wanderley Reis is professor of political science at the Universidade Federal de Minas Gerais, in Belo Horizonte, Brazil. He received his Ph.D. in political science from Harvard University and is the author of numerous books, including (with Francisco Zapata) *Modernización económica, democracia política y democracia social* (1993) and (with Guillermo O'Donnell), *A Democracia no Brasil: Dilemas e perspectivas* (1988). He received the 1985 Best Scientific Book award from ANPOCS, the Brazilian national social science association, for his volume *Politica e racionalidade* (1984).

Jennifer Schirmer is currently a 1994–1996 Henry Luce Fellow in Religion and Public Policy at the Center for the Study of Values in Public Life at Harvard Divinity School. She is the author of numerous articles on issues relating to human rights, social movements, and gender and of the forthcoming book *A Violence Called Democracy: The Guatemalan Military Project 1982–1992.*

Kathryn Sikkink is associate professor of political science at the University of Minnesota, where she teaches courses in comparative politics and international relations. She is the author of *Ideas and Institutions: Developmentalism in Brazil and Argentina* (1991) as well as of numerous articles on development, human rights, and transnational networks of nongovernmental organizations.

Catalina Smulovitz teaches politics at the Universidad de Buenos Aires and is an associate researcher at CEDES in Buenos Aires. She received her Ph.D. in political science from Pennsylvania State University and has published numerous articles on political parties, constitutional reform, legislatures, and human rights in Latin America's Southern Cone.

Rodolfo Stavenhagen is professor of sociology at the Colegio de Mexico and has served on the faculty of numerous universities throughout North and South America and Western Europe. His most recent books include *Derecho indígena y derechos humanos en América Latina* (1988), *Entre la ley y la costumbre: El derecho consuetudinario indígena en América Latina* (1990), and *The Ethnic Question: Conflict, Development and Human Rights* (1990).

Constructing Democracy

◀ 1 ▶

Introduction:
Human Rights and the
Construction of Democracy

ELIZABETH JELIN AND ERIC HERSHBERG

Profound changes swept Latin America during the 1980s. From an economic perspective these years may have been a "lost decade" for most countries; but in the political arena during this period, the basic institutional framework of democracy was established across most of the region. The politics of democratization and the political economy of adjustment and liberalization, as well as the relationship between the two processes, understandably galvanized the attention of scholars and public opinion alike. In contrast, transformations at the societal level attracted relatively little attention during the initial stages of Latin American transitions to democratic regimes. Of course, societal processes tend to evolve slowly, are more blurred and ambiguous than institutional changes, and often seem contradictory. However, with democratic mechanisms more or less in place in most Latin American countries, at least at a procedural level, the time has come to assess the implications of democracy at the level of society. We know a great deal about the institutional dimensions of such transitions, but how does the process of regime change and its aftermath shape the life chances of individual citizens and social groups? What factors will determine the prospects for constructing democracies in Latin America in which citizenship rights become extended beyond the formally political sphere?

MAJOR THEMES OF THE BOOK

This book moves beyond analyses of the process of transition itself to explore issues that are critical for understanding changing relationships between society and the political system in Latin America. Our principal concern is with the quest for human rights and the demand for justice, aspirations that are central not only to the moment of transition but also to the period when democratic institutions

1

have supplanted those of the dictatorships they replaced. In their explorations of contemporary struggles around issues of individual and collective rights, and in their examinations of competing claims about justice and citizenship, the chapters in this volume exhibit a common concern with the character of democratic life in Latin America, today as well as in the future.

By the 1990s, social scientific studies of transitions from authoritarianism were facing increased criticism for their failure to grapple sufficiently with the societal dimension of democratization (e.g., Fox, 1990; Waylen, 1994). In hindsight it is apparent that the previous decade's preoccupation with issues of institution building did indeed come at the expense of considerations of the composition and role of collective actors in democratic societies, particularly those collective actors representing the so-called popular sectors. The political science literature was concerned principally with interactions among elites and with specific types of institutional arrangements conducive to stable democratic governance. Connections between democratization at the regime level and societal democratization were largely overlooked. To the extent that these matters entered the discussion at all, it was in the context of the potential that regime change opened up for the subsequent democratization of other spheres of social life (Kaufman, 1986; Przeworski, 1986).

But criticism of the transitions literature for overlooking the multiple dimensions of democratization must be tempered by a recognition of the circumstances facing observers of Latin American societies during the period in question. The pernicious effect of the dictatorships on the possibility of securing the most basic human rights—those associated with life and with the physical integrity of the individual—amply justified the preoccupation with identifying strategies for overcoming these regimes and inaugurating more open and competitive political orders in which civilian authority would be ensured. It is nonetheless striking that the classic studies of democratization in Latin America have made no mention of authoritarian relations based on differences of gender, ethnicity, or race in a region characterized by vast inequalities along these and many other dimensions.

Experience of the past several years underscores the commonsensical observation that transitions to democracy entail much more than the (re)construction of institutions and the dismantling of nondemocratic forms of exercising power, whether authoritarian, corporatist, or coercive in nature.[1] Democratization involves changes not only in society but also in political institutions: It requires the emergence of new sets of rules governing the distribution of power, respect for individual rights, and recognition of social actors. People have to adopt beliefs and practices embedded in the notion of democracy and, at the same time, must learn how to act within the new institutional framework. For their part, political leaders and dominant classes have to acknowledge the rights and identities of diverse social actors. The fundamental challenge during the posttransition period is to combine formal institutional changes with the expansion of democratic practices and to create a culture of citizenship encompassing individual and collective actors across the entire spectrum of the diverse social and cultural landscape of contemporary Latin American societies.

There is ample precedent for observers of Latin America to turn their attention to social questions. Until the 1980s, analyses of the region frequently focused on expansion of the rights associated with the idea of social citizenship. Concern with the development of social rights guided the enlargement of the public sector during populist and postpopulist regimes at the same time that it fostered the development of social movements and popular demands upon the state by a wide range of groups. Composed of peasants and workers initially, and of women, neighborhood residents, or youth later on, these movements remind us that the expansion of social citizenship in Latin America was a historical process marked by highly contradictory features: The expansion was driven in part by deeply rooted patterns of clientelism and political patronage characteristic of populism, but the top-down social relationships associated with such patterns coexisted with pressures exerted from below toward both a more democratic distribution of power and for greater participation. These pressures grew stronger over the years as the region witnessed the development of new and more autonomous social actors.

The expansion of social citizenship was a central theme in the analytical perspectives that predominated in Latin America throughout the 1970s. Adherents of these perspectives exhibited relatively little concern for expanding the basic rights of the individual—rights they at times dismissed as merely formal, "liberal," or "bourgeois." They also attached little importance to the collective rights of ethnic and indigenous groups, often dismissing them outright with the ideological justification that the quest for equality needed to overshadow all other considerations. Yet the harshness of human rights violations by the military dictatorships that ruled much of the region during the 1970s, and that persisted in some countries well into the following decade, gave rise both to a significant human rights movement and to the revalorization of "formal" democracy. Rooted in struggles against dictatorships, these movements stimulated unprecedented activism around issues of human and civil rights.

The ensuing shift in focus affected both the content of societal demands and the perspectives of social scientists who analyzed processes of democratic transition. Whereas it was once commonplace to differentiate among civil, political, and social rights, and to conceptualize citizenship primarily in terms of social rights, in the 1980s basic human and civil rights could no longer be dismissed or taken for granted. Instead, they became the center of political activism and intellectual preoccupation. Calling on the state to guarantee and protect individual rights, and insisting that public officials be held accountable for their actions, social actors articulated new demands that were pivotal to the process of rebuilding democratic institutions or, in some countries, of constructing such institutions for the very first time.[2]

Particularly in the Southern Cone, these developments are best understood when we recall that the impact of human rights violations was not limited to the popular classes. Indeed, the middle and upper classes were victimized as well. The popular sectors had always been targets of violence from above; it was an inescapable feature of everyday life, one to which they had somehow grown accustomed, though by no means always acquiescent. The middle and upper classes, in contrast, had rarely needed to insist that the state acknowledge their citizenship rights, since historically their civil, social, and political rights had largely been assured. This scenario changed during the 1970s, as the rights of relatively privileged groups became increasingly less immune to the predations of authoritarian rulers. To an extent unprecedented in many countries, these groups were compelled to express their grievances and to articulate demands against the state. The fact that rights violations cut across all segments of the social structure, albeit to varying degrees, implied a widened social basis for concern about rights, for demands that they be respected, and for solidarity among the diverse victims of abuses by the state.

The transition to democracy in much of Latin America thus coincided with, and was partly stimulated by, a significant increase in the scope and variety of popular mobilization around issues of individual and collective rights. At the same time, the transition to democracy took place under conditions of profound social change. Particularly noteworthy was the trend toward growing inequality that prevailed throughout the region in the 1980s and has continued in most countries to the present. These circumstances suggest a need to examine the linkages between the characteristics of the political system and the evolving concerns of citizens in their everyday lives.

Conceptually, the societal issues raised by the process of democratization can be approached from at least three perspectives: first, in terms of equity and social inequalities; second, in terms of the nature of social struggles seeking to define the contents of democracy; and third, in terms of the process by which individual and collective actors are formed, particularly through the emergence and consolidation of citizenship. Let us consider each of these briefly.

The first perspective, concerning equity and social inequalities in the democratic process, pertains to the distributive effects of economic adjustment policies that have been implemented throughout Latin America in recent years. Most analyses of the topic stress the social costs of adjustment and the deepening of social inequality that accompanies it, and highlight the limitations of social policies that serve as mechanisms to compensate for the differential effects of economic changes. The burden the crisis places on women, the old, and the young, as well as the increase in social polarization, entailing the endangerment of working and living conditions at one extreme of the social hierarchy and income concentration at the other—these are two of the key issues raised by such an approach.

An alternative way to analyze the relationship between democracy and equity is to look into the effects of poverty, marginalization, and violence on respect for human rights. Violations of human rights do not cease automatically at the moment of democratic transition: The weaknesses of nascent democracy are accentuated when large sectors of the population live in poverty and marginality. As

Paulo Sergio Pinheiro, Malak Poppovic, and Tulio Kahn (1993: 3) concluded after reviewing worldwide quantitative and qualitative data, "Political democracy is fragile as long as basic economic rights cannot be guaranteed." Indeed, it comes as no surprise that social demands based on inequality and exclusion, which persisted in a subdued and hidden way during the moment of political transition, have reemerged as fundamental issues of protest and mobilization during the 1990s.[3]

The second theme perspective concerns social struggles around competing definitions of democracy and its contents. Emphasis here is on the contrast between the optimistic expectations placed on the process of transition to democracy and the often frustrating reality of the workings of the institutional system. The resulting disenchantment reflects difficulties inherent in the democratic process, but also specific obstacles derived from the context in which processes of transitions have taken place in Latin America. Under current circumstances of economic globalization, the relationship between political and economic systems involves complexities that are beyond the scope of this chapter. Yet the deep tensions that exist between capitalism and democracy—or more generally, between markets and states—are evident in a wide range of social conflicts. These tensions will have to be eased through the design of democratic institutional mechanisms, but this is no easy task given that secular trends are fostering ever greater inequalities.

Whatever initial expectations might have been regarding the connections between political democratization and social democratization, we now know that there exists no automatic or linear relationship between the formal functioning of democracy and the democratization of society, whether defined in terms of equity, participation and citizen control, or expansion of individual and collective rights. Nor does a democratic system ensure that actors and practices will in fact be democratic, or that democratic ideologies will prevail. Relationships among the relevant variables, as well as their sequencing and timing, turn out to be contingent and often erratic; change takes place slowly and is rarely unidirectional. In short, democratic outcomes are inherently provisional and uncertain (Przeworski, 1986), insofar as they are the result of a continuous social struggle about the distribution of socially valued resources and about the design (and redesign) of institutions intended to channel social conflict.

The third perspective centers on the social and cultural bases or components of a democratic society. To become active and responsible citizens, people require opportunities to develop special skills. Such opportunities, in turn, depend on access to public spaces and institutions. Hence we see the relevance of analyzing the notion of citizenship as well as the societal processes and mechanisms that foster the skills associated with it.

ORGANIZATION OF THE BOOK

This book takes as its point of departure the transition from military dictatorships to democratic political regimes that occurred in most Latin American countries at various times during the 1980s. Part 1, devoted to the political dimensions of transition processes, focuses on the processes by which issues of human rights and accountability for rights violations shaped relationships between civilian and military actors. The new regimes implemented a variety of strategies designed to confront these issues and thereby permit a return to "normal" politics. To ensure that the crimes carried out during the dictatorships would never be repeated, civilian supremacy over the armed forces had to be reasserted as a basic principle of the new institutional order. As demonstrated by Carlos Acuña and Catalina Smulovitz in Chapter 2 and by Manuel Antonio Garretón in Chapter 3, the ways in which this aim was accomplished in various countries had enduring consequences for the relative strength of competing actors in the new political system. In this sense, coming to grips with the past constitutes not only an obligatory moment in the transitional process itself but also a critical juncture in establishing the contours of the sociopolitical order. Some actors are empowered in the process, whereas others find their resources diminished. Prospects for extending the momentum of democratization beyond the sphere of political institutions— that is, for building a more robust democratic citizenship—are inevitably conditioned by the strategies chosen to deal with the past as well as by the distribution of political resources they engender.

It is well known that the centrality of human rights issues in these transitions, and for that matter the timing of the transitions themselves, was largely a function of the international context, including the network of nongovernmental solidarity organizations, the actions of governments, and the role of international organizations. This international dimension, which has received little systematic attention in the literature on human rights and transitions, is taken up in Part 2 of the book. Once again, we find that international pressures have influenced not only the timing and extent of transition from authoritarian rule but also the nature of governance in the aftermath of regime change. Accordingly, in Chapter 4, Kathyrn Sikkink traces the evolution of the international human rights network and assesses its impact on particular countries in various periods. In turn, Jennifer Schirmer, in Chapter 5, offers a case study of one instance in which international factors promoted a transition of sorts; yet human rights abuses persist as a result of the capacity of the Guatemalan military to appropriate the discourse of democracy articulated by outside actors. Both of these authors recognize that outside pressure cannot guarantee respect for human rights, though it may provide powerful incentives for dictators to alter their behavior and, in some instances, to cease their violations of human rights. The authors also concur in their emphasis on the challenges that the present conjuncture poses for the international human rights network and for the governments and nonstate actors that constitute it. The network gathered strength during a phase in which it could target its efforts directly toward openly authoritarian states engaged in rights abuses. Today, in contrast, obstacles to the exercise of citizenship rights are more ambiguous and complex, and require new strategies of pressure and encouragement from advocates of the expansion of rights, whether located domestically or abroad.

The third and fourth parts of the book deal primarily with societal issues, connecting the discussion of human rights during processes of transition to the ensuing challenges of extending citizenship rights across all segments of the population. Racism, ethnic and gender discrimination, and nonpolitical violence are dimensions of the social landscape with deep historical roots. Rethinking these phenomena from the perspective of human rights implies a need to reconsider the very notion of what constitutes human rights; it also brings forth the imperative to incorporate more fully the collective dimensions of rights and their structural underpinnings.

Accordingly, the two chapters in Part 3 confront the theoretical challenges of linking issues of human rights with democracy and citizenship, on the one hand, and with markets and capitalism, on the other. In chapter 6, Elizabeth Jelin analyzes the construction of citizenship from below in order to illuminate the meaning of democracy as people experience it in everyday life. In particular, she explores the means by which individuals who are formally defined as citizens put their citizenship into practice. Jelin recognizes the vast distance separating the formal sphere of law and the ways in which social subjects actually perceive and act according to their rights. But if citizenship is about rights, it necessarily entails responsibilities and civic commitments as well; thus Jelin analyzes the institutional and sociopsychological foundations upon which socially responsible practices are most likely to flourish.

In turn, Fábio Wanderley Reis argues in Chapter 7 that there is an underlying affinity between democracy and capitalism to the extent that the former can attenuate conflicts inherent in the latter; but he also suggests that Latin American democracies will meet this challenge only if the states in the region are endowed with the capacity to regulate the market. Despite the underlying egalitarianism of the market, Reis cautions that the oligopolistic relations of power that prevail in contemporary Latin America could prevent the smooth functioning of markets, thereby generating virtually insurmountable barriers to the exercise of citizenship rights by individuals and groups who find themselves excluded from the market. He argues that it is only through the construction of a decidedly "nonminimalist" democratic state that this adverse outcome can be avoided.

The chapters in Part 4 of the book are concerned with the structural dimensions of rights and citizenship. Whereas traditional conceptualizations of human rights reflected an individualistic notion of rights, these chapters situate the discussion of human rights in the challenges faced by communities of people in contemporary Latin American societies. To speak of *cultural* rights is to refer inevitably to groups and communities: the rights of various peoples to live as they choose, speak their own languages, wear their own clothes, pursue their own objectives, and receive fair treatment from the laws of the nation-state in which they happen to make their residence (almost invariably as "minorities").

As Rodolfo Stavenhagen shows in Chapter 8 in his analysis of the rights of indigenous peoples, individual rights may sometimes enter into conflict with collective rights. Respect for universal human rights does not guarantee satisfaction of people's collective rights, nor does the right of a people to pursue the lifestyle it chooses ensure that the individual rights of some of its members will not themselves be denied in the process. How is it possible to escape this dilemma? Contemplation of an agenda for the advancement of ethnic rights implies a profound departure from the original notion of human rights, conceptualized historically in an abstract way and with a bias toward universality and individual subjects. The statement that indigenous peoples and minorities have rights specific to their ethnic identity, then, suggests that the very notion of "human rights" can acquire meaning only in specific cultural circumstances, which themselves become preconditions for, and constitutive of, human rights.

Discussions about the human rights of traditionally oppressed or marginalized groups of the population—namely, indigenous peoples, racially or ethnically defined "minorities," and women—signal recognition of a history of discrimination and oppression and call for proactive measures to reverse situations of injustice. Such discussions also share an underlying critique of the individualistic and universalistic definitions of human rights and their identification with Western and masculine values. Beyond this initial commonality, however, the paths diverge. In the ethnic context, the critical task is to interrogate the individual or collective nature of rights. The Brazilian myth of racial harmony, debunked by Carlos Hasenbalg in Chapter 9, fits neatly into this category as well. In contrast, as Jelin argues in Chapter 10, the analysis of women's rights requires an approach in which rights are (re)conceptualized in the context of both gender relations and the tension between public and private spheres.

In Chapter 11, Teresa P.R. Caldeira analyzes a human rights problem that is growing not only in Brazil but across much of Latin America, despite the widespread trend toward political democratization. The extralegal violence visited upon common criminals, as well as upon those the public perceives as potentially criminal, highlights the degree to which the most basic human right—the right to life—remains unprotected for significant sectors of society. Accordingly, Caldeira reintroduces the theme of state violence, which was at the core of human rights activism under conditions of dictatorship. The victims are not political dissidents now but common criminals, whose rights are easily forgotten and who elicit scant sympathy from populations plagued by fear of violent crime. Indeed, the widespread association that Caldeira has discovered between criminality and marginality underscores the human rights implications of the increasing social and economic polarization that has beset most Latin American countries in recent years.

All of the chapters in this volume engage contemporary debates stemming from shared concerns about the continued obstacles to the practical realization of citizenship rights and, hence, to the extension and deepening of human rights to all peoples, in Latin America and beyond. In so doing, they actively explore both existing and potential paths toward the emergence of civil societies based on more robust conceptions of human rights and more inclusive conceptions of citizenship. It is primarily to that task of deepening democracy, no less daunting than the one faced by human rights movements and by the advocates of democratic transitions a decade ago, that the authors of these chapters direct their contributions. The fact that their perspectives sometimes vary, leading to divergent interpretations of the prospects for overcoming particular obstacles to democratic construction, should not obscure their shared commitment to this overarching goal.

The final chapter of the book does not aspire to be either a synthesis of empirical findings or a definitive statement of our conclusions. Rather, we have endeavored to highlight some points of convergence and disagreement among the various chapters. These points we believe, constitute the agenda for research and, more important, for actions seeking to imbue Latin American democracies with justice and the fullest possible range of citizenship rights in the new millennium.

Notes

1. Obviously, not everyone has to learn something entirely new. Some people retain memories of democratic practices from the past and have only to reenact them. Yet for the most part Latin American dictatorships endured long enough to ensure that younger generations never had the chance to learn democratic practices; and even where democracy has existed "on paper," the democratic ethos and culture have remained weak. Decades, even centuries, of arbitrary rule and cultural patterns of submission to hierarchical patterns of interpersonal relations—involving patriarchy in the family, subordination of ethnic minorities, and so on—have left a legacy that is highly resistant to change.

2. The trend toward increasingly broad definitions of human rights is illustrated by the degree of international attention given since the late 1980s to issues of collective rights of peoples. The demand for such rights is justified by "structural violations" of rights and the recognition of nationality and ethnicity as legitimate principles upon which to seek autonomy. Structural violations of this sort have reached tragic levels in the former Soviet Union and Yugoslavia, as well as in parts of Central Africa, particularly Rwanda.

3. Social outbursts, such as the Caracazo riots in Venezuela and the raids on supermarkets in Argentina during periods of hyperinflation, have been isolated and sporadic. Nonetheless, the 1994 uprising in Chiapas and the continuing tensions in Mexico and elsewhere relating to the distributive implications of neoliberal reform underscore the potential ways in which these hidden conflicts might surface. It is notable that, in Chiapas, social, political, cultural, and economic cleavages have coincided, and that the discourse of human rights has become the lingua franca accepted and understood by all actors.

References

Fox, Jonathon (ed.). (1990). *The Challenge of Rural Democratization.* Special Issue of *Journal of Development Studies.* London: Frank Cass.

Kaufman, Robert. (1986). "Liberalization and Democratization in South America: Perspectives from the 1970s." In Guillermo O'Donnell, Philippe Schmitter, and Laurence Whitehead (eds.), *Transitions from Authoritarian Rule: Prospects for Democracy.* Baltimore: Johns Hopkins University Press.

Pinheiro, Paulo Sergio, Malak Poppovic, and Tulio Kahn. (1993). *Poverty, Marginalization, Violence and the Realization of Human Rights.* São Paulo: Unpublished mimeo prepared for the World Conference on Human Rights, Vienna (June).

Przeworski, Adam. (1986). "Some Problems in the Study of the Transition to Democracy." In Guillermo O'Donnell, Philippe Schmitter, and Laurence Whitehead (eds.), *Transitions from Authoritarian Rule: Prospects for Democracy.* Baltimore: Johns Hopkins University Press.

Waylen, Georgina. (1994). "Women and Democratization: Conceptualizing Gender Relations in Transition Politics." *World Politics* 46, no. 3 (April): 327–354.

PART ONE

Settling Accounts with the Past: Human Rights in Processes of Regime Transition

2

Adjusting the Armed Forces to Democracy: Successes, Failures, and Ambiguities in the Southern Cone

CARLOS H. ACUÑA AND CATALINA SMULOVITZ

The literature on the recent dictatorships of the Southern Cone rightly emphasizes the importance of socioeconomic reform as a rationale for the military government and for repression. "National security doctrine" shaped the logic of repression and the short- and medium-term political projects of the military. The crisis of Keynesianism and of the semiclosed accumulation model, coupled with the rise of neoliberalism, also help to explain the nature of social conflict and the design of political-institutional structures meant to ensure the reproduction of a "Western Christian" order and the stability of a new accumulation model. Although the dictatorships in Argentina, Brazil, and Chile shared the overall features of this model, a comparison uncovers important differences among them in terms of political projects and strategies of repression. The technique of "detention-disappearance" was widespread in some cases, whereas mass detention predominated in others; constitutional reforms were attempted only in some countries; and efforts to alter the party system not only differed radically but also met uneven degrees of success. These variations reflect the very different logics of political struggle that characterized each of these regimes. In turn, these rationales determined dissimilar exit and transition formulas, as well as variations in key aspects of the political struggle in the emerging democratic regimes.

Through a comparative analysis of Argentina, Brazil, and Chile, this chapter explains why there are different paths of integration of the Armed Forces in the new democratic regime, even though the military in all cases sought to have an institutional role in overseeing the successor regime. The path of military integration defined much more than the extent of democratization of civil-military relations. Indeed, it led to different types of democracy.

ARGENTINA: FROM GOVERNMENT TO SUBORDINATION

The Political Project of the Armed Forces and Its Effects on the Democratic Opening

Between 1955 and the democratic transition in 1983, Argentina experienced a cycle of instability involving several regime changes and chronic uncertainty about fundamental policy choices. Amid this climate of political instability, however, aspects of continuity were evident. Most notably, although Peronism remained a de facto electoral majority, during much of the period the Argentine Armed Forces did not allow Peronist candidates to control key institutional spaces. In 1972, a conflictive and violent social situation combined with demands for a democratic opening to compel the Armed Forces (then in power) to grant free elections. For the first time since 1955, a Peronist victory was permitted at the national level. The Peronist government that took office in 1973 was ousted by the Armed Forces in March 1976, in the context of a deep economic, social, and political crisis.

The military attributed the Argentine crisis not only to guerrilla activity, a "lack of control" over trade union activity, and Peronism but also to the semiclosed economy, subsidized industry, and the "politicization" of the intersectoral transfer of resources. These concerns shaped the evolving political strategies of the military leadership during three clearly different stages of its rule. During the first stage (1976–1978), the main goal was to violently subordinate society to state control. The aim of the second stage (1978–1982) was to craft the future political order. And the third stage (1982–1983) was characterized by the pursuit of "minimal goals" in a context of crisis and retreat of the Armed Forces from government.

Immediately after seizing power, the Junta Militar announced the dismissal of constitutional authorities, modified the rules of political competition and the functions of governmental powers, and established regulations for the operation of state institutions. It also dissolved the National Congress and the provincial and municipal legislatures, granted legislative powers to the Executive, altered the composition of the Supreme Court and of the Higher Provincial Courts, and placed all judges "under commission." Finally, it eliminated freedom of assembly and suspended political parties, outlawed the political activity of trade unions, restricted the freedom of the press, and decreed swift indictments through military courts for cases of disruption of public order.

Yet it was the nature and magnitude of illegal repression that set this case apart from previous dictatorial regimes. The Comisión Nacional sobre la Desaparición de Personas (CONADEP) documented the disappearance of 8,960 people and estimated that the number of victims exceeded 9,000. Amnesty International's estimate surpassed 15,000, whereas other human rights organizations have maintained that the victims numbered as many as 30,000.

The Junta Militar empowered itself to designate the president, members of the Supreme Court, and all other government officials. The state apparatus was divided into various jurisdictions assigned to the three branches of the military: army, navy, and air force (Fontana, 1987). Each was entitled to one-third of the government positions. These provisions were intended to avoid intramilitary conflicts in presidential succession as well as the personalization of power that had characterized earlier military governments.

As decided during the planning of the coup, repression of terrorism was to be clandestine. It was to be used not only to neutralize but also to physically exterminate the militant opposition, regardless of whether it was involved in armed struggle (Camps, 1981; Mignone, 1990; Frontalini and Caiati, 1984: 32–33; Guest, 1990: 21–22; Uriarte, 1992: 97). In this way, subsequent civilian governments would be prevented from releasing regime opponents who then could mount, as in 1973, a political counteroffensive.

The clandestine nature of repression had various objectives: to delay protests and international pressures of the kind that confronted the Chilean dictatorship, to prevent potential constraints on military power, and to paralyze popular reactions through terror. Yet the Comandantes (commanders of all the Armed Forces) were aware—French and American military specialists had so warned them—that as a consequence of the clandestine nature of repression, sectors of the Argentine military would probably gain organizational autonomy, which they might use to obtain economic benefits. The chosen type and structure of repression carried the seeds of corruption and of breaches in the chain of command. It offered high political benefits and military efficiency in the short term; and in the medium term it set the structural bases for the erosion of military institutions.

Initially, the magnitude of repression and the inaction of political parties, trade unions, the church, and the press left citizens helpless. During the first months after the coup, some groups and organizations[1] denounced the repression, but for the most part the regime could limit public visibility of the accusations. In the international arena, however, the impact of the charges could not be offset so easily. Toward the end of 1976, an Amnesty International mission visited Argentina, and U.S. military aid was cut when the Carter administration took office shortly afterward.

The second stage of the Argentine military regime began in 1978, when the junta believed that a military victory had been achieved. The next four years were devoted to designing the future political order. Implementation of the government's vision required civilian approval of the policy of repression and a political agreement not to review the past. The first attempt to "whitewash" the government's repressive policies involved an international organization, the Comisión Interamericana de Derechos Humanos (CIDH), which was appointed by the Organization of American States (OAS). The government hoped that a visit by the CIDH could prove its contention that repression was part of a necessary but limited "war" that had already ended. The report that followed the visit in 1978 was much more critical than the Armed Forces had expected, however, and did not enable them to close the case. In 1979, the junta initiated the "Political Dialogue" in an attempt to reorganize political activity under its tutelage (Acuña, 1980;

González, 1991). According to the Armed Forces, their "victory in war" granted them the right to claim a permanent institutional role. They envisioned tutoring a future democratic regime, in which a friendly leadership would guarantee the continuity of their policies and presence in government.

Between 1980 and 1982, the military government confronted increasing political and economic difficulties, which limited its capacity to impose its conditions on the rest of the political and social actors. The Nobel Peace Price awarded to Adolfo Pérez Esquivel in 1980 gave national legitimacy to the demands and activities of the human rights movement, forcing the full spectrum of political and social actors to make public statements on an issue that many preferred to avoid. The presidential succession of 1981, in which General Roberto Vìola replaced General Jorge Rafael Videla, soon resulted in a palace coup and the presidency of General Leopoldo Galtieri. Although the coup indicated the incapacity of the Armed Forces to preserve the political stability that they pretended to guarantee, it also revealed the depth of intramilitary tensions. The size of the external debt, the decrease in the investment rate, the recession, growing inflation rates, and the growth of the opposition's capacity to mobilize—all were evidence of a crisis that would have significant middle- and long-term consequences.

Whatever the cause of the invasion of the Malvinas Islands in early 1982, the military defeat certainly had important consequences for the survival of the military regime.[2] Following this defeat, the government lost authority vis-à-vis society, and the intramilitary conflicts sharpened. In fact, the pact among the branches of the Armed Forces broke down, reducing the capacity of the military to negotiate with civilian sectors. As a result, the government was forced to revise its objectives: It abandoned the idea of establishing its own right-wing party and sought to negotiate with the opposition a way out of the crisis. Where the negotiations failed, however, the government imposed its will by decree.

In April 1983, the position of the military government with respect to human rights violations was established through the Documento Final (Final Document) and the Acta Institucional (Institutional Act). Accordingly, all military operations undertaken by the Armed Forces were to be considered acts of service and thus were not subject to punishment. After that, two weeks before the October elections, the military government sanctioned the Ley de Pacificación Nacional (Law of National Pacification or Law of Self-Amnesty), which granted immunity to suspects of acts of state terrorism, as well as to all members of the Armed Forces, for crimes committed between May 25, 1973, and June 17, 1982. Finally, in its last days of government, it passed a decree ordering the destruction of documents pertaining to military repression. With all these acts, the strategy of retreat implemented by the Armed Forces actually confirmed the centrality of the human rights question for the military, defining human rights as the key issue of the agenda of the transition.

There was no social explosion or radicalization of social demands during the process of liberalization. The Peronist candidate, taking for granted his electoral victory and preferring to minimize future confrontations with the Armed Forces, saw no need to make an effort to attract the constituency that had rallied around the demands of human rights organizations. The Radical Party candidate decided to set himself apart on the human rights issue, in contrast with the other candidates who preferred to remain ambiguous. To the surprise of many observers, the strategy of the Radical candidate proved successful: Raul Alfonsin won the presidential elections of October 1983.

Civil-Military Relations in Argentine Democracy: From Conflict to Subordination to Constitutional Power

To satisfy the demand for justice that had set the tone of its electoral campaign, the Radical government designed a strategy that aimed simultaneously at sanctioning members of the Armed Forces who had committed violations of human rights and at incorporating the military into the democratic arena. This strategy implied the use of military courts for high-ranking members of the Armed Forces and of civil courts trials for those responsible for violations of human rights. In this way, it was expected, the government would fulfill electoral promises without becoming an enemy of the Armed Forces. The government's plan included repeal of the so called Law of Self-Amnesty and enactment of a new law that was to specify both the scope of penal liability and the jurisdiction in which the trials were to be held.

Congress approved the repeal of the Law of Self-Amnesty in December 1983. Nevertheless, the government's strategy encountered its first problems when Congress sanctioned the law known as Reform of the Military Code, which gave the Supreme Council of the Armed Forces the right to prosecute military personnel, established a mechanism of automatic appeal in civilian courts, and precluded the indiscriminate use of the concept of "due obedience" in cases of infamous and aberrant crimes (*delitos atroces y aberrantes*). This last clause prevented the government from limiting *ab initio* the scope of the trials. Furthermore, in September 1984, when it became evident that the Supreme Council would not purge the military on its own, the Federal Appeals Court of Buenos Aires took the case into its own hands. For the next few months, the political logic that had governed the conflict until then was superseded by juridical logic.[3]

The juridical logic, openly presented and publicized, lent credibility to the narratives of the past and put the accounts of the witnesses beyond suspicion. In fact, the trial turned out to be an effective mechanism for the historical and political judgment of the dictatorship. Furthermore, and contrary to the expectations of the government, it reopened the "human rights question" instead of closing it.

After the trial, Alfonsin responded to increasing pressure from the Armed Forces by taking steps to restrict the scope of the verdict and to ensure military acquiescence. These moves included three measures: the Instrucciones a los Fiscales Militares (Instructions to Military Prosecutors), the Ley de Punto Final (Law of Fullstop), and the Ley de Obediencia Debida (Law of Due Obedience).

The Instrucciones were intended to reduce radically the number of prosecutions, by exempting from accountability those cases in which people accused of torture, kidnapping, or murder could prove that they were acting according to orders. This first initiative to close the question politically did not succeed, owing to opposition in the Peronist Party, among sectors of the Radical Party, in the human rights organizations, and in the Federal Court of the federal capital.

The Ley de Punto Final approached the issue from another angle, by establishing a deadline for summoning the presumed violators of human rights. When the law was approved in December 1986, seven Federal Courts suspended their January holidays to work on the pending cases. By February, when the deadline set by the law was approaching, more than 300 high-ranking officers had been indicted. Thus, although the president secured passage of the Ley de Punto Final, the practical consequences of the law signaled a political failure.

The Ley de Obediencia Debida was approved shortly after the April 1987 uprising of the *carapintadas,* who opposed the human rights policies of the Radical Party. The uprising brought to light the strength of ultramilitary grievances and the lack of command exercised by civilian authorities or the army chief of staff. At the same time, a wide and generalized mobilization of civil society demonstrated the strength of public repudiation of the possibility of a return to military government.

Following the "Easter Rebellion," a new front of conflict was opened in the relationship between the government and the Armed Forces. The human rights dispute overlapped with the conflict over what should be done with participants in military rebellions, a conflict that actually masked the ability of the emerging rebel sectors to influence the army's decisions. The preeminence of this new dispute modified the relative weight of the issues at stake. The dispute about how to penalize those responsible for violations of human rights was overshadowed by the need to restore the chain of command within the army. The government was ready to give up prosecutions for human rights violations, but neither the government nor important sectors of the Army High Command were willing to bend to the demands of the *carapintadas,* since doing so would reinforce their political power within the military.[4]

The *carapintadas* expected that a victory of the Peronist candidate in the 1989 elections would elevate their political standing and gain dismissal of the sanctions imposed by the army chief of staff as well as a governmental position for their leader, Colonel Mohammed Seineldín. On October 8, 1989, Carlos Menem, victorious and already in power, announced a first presidential pardon. Among its 277 beneficiaries were military personnel involved in violations of human rights or convicted for their role either in the Malvinas War or in the military uprisings during the Radical government. Also included were civilians who had been condemned for guerrilla activities. The ex-commanders Jorge Rafael Videla, Roberto Viola, Emilio Massera, and Armando Lambruschini were excluded from that pardon, as were Generals Ramón Camps and Carlos Suárez Mason and the head of the Montoneros, Mario Firmenich.

At first glance it seemed that the *carapintada* leaders had obtained the results they were after. The pardon spared them condemnation by civilian courts, but it did not allow them to obtain impunity in the military scene, since it did not reverse the sentences set by the army chief of staff.

Disenchanted with Menem, with some of their own members (who were shifting toward participation in institutional politics), and with a dwindling military influence and decreasing control over active units, the *carapintadas* made a last-ditch effort to gain control of the army chief of staff. The last uprising, on December 3, 1990, was the most violent, and the repression was bloody. The end of the rebellion marked the defeat of the *carapintadas* in the military arena and their neutralization in the political system.

A few days after the rebellion and its defeat, a second pardon was made public. It included the first two military juntas as well as Generals Camps, Suarez Mason, and Richieri, together with Firmenich and a few other civilians. The new round of pardons reaffirmed the "menemist" strategy of forgiving past rebellions while punishing present and future disobedience. At the same time, it strengthened the army chief of staff, preventing the *carapintadas* from becoming once again the spokespersons for military causes.

This brief analysis of the Argentine case allows us to reach several conclusions. First, criminal prosecution of those responsible for human rights violations did not have the effects intended by the executive, inasmuch as the process's two central goals were not met: Neither the number of military men to be prosecuted was limited, nor was the self-purging of the military achieved. Meanwhile, the human rights organizations and the political opposition were largely unsuccessful, and the judiciary saw its primary goals frustrated; yet the Armed Forces failed to reach their main objective of preventing either the trials or societal condemnation. In that sense, the transition in Argentina did not satisfy the central aims of any of the actors involved in the political struggle over human rights.

Up to now, the Menem government seems to have experienced the greatest degree of success. Arriving late on the scene, Menem was able to strike a deal, pardoning those accused and convicted for human rights violations or military uprisings in exchange for a commitment on the part of the military to obey the civilian government. Free of the electoral obligations that had constrained Alfonsin, Menem tried to solve the "military problem" by strengthening the army chief of staff while at the same time negotiating with the *carapintadas*. Yet the success of this strategy was also partial. It did not stop the rebels from resorting to armed conflict, but it did manage to prevent the insurgents from using forces loyal to the army chief of staff, thereby restoring the chain of command. The harshness of the punishment imposed on the officers who participated in this last uprising set the rules that would define Menem's relationship with the military: All crimes committed in the past would be pardoned, but present or future disobedience would be punished, and severely.

The Present and Future Roles
of the Armed Forces in Argentina

The position of the Armed Forces today is not the product of contingent factors. The Armed Forces have confronted the worst of possible scenarios: the trials and the conviction of its leadership for the repressive methodology it had employed. Even though the chief of staff succeeded in gaining the pardon and triumphing over the *carapintadas,* it could not prevent the profound redefinition of its role brought about by the trials; nor has it been able to neutralize the costs and risks resulting from the politicization of military institutions.

The experience in government from 1976 to 1983 took a high toll on military authority. Systematic violations of human rights generated strong resentment among the majority of the population against the military, and in this sense the trials only accentuated an existing tendency in Argentine society. In addition, the deep socioeconomic crisis that resulted from the economic policies of the military produced resentment among the popular sectors. One consequence was the alienation of important segments of the bourgeoisie, which traditionally had constituted the core of the political and economic alliance that lent social support to military governments.

The internal confrontation that originated during the week of Easter unveiled a new scenario for conflicts involving the military. In contrast with past conflicts, in which the internal divisions cut across ranks, this confrontation took place between low-ranking officers supported by noncommissioned officers, on the one hand, and "the generals," on the other. This "class struggle" threatened the military as an institution, since a victory of the *carapintadas* would have implied the discharge of most high-ranking personnel, whereas the victory of "the generals" meant the dismissal of the lower ranks.

The Armed Forces emerged from this experience with a strong sense of social and political isolation. They also found themselves in a state of acute internal crisis. In such a context, those who defeated the *carapintadas* could not afford to risk again their institutional survival through political intervention. Therefore, as a consequence both of the crisis that the Armed Forces started to suffer during their own administration and of the political and legal ramifications of the struggle over human rights, the Armed Forces lost the incentive to challenge constitutional governments. Of course, their diminished capacity to threaten democratic regimes does not imply the absence of conflicts with civilian governments over issues such as budgets, distribution of funds, and the definition of military functions.

The role of the Argentine Armed Forces has also been affected by the transformation of the international scenario as well as by the crisis of the state. The end of the cold war resulted in the disappearance of the "communist threat," eroding one of the traditional arguments used to justify preventive military interventions in politics. The MERCOSUR agreements and the peace agreements with Chile have resulted in the transformation of old scenarios of conflict and in the conversion of former potential enemies into allies. Moreover, the recent political and economic realignment with the United States has resulted in a dismantling of important military projects.

These changes are reflected in a series of legal modifications that reveal the new political and institutional position of the Armed Forces. Since 1983, the president has concentrated power as chief commander of the Armed Forces, eliminating the historically established large quotas of power and autonomy of the military elite. And the 1988 Ley de Defensa (Defense Law) restricted the duties of the Armed Forces to defense in cases of external aggression.[5]

Finally, the crisis of the state and the continuing process of economic restructuring have resulted in a significant decrease of military participation in economic activities. Many army barracks have been dismantled, several military enterprises have been privatized, and the number of nonprofessional personnel has been substantially reduced. Together, these developments have led to a radical transformation of the power of the Armed Forces as a political actor.[6] The 1994 governmental decision to eliminate the draft, in favor of relying on a much smaller "voluntary" army, can be taken as a further indication of societal disaffection toward the military and its increasing isolation.

BRAZIL: FROM AUTHORITARIANISM TO A DEMOCRACY UNDER MILITARY TUTELAGE (*MA NON TROPPO*)

The Policies of the Brazilian Authoritarian Regime

Of the three military governments under examination here, the Brazilian Armed Forces stayed for the longest period in government (1964–1985). This fact suggests that the design of medium- and long-term policies and goals took place in Brazil in an ideological and economic context different from that in Argentina and Chile. The goal of the military government in Brazil was to consolidate a model of capitalist accumulation—in which the state, along with oligopolistic groups composed of local and multinational capitalists, played a central role— based on an industrial development that could substitute imports and reach export capacity. The dismantling of popular organizations was the political prerequisite to forcing the necessary transfer of resources to the bourgeoisie.

In contrast with the Chilean case, at the time of the 1964 coup the Brazilian Armed Forces confronted a party system and a democratic order only recently developed and with strong elements of authoritarianism. The coup took place amid mobilizations of the middle class and of the Catholic Church against President João Goulart. Military intervention was supported by a number of political parties. These circumstances induced the Armed Forces, in a first stage, to try to govern without radically modifying the party system. General Humberto de Alencar Castelo Branco kept the Parliament functioning, and, a short time after Goulart was removed, Castelo was named president by a Congress purged without much repression.[7] It was only in 1965, after the opposition had won the congressional elections, that the Armed Forces, confronted with the division of the political forces that supported them, "dissolved" the parties and the multiparty system.

The dissolution of parties did not entail the closing down of the national Congress, in which a bipartisan system began to emerge. The unification of right-wing forces and government "favors" allowed the official Aliança Renovadora Nacional (ARENA) to hold the majority in the Congress and in most state legislatures. The opposition, unified in the Movimento Democrático Brasileiro (MDB), became part of a game in which it was unable to become a majority and could control only a few states. This peculiar relationship of the military government with the "representative" system was maintained until 1979, when the political system was "reopened" to multiparty competition.

The political strategies of the military were effective at first, but during a second stage, from 1968 to 1974, the systematic political and economic exclusion that characterized the policies of the military regime led to a deepening of the conflict with the opposition that was not integrated in the bipartisan game. The average annual growth rate, which in 1962–1967 was 3.7 percent, rose to 10.1 percent during 1968–1974. This process was accompanied by a consistent distributive exclusion: The income of the poorest half of the population fell in relation to the total national income from 17.4 percent in 1960 to 14.9 percent in 1970 and 12.6 per cent in 1980, whereas the income of the richest tenth of the population grew in those years from 39.6 percent to 46.7 and 50.9 percent, respectively.

Meanwhile, even though ARENA had won the 1966 and 1970 elections and widened its electoral margin, the system started to show signs of an imminent crisis of representation. From 1968 on, student and worker mobilizations grew, and guerrilla organizations emerged and continued their operations. Social support for these groups was limited, as were their prospects for success. Yet their political weight was strong. Consequently, the government, now in the hands of Emilio Garrastazu Médici, was able to increase repression and set up a strong intelligence and security apparatus that consolidated its political presence within the state and the Armed Forces. In this context the elections of 1970, won by ARENA, were a clear indication of a crisis in the bipartisan system: The vote for the opposition MDB failed to exceed the number of blank ballots.

The third period began in 1974 with the government of General Ernesto Geisel (1974–1979), who started a "slow, gradual, and certain" process of political relaxation. His administration began precisely at the time when the MDB had managed to recover its role as a channel of expression for the opposition, and when the oil crisis and the increase in imports promoted by the industrial expansion had led to inflation, though without affecting the rate of growth. This situation led the military regime to search for greater national autonomy, to guarantee its sources of supply, and to pursue markets for Brazilian exports. During this process, the war industry, which by then was growing steadily, played a strategic role—for instance, by arranging exchanges with Iraq. Another significant event of the Geisel years was the denunciation in 1976 of the 1952 military cooperation treaty signed by the United States and Brazil. The Brazilian government used U.S. criticism of Brazilian human rights policy to denounce the treaty, thereby countering American pressure to block Brazil's access to nuclear technology.

The Brazilian government also increased the concentration of power in the Executive to ensure control over the liberalization process. After taking on the repression of guerrillas, the security apparatus broadened its political control over the government and the army, and was quite harsh in responding to the plans of political liberalization. Geisel also reacted against the advances of the opposition with a set of measures intended to maintain control over the Congress. Finally, the president restricted the influence and autonomy of Executive advisory departments with private business participation.

This concentration of power implied the closure of channels for participation by capitalists, redefining the meaning of state power in the minds of entrepreneurs: If in the past the state had been seen as an ally with common interests, it was now regarded as a dangerous boss. A breakdown of the alliance between the Armed Forces and the entrepreneurs ensued, and the democratic opening was accelerated.

The repression initiated in 1968 did not stop in 1974–1979: Political and labor union groups were affected by government measures, and the incidence of detention-disappearances increased. Paradoxically, it was during the time that the security apparatus was being dismantled that the highest number of detention-disappearances took place in Brazil. In fact, this repression was the reaction of the security apparatus against the curtailment of its power and against the gradual and controlled liberalization proposed by Geisel. The detention-disappearance of members of the opposition was intended to undermine the political negotiations between the government and the opposition. Activism of human rights organizations was now on the increase.

The substitution of Geisel by General João Baptista Figueiredo in 1979 led to a deepening of the liberalization process. A first amnesty was passed, political prisoners were freed, and exiles and well-known politicians were allowed to return to the country. The amnesty included military personnel accused of human rights violations, but not those who had been imprisoned for guerrilla activities or members of the military who had been dismissed for political reasons. The pardon blocked the possibility to punish crimes perpetrated by the dictatorship. After it was passed, the majority of the political leaders considered the question of human rights "closed."

From that moment on, the opposition concentrated on reinitiating political and partisan activities. Between 1979 and 1983, Figueiredo accelerated the *abertura,* taking the initiative so as to maintain control over the form and content of the transition. Reproducing the dynamics implemented by Geisel, openings and concessions to opposition groups were linked to the repression of opponents who were mobilizing beyond the scenarios proposed by the government. The forced bipartisan system was dissolved: ARENA transformed itself into the Partido Democrático Social (PDS), and the MDB, which remained the main party in opposition, became the Partido do Movimento Democrático Brasileiro (PMDB).

The government knew the risk of opening the political system. The consequences could include increased mobilization of labor unions (at this stage the massive ABC strikes were taking place) as well as political fallout from the reorganization of the party system. Accordingly, liberalization was accompanied by increased social repression: "National security" laws were maintained, and electoral laws were modified to ensure the majority of the PDS in the Senate. Although the government's party commanded only an electoral minority, it never lost control over the Senate during the process of transition.

During the 1982 elections, in a context of considerable social mobilization that pushed the government and the political parties to accelerate the transition, the MDB obtained the majority in the House of Representatives as well as control of a number of state governments. In 1983, popular pressure erupted on the political scene with a campaign to force "immediate direct elections" (Diretas Ya!). Although the vote in favor of direct elections gained a majority in Congress, the government party did not provide the necessary quorum and the initiative was defeated amid military threats to declare a state of emergency if direct presidential elections were ratified. At the time of the vote, the military surrounded the Congress building with troops and tanks. Despite strong popular pressure, leaders of the major opposition parties that had participated in the movement for direct elections accepted the defeat.

A process of negotiations soon followed, however, with an agenda of indirect presidential elections and the guarantee of an ordered and definite retreat of the military. Rejecting the candidate that the military government tried to impose, reformists in the official party joined the moderate opposition to form the Aliança Democrática (Democratic Alliance). This new party was made up of members who had split from the PDS, led by José Sarney, and the PMDB, led by Tancredo Neves. Figuereido's government thus was left politically isolated. It had little choice but to negotiate an exit with Aliança Democrática, which seemed likely to win the elections and whose moderate candidates were acceptable to the Armed Forces.

Among the goals sought by the Armed Forces during this transition process were the following: (1) Military personnel would not be condemned for political crimes (e.g., torture, kidnapping, and murder); (2) officers dismissed for political reasons would not be reincorporated; (3) the repressive apparatus would be maintained, and Figuereido would name new security and intelligence heads, who in turn would keep their functions under the civilian government; (4) the Armed Forces would designate the military cabinet ministers (one for each branch, one for Intelligence, another for the Casa Militar, and a sixth for the chief of staff); (5) the Constitution of 1967, with its 1969 amendments, would be retained until a new constitution was approved; (6) the body in charge of revising the Constitution would not be chosen by direct elections but, rather, would consist of the incumbent members of Congress; and (7) the constitutional reform would be restricted to issues that did not affect "national security."

The good relations between Tancredo Neves and the Armed Forces guaranteed most of the military goals and neutralized the risks involved in the transfer of government. In 1985, Tancredo Neves and José Sarney were elected by the Congress as president and vice-president of Brazil, respectively. The sudden death of Tancredo before he took office placed in the presidency of the first civilian government since 1964 a politician who, until the previous year, had been an important member of the military government party.

Transition and Democracy in Brazil: A New Regime with the Armed Forces Maintaining Their Traditional Role

The civilian government called a National Assembly and passed an amnesty for civilian and military opponents of the regime. This law allowed the reincorporation of civilians to positions from which they had been discharged; it also gave seniority-based promotions only to lower ranking officers, who were not reappointed or otherwise compensated. A third amnesty was passed in 1988, applying to officers who had been discharged between 1946 and 1985.

During his first year of government, Sarney kept the cabinet designated by Tancredo; it had a democratic and even progressive profile. When the Cruzado Plan failed in 1986, however, differences with the PMDB (the party of Tancredo Neves) became wider, and the PMDB started to discuss the possibility of shortening the presidential term. Sarney was able to end his term in office, but the scant political support of his own party, the PMDB's closing of ranks with the opposition, and the loss of the majority in the Congress transformed the Armed Forces such that it became almost the sole support of the government's policies. The result was a friendly military tutelage over the Executive.

The 1988 constitutional reform once again generated important expectations and mobilizations in civil society. At the same time, the Executive and Congress clashed over control of the constituent assembly. Pressure from popular organizations led to the inclusion of an array of social and individual rights in the new constitution, which also contained a clause declaring torture a "crime without prescription." Furthermore, the new constitution suppressed a key symbol of the military regime, the Conselho de Seguridade Nacional (National Security Council, or CSN)—a presidential advisory committee with high-level military participation—and replaced it with the Conselho da República (Council of the Republic, or COSERE) and the Conselho de Defensa Nacional (National Defense Council, or COSENA). These new institutions incorporated constitutional powers other than the Armed Forces and the Executive.

During the constitutional process, an effective military lobby was able to maintain the role of the Armed Forces in guaranteeing these constitutional powers.

Thus, according to the new constitution, if demanded by any of the constitutional powers, the Armed Forces could intervene in the democratic process to guarantee law and order. In this way, the possibility of a military intervention in issues related to internal security was legitimated, and the Armed Forces were granted a tutelary role. Owing to military pressure, an attempt was made to replace military ministries with a civilian minister of defense.

In the new institutional scheme, Congress does not have the power to nominate the leading officers of the Armed Forces, who to this day are chosen by the president; furthermore, there are no institutionalized parliamentary controls over military intelligence organizations. Beyond the institutional prerogatives retained by the Armed Forces after the inauguration of the civilian government, even following approval of the new constitution, the role of the Armed Forces in Brazilian politics reveals itself not only in their continuous interference and ability to influence economic, political and social policies but also in their capacity to keep "closed" the issue of human rights violations.

The 1990 direct presidential election of Fernando Collor de Melo, held according to the rules established by the new Constitution, marked the end of the democratic transition. Heading an alliance of center and right-wing parties, Collor's election constituted an impediment to the growth of the left, yet his legitimacy and political power were independent of support from the Armed Forces. Collor enjoyed a greater degree of freedom in his actions regarding the military. Even though he did not modify the political and institutional bases that defined the tutelary role of the Armed Forces, he reformed some of the mechanisms that the military considered important for their strategies.[8]

Brazil's significant arms industry had already been affected by the general economic crisis during the Sarney administration. The state's reduced ability to subsidize arms exports decreased productive capacity and led to diminished funding for Brazilian nuclear projects. Confronted with the economic crisis and its effects on the arms industry, Collor concentrated military industrial resources in the areas of research and high technology. This decision led to a debate over the privatization of that part of the industry managed by the military, a debate that hinges on the assumption that strategic projects, such as the construction of nuclear submarines, would be maintained without consideration of cost.[9] Thus, even though the Brazilian Armed Forces have less institutional autonomy for deciding their economic policy than does the Chilean military, their resources and capabilities have not been affected to the same extent as have those of the Argentine military. Their industrial structure is still strong, and they maintain their status as a significant geopolitical presence in the South Atlantic and throughout the Third World generally.

Both the economic situation and the political role of the military were changed by the policies of the Collor administration. Whereas the former implied salary cuts, the latter meant the loss of institutional space and a reduction of political power. Now that the East-West conflict and frontier tensions (particularly with

Argentina) have ended, areas of strategic preoccupation are restricted to those related to maintaining Brazil's presence in the South Atlantic, redefining its relationship to the main world powers, securing territorial integration (in the framework of problems posed by many different groups of Indians with respect to recognition of the "Yanomami Nation"), avoiding the "internationalization" of the Amazon, and reducing the drug trade.

The political crisis culminating in the impeachment and resignation of President Collor demonstrated that even though the military tutelage continues to be a constitutionally legitimized threat, the possibility that the Armed Forces will exercise this role is relatively small—not only because the political scenario for its exercise has narrowed, but also because the costs of intervention have increased. Given the specific development of the transition process in Brazil, the Armed Forces support the stability of the democratic regime. Conflicts over issues such as the budget are framed within the established rules of the game. The possibility that social and economic crises will result in social unrest does not lead the Armed Forces to consider a new military intervention as a feasible option. Their role in such a contingency would undoubtedly conform to the legal mechanisms that authorize their intervention. Thus, even if the institutional prerogatives remain in place, the political behavior of the Brazilian Armed Forces seems to be shifting toward a very weak (and dwindling) tutelage—a *tutelage ma non troppo*—over the constitutional powers. In this way, Brazilian democracy regains three old traditions: a certain measure of military tutelage, extensive economic exclusion, and systematic social repression.[10]

CHILE: FROM AUTHORITARIANISM TO DEMOCRACY UNDER MILITARY TUTELAGE

The Politics of the Chilean Authoritarian Regime

On September 11, 1973, the Estado de Compromiso (Compromise State, or EC), which since 1932 had guaranteed the political stability of the Chilean regime, came to an end. In that arrangement, party representation—with the political spectrum divided roughly in thirds—led to a political dynamic that was based on alliances between the center and either the right or the left, thus guarding against the risk of polarization or of an "extremist" government. Given the central position of the Chilean state in the production and distribution of resources, the EC enabled the various political and social forces to defend their political and economic interests, whereas the division of the party map into thirds necessitated the building of government coalitions that included one or the other extreme, thus neutralizing risks. Such a political dynamic allowed for the gradual introduction of political and economic reforms, while simultaneously producing stability. In contrast with the Brazilian and Argentine cases, Chile showed from early on a strong party system capable of mediating social conflict through party politics. Furthermore, and in contrast to the scenarios in Argentina and Brazil, Chile's political parties themselves were in control of the political dynamics of the state; for instance, they proscribed the power of the Communist Party when it opted to organize rural workers. In this way, they not only avoided the "moderating interventions" of the Armed Forces that characterized the history of the other two countries but also encouraged the military to concentrate on matters of professional development.

Why did this dynamic break down in 1973? The answer lies in the 1964 victory of the Christian Democratic Party (DC), which produced a revolution in the Chilean political scheme. The DC won a majority on its own, gaining the support of a large number of right-wing voters and replacing the Radical Party as the party representing the center. For the first time, a protagonist of the center did not need alliances to gain power. For both the left and the right, this hegemonic center posed a threat: It could compete with the left over the ideals of social justice, and it threatened the right with an agrarian reform plan that included the organization of rural workers.

The 1970 elections were a second shock to the continuity of the Compromise State. The risk of a leftward turn in the DC led to a unification of the right, which put forth its own candidate. Furthermore, the hegemonic ambitions of the center discouraged the search of a center-leftist coalition. Under these conditions—the shift of votes of the right toward its own candidate, the absence of an alliance between the new center and the left, and the ability of the left to maintain its own voters—the 1970 elections gave a surprising victory to the Unidad Popular (UP), which took office without the need for alliances. Although it lacked a majority in Congress, the UP government decided to go ahead with its project of socialist modernization. After some time, the social and political opposition was able to transform its resistance to the socialization of the means of production into a constitutional conflict. In September 1973, in a context characterized by the delegitimation of the democratic system as well as by growing polarization and political mobilization, the Chilean Armed Forces overthrew the UP government in the name of the constitution.

From that moment on, a military regime governed Chile. It ousted all representative authorities, prohibited elections as a mechanism for access to public positions, outlawed and dismantled political parties with a long historical tradition, persecuted their leaders, and severely restricted freedom of association and speech. High-ranking officers were appointed to government positions. And General Augusto Pinochet, together with officers chosen by him and a junta consisting of the commanders of each military branch and of the *carabineros,* took over the political decisionmaking process. The persecution and death of those people the regime defined as its opponents were pursued systematically. In some cases, this process took place publicly and on a large scale, with the intention of paralyzing possible reactions. In other cases, it occurred in a clandestine and selective way.[11]

Several authors have emphasized the reactive character of the first stage of the Chilean military regime. Between 1973 and 1974, the regime's main goal was to destroy the experiment of Unidad Popular and to dismantle the party structure. The deep political and social crisis that preceded the 1973 coup gave way to an intense and prolonged repression. The political and social actors who felt threatened by the reforms implemented by the UP government supported the military repression—some openly, others silently. Insofar as the military government concealed its intention to change the foundations of government and state, it could count on the support of the DC, which in turn saw the military administration as a means to restore the public order "subverted" by the UP government.

In 1975, the military government made its initial move toward the economic neoliberals. The conversion from a reactive to a foundational coup had several consequences; at once redefining the government's goals and policies, its alliances and supporters in the old party spectrum, its policy within the Armed Forces, and its relationship with the Catholic Church.

Pinochet's main goal during the second stage of the regime, in 1976–1980, was to consolidate the internal front. The international challenges being posed at the time[12] were not unrelated to this choice of goal, which was further motivated by the need to strengthen Pinochet's personal leadership. (In 1978, Pinochet had displaced General Gustavo Leigh and the Air Force Main Staff.) During this period, the Dirección Nacional de Inteligencia (National Intelligence Directorate) was replaced by the Centro Nacional de Inteligencia (National Information Center), and the repressive apparatus became institutionalized. In 1978, a plebiscite was called to support the government and to condemn the denunciations of human rights violations that had been voiced at the UN. Once the results of the plebiscite strengthened the government's position, an amnesty law was passed in order to avoid eventual trials for those who had participated in the repression.[13] This second stage ended in 1980 with the consolidation of Pinochet's leadership through a plebiscite that ratified the constitution proposed by the military regime.

Although the Constitution of 1980 contemplated a return to open elections in 1989, it also established a mechanism for succession that ensured the continuity in power of the military leaders, of the Judiciary, and of the commander in chief of the army until 1997.[14] In addition, it limited the power of future civilian governments through the creation of nonrepresentative institutions and of a National Security Council that ensured a continued military role in surveillance and repressive functions. As Manuel Antonio Garretón emphasizes in Chapter 3 of this volume, this constitution shaped the subsequent dynamics of the Chilean process in fundamental ways. The inclusion of transitional provisions created a time limit for the dictatorship, provided legal mechanisms for its retreat, allowed the military government to constrain the opposition during the transition, and conditioned both the resources and the actions of the postdictatorial government (Barros, 1992). Thus, the internal consolidation of the regime helped to define the characteristics of the future democracy and of the Armed Forces' role in the future civilian government, while also strengthening the personal leadership of Pinochet.

Between 1981 and 1986, the Chilean regime confronted its greatest difficulties. The economic crisis that started in 1981 gave way to increased social discontent, which in 1982 and 1983 led to broadly based social mobilizations that combined human rights movements, social and church organizations, and opposition parties. The regime reacted by increasing repression. Continuous government violence spawned violent reactions from some of the protesting groups. The escalation of conflict resulted in diminished popular support for the mobilizations and, in the middle run, allowed the government to control the protesters' movements. The failed attempt against Pinochet's life in 1986 sealed the outcome of this wave of opposition. During that year and the previous one, the government was able to offset protests and to regain political and economic control.

However, the failure of the opposition strategy led to another outcome as well: From that moment on, the central goal of the parties' strategy was to achieve the unity of the opposition. Faced with the failure of confrontational strategies, the opposition chose to fight within the restricted legal margins offered by the military regime, organizing itself to challenge the government in a third plebiscite, in which the continuity of Pinochet as president was to be decided. However, it was only in February 1988, when the debate over the plebiscite began, that the opposition was able to unite around a common issue.

The decision to act within the margins defined by the military regime was a critical one: It defined the shape of the transition and conditioned the possibilities for action by the first postdictatorial government. The opposition was able to displace Pinochet from the presidency in 1989 at the cost of reducing its future scope of action. In contrast with other transitions, in which military governments had tried to preserve some of their prerogatives through negotiations with the opposition, the Pinochet government avoided discussion of many of these issues in the informal conversations that took place in 1988 and 1989. From the point of view of the military government, the restrictions imposed by the legal framework that the opposition had accepted and endorsed were such that new agreements became unnecessary. Consider, however, the reaction of the Concertación de Partidos por la Democracia, the political base for President Patricio Aylwin's government. Confident of its chances to achieve a parliamentary majority sufficiently large to offset the restrictions imposed by the Constitution of 1980, the Concertación chose not to debate these restrictions. The opposition's belief was that, by avoiding such discussion, it could avoid compromises that might restrict its future autonomy.[15] In the last months before the transfer of power, the forces of the Concertación agreed to one key point involving the future of the Armed Forces. When the Organic Law of the Armed Forces was negotiated, the parties agreed to maintain the budgetary autonomy of the military: Specifically, the military budget could not fall below its level of 1989, and the military would in addition receive 10 percent of income earned through copper exports. In contrast to the situations in Brazil and Argentina, where crises of the state significantly affected the military budget, the Chilean Armed Forces were able to isolate themselves from fluctuations of the national economy and to guarantee a budget ensuring operational autonomy and high salaries for their officers.

Transition and Democracy in Chile

From the very start of the Aylwin administration, the Concertación experienced the limitations imposed by the legal framework it had accepted. What became evident, inasmuch as it failed to obtain a substantial legislative majority, was "that from then on, it would obtain only what was possible" (Namuncura Serrano, 1991). Yet until the constitution and the Organic Laws passed by the military can be changed, the president will not be able to appoint the commander of the Armed Forces or remove any military commander without the permission of the Security Council; the military budget will not be set by elected civilians; the 1978 Amnesty Law will not be annulled or overruled; and the government will continue to confront nine senators appointed by the military (four of whom are ex–military commanders). The balance of forces in Parliament has also affected the government's capacity to pass and amend legislation. Even today, now that limited legal reforms have been achieved, the death penalty remains in place for crimes related to state security, military courts have jurisdiction over crimes committed by civilians, verdicts issued by the military regime are still in force, and political prisoners are still in prison.

Since those responsible for human rights violations could not be prosecuted, the government in 1990 formed a commission to investigate and establish the truth about violations that resulted in death. But even before the results of the commission were made public, the Unión Democrática Independiente, the Renovación Nacional, and members of the Armed Forces denounced it. At the same time, the commission report stimulated new demands to modify the Amnesty Law and to bring to trial those liable for crimes, even though they could not be sentenced. Yet General Pinochet and other military leaders repeatedly warned that they would not allow military personnel to be brought to trial. For its part, the Supreme Court, made up mostly of judges named by the military government, rejected in August 1990 a motion requesting the inapplicability of the Amnesty Law. In this way, the Court ratified the will of the military leadership. Toward the end of 1990, moreover, the army successfully opposed the implementation of measures that could have reduced its prerogatives.

The painstaking detail of the Rettig Commission Report, which was released to the public in early 1991, provided hard evidence in support of widely held suspicions about the extent and brutality of human rights violations during the dictatorship. Eager to make the most of an apparent opportunity to press the need for justice, the government responded to the Report by attempting to accelerate the reform of the Judiciary. This initiative met strong opposition, however, and was finally aborted when terrorists assassinated the right-wing leader Jaime Guzmán. The criminal attack allowed the right wing to regain the offensive and shifted the debate toward discussion of measures to guarantee internal security and order.

Once again, the debate over the need to review the past and to limit military prerogatives vanished from the agenda of democratic construction.

The Role of the Armed Forces in Chilean Democracy

Several distinct features set the Chilean case apart from those of Argentina and Brazil. In particular, the legal and institutional framework of Chile's transition constrained the first democratic government by legalizing, legitimating, and facilitating continuity of the Armed Forces in the new government.

The economic success of Pinochet's administration, combined with the support that the fear of a return to the pre-1973 period generated in significant sectors of the civilian population, restricted the effectiveness of the democratic forces. With the failure of strategies that went beyond the limits imposed by the military legality, the opposition opted for solutions that were based on accepting the boundaries defined by the military model.

Granted, the Concertación failed to obtain the parliamentary majority needed to overrule the restrictions imposed by the military government; one wonders why it opted for such a "minimalist" strategy. Was it not true, as Garretón points out in Chapter 3, that the Concertación government enjoyed sufficient political credibility to have been able to disregard some of these restrictions? Furthermore, given the international context, could the Chilean Armed Forces plausibly embark on a new reactive coup? The government's choice of a gradualist strategy cannot be attributed to cultural factors alone (i.e., to the Chilean legalist tradition). It is likely that a confrontational strategy would have broken the alliance of forces included in the Concertación. If this is so, the gradualist strategy reflected not only the threat of the Armed Forces and their party allies but also the constraints imposed by the composition of the governing alliance.

Compared to their counterparts in Argentina and Brazil, the Chilean Armed Forces fared better politically: They left government after a successful economic administration, part of the citizenry endorsed and legitimated a legal framework that placed them at the center of the institutional order, economic autonomy prevailed, internal conflicts were limited, and they did not have to relinquish their right to conduct domestic intelligence activities. At the same time, however, their growing political isolation, the personalization of Pinochet's leadership, the international context, and the fact that the civilian government has no intention of reversing the economic and social model imposed during the dictatorship have diminished the capacity of the Armed Forces to convincingly threaten a coup. Thus, although a more aggressive stance on the part of the democratic leadership could result in an intensification of political conflict, it would not necessarily imply the collapse of the institutional order.

Another major consequence of the political process inaugurated in 1973 has been the incorporation of the military as overseers of Chilean politics. Even if a tripartite system of parties reemerges, and even if the links between social and party representation are rebuilt, the military's continuing role as overseers of the system, imposed by the Armed Forces themselves with support from important sectors of Chilean society, precludes a return to the Compromise State.

CONCLUSIONS

The basic traits common to the authoritarian regimes of Argentina, Chile, and Brazil do not help to explain the political or repressive strategies implemented by these regimes, the different types of transitions that occurred, or the resulting democracies. All three military regimes did try to "normalize" the economy[16] and reinstate "order" in society through the resubordination of the popular sector. And to accomplish these goals, the Armed Forces of each country, as institutions, occupied the state apparatus. But no shared economic and social strategies can be inferred from these common political and social goals, nor did they lead to similar transitions or democratic orders.

The political plans implemented to achieve these shared goals depended in each case on (1) the previous experiences of the Armed Forces in government and the "lessons" they could learn from other international experiences, and (2) the structure of the political and social forces they confronted, particularly the structure of the party system.

The institutional role of the Armed Forces in the new democratic regimes was, in all three cases, a matter of conflict between political and military elites. The principal demands of the military regimes and the Armed Forces during the transition processes concerned, first, the granting of legal privileges that would save them from being taken to court for their past actions and, second, the institutionalization of legal prerogatives to guarantee their right to intervene in internal conflicts in case the "subversive" threat reemerged. The Armed Forces' success in obtaining these prerogatives varied. They invariably tried to preserve a tutelary role over the civilian government; but the process of political struggle that took place before, during, and after the dictatorship determined the way in which the Armed Forces were eventually integrated into the democratic system. These different patterns of integration in turn, had diverse consequences for the resulting types of democracy. Although democracy developed under military tutelage in Chile and Brazil, struggles over the form and scope of that tutelage are still being waged there. Argentina, meanwhile, has surprisingly been better able to subordinate its Armed Forces to the civilian power.

When the military regime is economically successful, the Armed Forces can direct the pace of transition and preserve the prerogatives they have obtained. In Argentina and Brazil, Congress discusses and approves the military budget, whereas in Chile the Armed Forces keep 10 percent of the income from copper exports, in addition to their regular budget (which, by law, cannot be inferior to the 1989 military budget). In Chile, the president cannot appoint or remove military commanders without permission from the National Security Council, whereas in Argentina the Senate approves the promotion lists of high-ranking officers. The Senate acts on the basis of a proposal made by the Executive, which in turn considers the proposal made by each of the forces. In Brazil, military promotions are decided by the Executive. In Argentina, there is a Ministry of Defense led by a civilian. This ministry manages the country's war industry. In Brazil, there are three military ministries; each is in charge of its own military industries and all are members of the national cabinet. In the Chilean case, the military presence in the civilian power structure is guaranteed through senators designated by the military, as well as through a National Security Council with the responsibility for guarding and controlling the political process.

In Brazil and Chile, the Armed Forces have constitutional rights to guarantee law and order. Thus, the possibility of intervention in internal security matters and of a military tutelary role over the constitutional powers is legitimized. In Argentina, the Law of National Defense explicitly states that the mission of the Armed Forces is to defend the nation in the event of foreign aggression. This rule was maintained in the Internal Security Law, which nevertheless allows for the Armed Forces to lend logistic support in matters of internal security. Several decrees passed in the last stage of Alfonsin's government and during the Menem administration have, once again, introduced some ambiguity into the scope of the intervention of the Armed Forces in internal conflicts.

The military prerogatives in these three countries also differ in matters related to the scope of action by military courts, the right to carry out internal intelligence activities, and the extent of legislative control over internal security agencies. Alfred Stepan (1988: ch. 7) has suggested a way to analyze civilian-military relations as a function of two variables: the degree and scope (maintenance/variation) of military *prerogatives,* on the one hand, and the degree and level of military *contestation* of civilian decisions, on the other. If we adopt a maximalist position regarding the notion of democracy, only those societies with low prerogatives and a low level of military contestation can be considered democracies.[17] However, since many regimes in Latin America have been and still are considered democracies despite medium levels of military prerogatives, we will adopt that intermediate level as our dividing line between democracy and authoritarianism. That is, in general terms, we will consider that a regime reaches the democratic condition when it has low or middle levels of military prerogatives. Comparing our three cases in these terms, we can draw the following conclusions:

First, Argentina shifted from *low* prerogatives and *high* contestation during the Alfonsin years to *low* prerogatives and *low* contestation in the Menem administration, implying that the existing *de jure* control over the military has shifted, resulting in both *de jure* and *de facto* control. Some restrictions to military prerogatives introduced in the first stage of the Radical government were eroded during the last stage of that same government (from 1989 on), with the creation of the COSENA and with the approval of decrees that reincorporate the Armed Forces into internal security activities. Nevertheless, the Argentine military is very different from the Brazilian and Chilean cases in terms of both the degree and the nature of its participation.

Second, Brazil moved from *high* prerogatives and a *medium* level of military contestation during the government of Sarney, to *medium* prerogatives and *low* contestation during the Collor and Itamar Franco administrations. Although some of the military prerogatives began to be reduced under Collor, the legislation still provides ample faculties for military tutelage. In particular, we must remember that although the military regime broadened many of those faculties, even before the 1964 coup the Brazilian Constitution had granted institutional functions for its Armed Forces that were absent in Chile and Argentina.

Third, at this writing, Chile has a *high* level of prerogatives and a *medium* level of military contestation of constitutional authorities. Thus, it is the country in which the Armed Forces have been the most successful in maintaining their prerogatives and tutelary role. Indeed, the magnitude of these prerogatives and the degree of military influence over certain areas of democratic control put into question the democratic character of the present Chilean regime. Chilean democracy can be considered "partial" or "incomplete," or as representative of a civilian regime that, despite having a democratically elected government, has yet to complete the process of transition to a democratic political order. Beyond semantic discussions or classifications, one or the other of these political scenarios may develop in Chile: Either the civilian administration will be able to accelerate and complete the reforms designed to diminish military autonomy and prerogatives, or the civilian leadership will respect the original plan of the Armed Forces and postpone completion of the transition to full democracy until 1997.

Today, more than ever, an understanding of Latin American democracies requires consideration of the Armed Forces as a political actor, irrespective of theoretical discussions about democracy. Inferences based on case studies and comparative analysis must replace assumptions that portray the behavior of the Armed Forces and its consequences as the product of a script written beyond the limits of the region. Yet it is also necessary to stop thinking about democracy as a static end point, whereby the political power of the Armed Forces, their relationship to constitutional power, and their impact on the type of democracy that each society may be consolidating reproduce the predictions of an abstract generic model. The struggle to redefine the political role of the military is one of many issues in the context of Latin American transitions demonstrating that not all roads lead to Rome—indeed, that democratic theory must accommodate the existence of various Romes.

Notes

This chapter is part of a research project on the integration of the Armed Forces of the Southern Cone into various democratic regimes. The project has been supported by the John D. and Catherine T. MacArthur Foundation, the Ford Foundation, and the North-South Center of the University of Miami. An initial product of this research is Acuña and Smulovitz (1991). We are grateful for the collaboration of Leonardo Perez Esquivel, Luis Alberto Quevedo, Pablo Frederick, and Néstor Restivo, who have assisted in the fieldwork.

1. Noteworthy examples include Madres de Plaza de Mayo, Familiares de Detenidos y Desaparecidos por Razones Políticas, Abuelas de Plaza de Mayo, Servicio de Paz y Justicia, Movimiento Ecuménico de Derechos Humanos; Asamblea Permanente por los Derechos Humanos, Centro de Estudios Legales y Sociales, and Liga Argentina por los Derechos del Hombre.

2. Several analysts have contended that this invasion was intended by the military leadership to freeze growing opposition and to overcome increasing levels of political and social tension. However, historical analysis of the conflict (see Freedman and Gamba-Stonehouse, 1992) indicates that the causes of the military adventure were only partially related to the internal situation and must be clearly distinguished from the aftermath.

3. The following punishments were handed down at the trial of the military commanders: life sentences for General Jorge Rafael Videla and Admiral Emilio Massera, seventeen years in prison for General Viola, eight years for Admiral Lambruschini, and three years and nine months for Brigadier Agosti. The members of the junta that governed between 1979 and 1982 were acquitted because the Court found the evidence against them to be inconclusive.

4. Three uprisings followed: "Monte Caseros," "Villa Martelli," and the last uprising of December 1990. They started as a consequence of the rejection by the *carapintada* sectors of the penalties set for them by the military cupula. Nevertheless, passage of the Law of Due Obedience deprived the *carapintadas* of potential support among the officers. With the recurrence of incidents in which the chain of command was being broken to advance factional interests, entailing great dangers for the future of the army, the sympathy that the *carapintadas* enjoyed among the higher-level officers started to erode.

5. Although the Defense Law explicitly prohibits participation of the Armed Forces in internal intelligence and security, following a guerrilla attack on military installations the Alfonsin government issued various decrees authorizing the Armed Forces to lend logistical support to the Security Forces.

6. For a comparative analysis of the evolution and significance of military industry and resources, see Acuña and Smith (1994).

7. More specifically, the brutality of this repression was significantly less than that in the Chilean or Argentine experiences during the 1970s, yet greater than that inflicted by the Argentine military dictatorship that planned the 1966 coup.

8. Collor dismantled the Servicio Nacional de Informaçoes (National Information Service), thereby neutralizing a structure that had been able to build a chain of command equivalent to that of the Armed Forces and that had placed representatives in all ministries and relevant government departments. He also reduced the military presence in the cabinet, removing three ministers from their office: the head of the Casa Militar, the head of the Joint Major Staff, and the head of Intelligence. In addition, Collor's administration secured passage of a law that regulates the rights of the constitutional powers to demand Armed Forces intervention in internal security matters. Currently, the Armed Forces can become involved in internal conflicts only if the Executive requests their intervention and if the Security Forces are overpowered. This law also states that only the highest authorities of Congress and of the Judiciary can ask the Executive to order military intervention in matters of internal security. Finally, Collor restricted military budgets, a measure that has resulted in conflicts over salaries between the Armed Forces and the government.

9. Note, however, that other projects, such as the development of nuclear explosives, were abandoned as part of the strategy that Collor initiated before signing the Tlatelolco Treaty with Argentina.

10. As of October, the recently inaugurated government, presided over by Fernando Henrique Careloso, promised significant steps to redress or correct these three traditions.

11. The public and massive character that distinguished the first stage of the Chilean repression, as well as the international reactions that it provoked, weighed heavily years later in the Argentine military's choice of repressive strategies. In particular, it "learned" that in order to defer international repercussions and isoltion, repression had to be mainly clandestine. Meanwhile, the Chilean military leadership "learned" from the Argentine military's experiences of the 1960s not to set deadlines for its intervention, so as not to be bound by promises and compromises.

12. These challenges included political isolation generated by foreign reaction to repressive policies, human rights policies implemented by the Carter administration, and the threat of military conflict with Argentina.

13. Keep in mind that most human rights violations in Chile took place between 1973 and 1978. Although repression grew significantly during later periods, it was from 1978 on that military repression became more selective.

14. These constraints are treated in more detail by Garretón in Chapter 3 of this volume.

15. The informal conversations that took place from 1988 on between the leaders of the government and the Concertación dealt with mechanisms for changing the Organic Laws and the constitution. These mechanisms gained implicit legitimacy when, in the 1989 plebiscite, the electorate voted in support of the opposition and against Pinochet's remaining in power.

16. Corradi (1982) notes that the distinctive feature of the authoritarian regimes in the Southern Cone was their capacity to exercise, simultaneously, the two types of systematic and generalized violence that characterize the contemporary world: the violence of the totalitarian state and the violence of the market. As is well known, the economic policies of the Brazilian military governments were not characterized by the neoliberalism that marked the two other cases.

17. The level of contestation is not essential to the definition of the democratic character of a regime. However, once a democratic regime has been established, the level and nature of military contestation of civilian decisions and policies become relevant to establishing the prospects for democratic consolidation.

References

Acuña, Carlos H. (1990). *Intereses empresarios, dictadura y democracia en la Argentina actual (O, por qué la burguesía abandona estrategias autoritarias y opta por la estabilidad democrática).* Buenos Aires: Documento de Trabajo CEDES, vol. 39.

———. (1980). "El 'Diálogo' del Gobierno." *Revista del Centro de Investigación y Acción Social* (Buenos Aires) 29, nos. 295–296 (August-September).

Acuña, Carlos H., and William C. Smith. (1994). "The Politics of 'Military Economics' in the Southern Cone: Comparative Perspectives on Arms Production and the Arms Race Among Argentina, Brazil and Chile." In Lars Schoultz, Augusto Varas, and William Smith (eds.), *Security, Democracy and Development in the Western Hemisphere.* New Brunswick, N.J.: Transaction/North-South Center.

Acuña, Carlos H., and Catalina Smulovitz. (1991). *Ni olvido ni perdón? Derechos humanos y tensiones cívico-militares en la transición democrática Argentina.* Buenos Aires: Documento CEDES, vol. 69.

Barros, Robert. (1992). "Dictatorship and the Rule of Law: A Chilean Exception?" Mimeo. University of Chicago (January).

Camps, Ramón. (1981). "Apogeo y declinación de la guerrilla en la Argentina." *La Prensa* (January 4).

Corradi, Juan. (1982). "The Mode of Destruction: Terror in Argentina." *Telos* 54 (1982–1983): 67.

Fontana, Andrés. (1987). "Political Decision Making by a Military Corporation: Argentina 1976–1983." Ph.D. dissertation, University of Texas, Austin.

Freedman, Lawrence, and Virginia Gamba-Stonehouse. (1992). *Señales de guerra: El conflicto de las Islas Malvinas de 1982.* Buenos Aires: Javier Vergara.

Frontalini, Daniel, and María Cristina Caiati. (1984). *El mito de la Guerra Sucia.* Buenos Aires: Centro de Estudios Legales y Sociales.

González Bombal, Inés. (1991). *El diálogo político: La transición que no fue.* Buenos Aires: Documento CEDES, vol. 61.

Guest, Ian. (1990). *Behind the Disappearances: Argentina's Dirty War Against Human Rights and the United Nations.* Philadelphia: University of Pennsylvania Press.

Mignone, Emilio. (1990). "Derechos humanos y transición democrática en la sociedad Argentina." Mimeo. New Haven: Schell Center, Yale University.

Namuncura Serrano, Domingo. (1991). "Derechos humanos en Chile: Tensiones cívico militares en el camino por establecer la verdad." Mimeo. Buenos Aires: CEDES.

Stepan, Alfred. (1988). *Rethinking Military Politics: Brazil and the Southern Cone.* Princeton: Princeton University Press.

Uriarte, Claudio. (1992). *Almirante cero: Biografía no autorizada de Emilio Eduardo Massera.* Buenos Aires: Planeta, Espejo de la Argentina.

3

Human Rights in Democratization Processes

MANUEL ANTONIO GARRETÓN

This chapter explores the problem of human rights in processes of political democratization—specifically, with reference to transitions from military to democratic regimes in the Southern Cone of Latin America. The analysis is historically bounded rather than general in its method of inquiry. Clearly, the construction of such an analysis cannot be undertaken without consideration of the diversity of human rights experiences; democratization in these countries is but one such experience.

Four central topics are examined here. The first pertains to the nature of the human rights problem in democratic transitions. The second and third topics concern, respectively, the measures that are carried out during such transitions and their impact on human rights outcomes. The last deals with the prospects for debates about human rights issues in processes of democratic consolidation.

It is worth noting at the outset that human rights are basically historical-cultural constructs centering on the "right to life." The values projected onto these constructs are attributed to life and become unrenounceable conquests for humanity. Recognition of these values is disparate from one era and culture to another, and generally takes into account the struggles to universalize values and principles that are initially the privilege of the particular groups that have articulated them.[1]

We should also recall that experiences of political democratization entail processes of democratic regime construction, which in turn can take a variety of different forms such as democratic foundations, transitions from an authoritarian regime to a democratic one, or extensions and deepenings of democratic institutions as they evolve from semi-authoritarian regimes or restricted democracies. The experiences of political democratization in the countries considered here include two fundamental processes: transition from authoritarian-military regimes, and consolidation of the democratic regimes that result from such transitions (Garretón, 1991a).

HUMAN RIGHTS IN TRANSITIONS TO DEMOCRACY

The first topic introduced at the beginning of the chapter concerns the nature of the human rights problem in processes of democratization. In Latin American societies of recent decades, abuses of the military regimes have led to human rights concerns among the population. This is not to deny the historical incidence of human rights problems. Rather, the systematic nature of repression under these regimes represents a step backward, one that has placed at the center of societal concern the problem of life in its elemental, almost biological dimension of survival or physical integrity. It is this regression that has been challenged in the name of human rights.

Central to the human rights problem in democratic transitions is the military regime that is left behind. Indeed, it is necessary to resolve in the present a problem of the past—namely, the human rights violations that occurred under the authoritarian or military regime, whose principal subjects were the victims of repression. The concern here is not so much with present and future conditions that would ensure the achievement of human rights (which are considered to have been secured with the disappearance of the military regime and the installation of a democratic one) as with the imperative to deal with an unresolved issue. In short, Nunca Más (Never Again) is less a program for the future than a denunciation of the past, since the future seems guaranteed by the very conditions that define all democracies.

Thus the human rights question is a problem not of the new regime itself but of inheritance, a legacy of the previous regime. It constitutes one of several authoritarian enclaves present in nascent democracy; yet it is not the only one. Indeed, postauthoritarian situations generally exhibit three other inherited enclaves. One of these is the institutional legacy—that is, the coexistence of democratic norms with constitutional or legislative provisions that limit democratic practice. A second enduring feature of the postauthoritarian landscape is its political actors, organizations, and social sectors, principally those in or linked to the military, which are not wholly integrated into the democratic game and sometimes even conspire against it. The third enclave is less characteristic of Latin American countries that experienced the "new authoritarianism" of the military than of societies in the region with no previous experience of democracy (including those in which authoritarianism has spanned several generations). It is the generalized presence of antidemocratic or authoritarian values, mentalities, and attitudes that characterizes this third enclave. (Garretón, 1989).

In processes of transition and democratization, then, the issue of human rights emerges in the context of the need to elaborate a comprehensive strategy to overcome several authoritarian enclaves that persist despite the experience of regime change. Whether explicitly or implicitly, this strategy recognizes the interconnectedness of these enclaves. Though at a given moment priority may be assigned to overcoming one or another, it is understood that authoritarian enclaves can be surmounted only if they are treated comprehensively. Failure to overcome these enclaves renders the transition incomplete and handicaps the new democratic regime. Indeed, if the enclaves persist, the tasks of democratic consolidation, which involve social democratization and modernization, and sometimes relatively profound economic reforms as well, are slowed or obstructed.

Yet this first dilemma involving issues of human rights in processes of political transition and democratization overlaps with another, creating what could be labeled the dilemma of two intertwined logics or rationalities. On the one hand, there is an ethical-symbolic logic, which proposes a radical solution suggesting the reconstitution of the situation that existed prior to the massive violation of human rights by authoritarian regimes. Given the practical impossibility of that position, however, the ethical-symbolic logic leads to demands for maximum truth, for the diffusion of information about the crimes that were committed, for trial and punishment of those who were responsible, and for the greatest possible institutional and symbolic reparation to the victims. This is a principle that cannot be achieved and whose utopian charge takes on all the ethical, epic, doctrinaire, and radical baggage of the ideology of human rights as it has developed in the West. The ethical-symbolic logic reflects the principle of all the struggles against authoritarianism and military regimes, struggles that privilege the actors expressed in and represented by human rights movements. Democracy becomes identified and confused with—indeed, subordinated to—human rights.

On the other hand, there is a politico-statist logic, which basically centers upon the conquest and maintenance of a democratic regime, considering such a regime not only the *sine qua non* for resolving the inherited human rights problem but also the guarantee of avoiding violations in the future. Here, the issue of human rights is subordinated to that of democracy, inasmuch as the central concerns are the carrying out and consolidation of the transition from authoritarianism to democracy. Those who emphasize this logic are more often political than social actors and, usually, are located within the state.

If the specter haunting the ethical-symbolic logic consists of forgetting and impunity, the greatest fear of adherents of the politico-statist logic is authoritarian regression. Taking the metaphor to its extreme, one can say that there is a hidden reciprocal blackmail between the two competing logics. Some will claim that the radical solution to the human rights problem invites authoritarian regression, whereas others will contend that if the human rights issue is not resolved, democracy will lack legitimacy. In the context of struggles against authoritarianism these logics appear fused, as the ethical logic predominates. Though ultimately rooted in the ethical logic, the political logic seems to predominate in the behavior of actors during transitions, with the ethical dimension being postponed until the moment of democratic inauguration. Once the transition has generated a democratic regime, however, the latent contradiction between these two principles is translated into open conflict between the state actor (democratic government) and the social actor (the human rights movement). The democratic movement and the human rights movement, previously identified as one, become divided by this contradiction, although of course the intensity of this conflict varies from case to case.

The considerations outlined here permit us to reflect on some general characteristics of the human rights issue. Ultimately, there cannot be, nor has there been historically, a definitive solution to the general problem of human rights violations under military regimes. The issue involves an irreparable historic ill. In this sense, no transition can be completely successful in dealing with this specific problem, even when the transition culminates in an authentically democratic regime and even when the democracy is consolidated. This is a problem that cannot be resolved, even when it ceases to be defined as a problem. Nevertheless, it is precisely the inclusion of human rights as part of the strategic challenge of overcoming authoritarian enclaves, and the simultaneous presence of the two logics outlined earlier, that makes possible the generation of criteria for evaluating and analyzing the different human rights solutions that societies have put forth in postauthoritarian situations. Stated differently, these solutions should be contextualized in terms of the means by which each democratization process has attempted to overcome authoritarian enclaves, and in terms of assessments of the degree to which different combinations of the two logics have generated partial success.

HUMAN RIGHTS POLICIES IN PROCESSES
OF DEMOCRATIZATION: THE CHILEAN CASE

Our second topic concerns actions that are carried out with regard to human rights during processes of democratization. In considering the experience of the Chilean democratic government, we recall that the program of the Concertación de Partidos por la Democracia, the political base for President Aylwin's government inaugurated in March 1990, was a classically radical program that highlighted the principles of *Truth, Justice, and Reparation.*[2] The concept of truth was aimed at the entire society, that of justice was directed at the military, and the reparation addressed the victims of human rights violations.

A first element of ambiguity in this relatively consensual program was the introduction of the concept of reconciliation, which has tended to be superimposed upon and at times to replace the concept of justice (Viera Gallo and Sánchez, 1988).[3] A second element of ambiguity arose with regard to the government's need to deal with the problem of political prisoners who remained incarcerated, in that discussions of amnesty could stimulate the military and its civilian bloc of support to advocate a general amnesty, thus closing the book on the question of human rights.[4] Finally, a third element of ambiguity arose from the degree to which the elements of justice and reparation were considered negotiable by the relevant actors.[5]

Despite the high priority given to human rights by such rhetoric, this approach to human rights issues did not form a part of any comprehensive strategy of overcoming authoritarian enclaves. As shown elsewhere (Garretón, 1991b), no such comprehensive strategy existed; instead, these enclaves were the subject of a piecemeal, tactical, and gradual approach. In other words, there was a failure to consider authoritarian enclaves in their entirety. Thus, although the principles and policies of the Aylwin government appeared quite radical, given the existence of a position and a proposal for addressing each enclave, in practice there was no overarching strategy for addressing the authoritarian legacy. This situation led necessarily to essentially reactive responses to demands and problems that arose conjuncturally at the level of the individual enclaves.

The process of dismantling the enclaves was bogged down as a result, yet important advances occurred in each of these dimensions. For example, in the case of the institutional enclave, no political-institutional reforms were advanced at the beginning of the government's term of office, and the democratization of the municipalities was achieved only during the middle of that period. As for the military enclave, although the political isolation of Pinochetism is undoubtedly a great achievement, it has not been accompanied by institutional modifications in civil-military relations.

This observation concerning the general treatment of the enclaves is also valid with regard to the specific problem of human rights: A basically ethical stance was taken initially, entailing creative and worthwhile responses accompanied by a solid position on the ethical and symbolic plane, but there was no coherent, comprehensive human rights strategy. Thus, the first problem that arose was that of the political prisoners. This problem forced the government to react defensively by enacting specific laws on the issue, which in turn provided an opportunity for the rightist opposition to propose a general amnesty. The broader effort to deal with human rights by means of the Commission for Truth and Reconciliation was another such reaction; but this one, inspired by the president, was not based upon a clear vision of the commission's potential achievements or foreseeable effects. Symptomatic of this lack of strategic clarity, as distinct from the vigor of the ethical position, is the fact that these reforms became mired in and partially absorbed by discussions of terrorism and personal security, issues that were placed on the political agenda primarily through the efforts of the rightist opposition.

This is not to deny the considerable action taken on the human rights front. Indeed, there have been great achievements, even though the expectations of organizations active in the field, and of the public more generally, have not been satisfied. It is useful to point out several factors that, considered in hindsight, provided the outlines of policy for dealing with human rights issues.

First, there was a highly worthwhile and consistent symbolic politics, emanating directly from the highest levels of the state, that sought to put an end to generalized trauma and underscored the dual idea of symbolic justice and reparation together with the reconciliation of society with the past. For example the beginning of the government's term of office was celebrated through dissemination of the names of detained and disappeared people from across the entire country, as well as through a dance performed by the female relatives; the vice-president inaugurated a monument to the victims in the central patio of the General Cemetery; and public television broadcasts revealed the human rights situation under the military regime. In this vein, the creation of the Commission for Truth and Reconciliation, also known as the Rettig Commission, was extremely important. Charged with investigating human rights violations that resulted in deaths or disappearances, the commission issued a widely disseminated report that enabled the government both to present the issue to the country and to request a national response (Garretón, 1991b). This report analyzed the causes of human rights violations; described these violations accurately; examined the behavior of the security services, the Armed Forces, and the Judiciary; and proposed a series of measures designed to prevent the recurrence of such violations. The report also led to creation of a public agency charged with conducting further research on the fate of missing people.

Second, a series of institutional measures have addressed directly some of the most urgent human rights problems. Laws and constitutional reforms have been enacted with the aim of reaching a judicial solution, albeit a partial one, to the problem of political prisoners (a solution that hinges on restoration of the president's capacity to pardon). During the Aylwin administration 135 pardons were conceded. By January 1994, only 12 people imprisoned on political grounds by the military regime were still in jail, and 5 applications for pardons were pending (Fundación de Ayuda Social, 1994).

Similarly, a partial reorientation of military justice has occurred, making it possible to conduct some trials through civilian courts rather than through military tribunals. Nonetheless, many of these cases remain under the jurisdiction of military courts, a situation that deteriorated even further following military pressures in late 1993. According to certain reports disseminated by human rights organizations (Fundación de Ayuda Social, 1994), civilian judges have abstained from calling upon military officials to testify in human rights cases. In the same reports, military courts are accused of having defended their prerogatives vis-à-vis civilian tribunals, and the Supreme Court is described as having repeatedly endorsed military court decisions to apply the Amnesty Law to specific cases without pursuing investigations.

Laws have also been enacted to provide legal reparation for victims of repression under the military regime, including people driven into exile, people driven from their jobs in public administration, and families of the missing and disappeared. In particular, the Aylwin government created the Oficina Nacional del Retorno (National Office for the Return), which has helped more than 18,000 exiles and their families to return to Chile (Revista Ya, 1994). These individuals, numbering more than 50,000 in all, have benefited from a wide range of compensatory measures, including legislation on eduational and degree equivalency, exemptions from customs duties for home and work tools, loans for economic projects linked to their occupations, medical services, and scholarships. The same benefits were made available to exiles who returned to Chile on their own, without assistance from the government's program.[6]

For those people expelled from the public administration, the reparation process has been very slow and the benefits in terms of social security have been more symbolic than effective. Their difficulties in gaining access to these benefits, as well as the poor quality of the benefits themselves, have resulted from the manner in which the reparation law was approved. In fact, the right wing opposition was more interested in receiving credit for the law than in providing reparations for human rights violations. Experience has shown that this law must be reformed if its objectives are to be fulfilled.

One of the most controversial measures of the reparation policy was the legislation on economic compensation to families of victims listed in the Rettig Report. The report precipitated not only judicial reconsideration of several cases included in its study but also the creation of an agency to continue investigations and to pursue the reparation issue within the restrictive legal framework.[7] The most significant cases of human rights violations not covered by the 1978 Amnesty Law remain under consideration in the courts. Their outcomes will likely vary, depending on the judges hearing the case and the erratic rulings of the higher courts. We will return to this point later in the chapter.

In the meantime, it is worth noting a series of measures that are being studied, discussed, or partially applied, based on the range of human rights concerns inherited from the old regime. These include parliamentary discussion of proposed judicial reforms, very slow and gradual restructuring of the security services, and the incorporation of the subject of human rights into educational curricula.

The Institutional Problem

Two critical problems must be taken into account in order to explain the limited extent of human rights policies in Chile and the obstacles they have confronted. The first is institutional; the second, political. The institutional problem constrains policy options and undermines the political will for achieving the program of Truth, Justice, and Reparation. The political problem, in turn, greatly hampers efforts to change the institutional framework. Notwithstanding the significant advances that have taken place to date, particularly in terms of truth and reparation but also along the ethical-symbolic dimension, we must recognize that the institutional limits make impossible a real policy of justice.

One aspect of the institutional problem is the juridical framework. Recall that the democratic government inherited the institutional framework set up by the military in order to prevent any policy designed to punish, or even to investigate, the crimes committed by the authorities during the Pinochet regime. Two provisions are central to this framework. One is the 1978 Amnesty Law, which covered the period from 1973 to 1978. The heyday of Pinochet's secret military police, the Dirreción Nacional de Inteligencia (DINA), this period was characterized by harsh repression of the dictatorship and widespread disappearances. The other provision is the series of norms that assigned specific privileges to military courts, both in cases concerning members of the military and in some offenses perpetrated by civilians.

The second aspect of the institutional problem concerns the behavior of the courts. The composition of the Supreme Court has not changed; indeed, the country's highest tribunal retains the ideological biases that prevailed during the years when it routinely upheld the arbitrariness of the military government. The erratic and indulgent attitude of the Court toward offenses by the military is demonstrated by the fact that almost all of its trials have resulted in impunity for the accused officers. This attitude on the part of the Supreme Court has tended to discourage Appellate Court judges from persisting in their investigations and judicial inquiries into human rights issues. At the same time, the continuing requirement that Military Tribunals conduct all trials involving the military ensures that cases are closed without investigation, since military judges invariably invoke the 1978 Amnesty Law.

The foregoing suggests little hope for the prospect that the judicial system will play a constructive role in ensuring that justice is served in cases of human rights violations under the military regime. However, crucial changes occurred in 1994 as a result of honest interventions on the part of some judges who, remaining within the strict boundaries of the law and the existing institutional framework, have opened a road to justice that could destroy the structure of impunity built by the military and its allies in the Judiciary. In two different cases concerning missing people, an Appellate Court judge has challenged the legitimacy of the 1978 amnesty, based on the argument that international pacts signed by Chile (namely, the Geneva Pact and the International Agreement on Civil and Political Rights) prevail over national laws, particularly in a situation that was tantamount to civil war.[8] These pacts state that inhumane treatment of prisoners and such crimes as disappearances cannot be subject to the Amnesty Law. The Supreme Court has yet to reach a definitive position regarding this ruling, but clearly the door has been opened to a review of old cases in which the Amnesty Law had resulted in impunity for perpetrators of human rights violations.[9]

Two other important cases illustrate the degree to which human rights policies depend on the attitudes and behavior of judges and on the role of the Supreme Court. One concerns the *degollados,* three communist leaders who were decapitated in 1985 in a case involving the high command of the police. A serious investigation was performed by a judge who did not turn over the case to military justice, but the Supreme Court's decision is still pending as of December 1995. The current expectation is that the case is unlikely to generate as rigorous a judgment as the evidence would seem to demand.

The second case, involving the murder of former Foreign Affairs Minister Orlando Letelier and his secretary, Ronni Moffit, perpetrated in 1976 by the DINA in Washington, D.C., is considered highly symbolic by both the government and the military. Crucial to relations between the United States and Chile, as well as between the Chilean government and military, this case was explicitly excluded from the Amnesty Law because of pressure by the U.S. government. Yet the Supreme Court would not approve a U.S. extradition request once the director of the DINA, General Manuel Contreras, was determined to have been responsible for this terrorist act. The Letelier family initiated a trial in Chile, with support from the Aylwin government. After three years of investigation, Judge Adolfo Bañados sentenced General Contreras and an accomplice to prison terms of seven and six years, respectively. As the case awaits appeal, General Contreras also faces accusations by the Italian government of involvement in the attempted murder of the former minister of the interior, Christian Democrat Bernardo Leighton. The Supreme Court upheld the sentences, even though it was subject to extreme pressure from the military, which invited General Contreras to official ceremonies despite Judge Bañados' ruling and expressed "preoccupation" over the prospect of his being jailed. By January 1995 these circumstances had already created an important political problem, and tensions remained after the Supreme Court decision. Whereas Espinoza promptly began serving his sentence in a special military prison built specifically to house officials charged with human rights abuse, for most of 1995 General Contreras managed to avoid imprisonment through a protracted and politically charged confrontation with the government. Having been admitted to a naval hospital far from Santiago, he remained beyond the reach of civilian authorities until late October when, in a major triumph for the principle of constitutional rule, he began serving his sentence.

Changes in the judicial sphere and the constructive attitude of several judges have the potential to move the Judiciary beyond the complicity with which it has acted in recent decades, thus increasing the possibility that greater justice will be achieved in human rights cases. But this solution within the judicial branch itself is insufficient in the absence of reforms designed to adjust the institutional framework to democratic conditions. Such reforms would have to include a reinterpretation or abandonment of the 1978 amnesty, the adaptation of national laws to the terms of international accords, and a drastic curtailment of the prerogatives of military courts. Of course, all of these measures depend on political factors.

The Political Problem

Behind the institutional problem lies the political one. At stake is the capacity of the democratic government to change the institutional framework, to reform the Judiciary, and to neutralize pressures from the military in order to carry out its program of Truth, Justice, and Reparation without abandoning the goal of reconciliation or weakening democratic legitimacy.

An initial obstacle is found within the coalition of parties that support the government, for the coalition is torn between the two logics referred to at the outset of this chapter. On the one hand, the alliance—especially the left-leaning parties of the Concertación—represents the victims of human rights violations under Pinochet. On the other hand, the Concertación itself supports a government that not only must avoid an authoritarian regression and overcome authoritarian enclaves but also must achieve an ambitious program of modernization and social democratization. The way in which these two logics are internalized and understood is different for each component of the coalition, depending largely on experiences prior to the transition.

Two additional obstacles are perhaps more important and more difficult to overcome. First, in order to enact legislation to change the institutional framework, the Concertación must reach agreements with the rightist opposition. This is so because the electoral system, in combination with the continued presence of senators appointed by the Pinochet regime, prevents the Concertación from gaining a congressional majority, even though it receives a majority of votes cast in elections. Yet cooperation from the two major parties of the right—the *Unión Democrática Independiente* (UDI) and the *Renovación Nacional* (RN)—is highly uncertain. The UDI, in particular, but also important sectors of the RN insist on remaining loyal to the "legacy" of military government. In practice, this insistence engenders a highly skeptical attitude toward human rights issues and a desire not to risk any change that would diminish the impunity of the military. Although some sectors of the RN also proclaim a commitment to democratic consolidation and are sensitive to the problem of past abuses of human rights, they remain a minority of the right. The attitudes and alliances of the rightist parties will likely combine to deny a congressional majority in support of institutional changes that can bring about a definitive solution to the human rights problem.

The other obstacle is even more complicated and serious. Because no institutional change has taken place within the military, Pinochet remains commander in chief of the Armed Forces, and some officers involved in human rights crimes have not yet retired. As a result, the Armed Forces, particularly the army, have given no sign of self-criticism or repentance over past behavior. On the contrary, they constantly recall their actions with pride and acknowledge only certain rare "excesses" that have already resulted in punishment. It is difficult, indeed, to generate a real and comprehensive solution to the human rights problem when the key actor refuses to recognize its responsibility. In this situation, reconciliation—that is, of Chileans who had been divided into human rights violators and victims—seems impossible.

TAKING STOCK: TRUTH, JUSTICE, AND REPARATION

The third topic introduced at the outset of this chapter concerns the impact on human right outcomes of measures taken during democratic transitions. Although the Rettig Report contained a significant amount of widely disseminated information on the issue of truth, as well as on the topic of reparation, it referred only to cases of disappearances or assassinations. To be sure, the report stimulated a wide range of subsequent inquiries that have sometimes uncovered the facts about specific disappearances and murders. But because the Amnesty Law grants immunity for all offenses committed from 1973 to 1978, judges have an easy pretext for avoiding investigations. An important demand of human rights organizations, with support from political leaders, has been the repeal of the Amnesty Law. A petition drive sought to generate pressure toward this end, yet the Aylwin government proved reluctant to take concrete action. Despite its endorsement of an interpretation of existing law that would permit investigation, the government has chosen not to propose specific legislation intended to achieve this objective.

Thus, whereas some advances have occurred in the areas of truth and reparation, the issue of justice, entailing the punishment of guilty parties, has least fulfilled the expectations of the public and of the principal social actors involved in human rights.

In this regard, it is interesting to consider some public opinion data evaluating the human rights situation. In a poll conducted at the end of 1991 with a sample from several cities, people were asked what missing factors prevented Chile from having a true democracy. The largest number of respondents (26.1 percent) indicated the prosecution of those guilty of human rights violations, surpassing the numbers who cited a change in the electoral system (24.3 percent), termination of the permanence in power of the commander in chief of the Armed Forces (22.4 percent), elimination of designated senators (15.4 percent), resolution of the problem of political prisoners (3.7 percent), and elimination of the National Security Council (2.1 percent). The rate of nonresponse was 6.1 percent. A year later the identical question yielded similar results, with prosecution of the guilty the first issue mentioned as a deficit for democracy (24.5 percent), comparable only to the proportion of respondents who believed that no factors were missing (24.2 percent) and far above the proportion responding to other issues (Garretón, Lagos and Méndez, 1992). By 1994, the latter percentage had reached 29 percent, but preliminary data also suggest that an increasing portion of the population believes that problems of human rights left over from the military regime constitute the most serious issue affecting the democratic regime (Garretón, Lagos, and Méndez, 1992).

Another survey, conducted in Greater Santiago in April 1992, found similar results concerning the public's expectations about human rights and its frustration with outcomes. Specifically, the government's record on confronting human rights violations committed under the military regime was assessed as follows: 17.9 percent of the respondents believed that the truth had been clarified and justice carried out; 53.3 percent believed that there was truth but no justice; 16.2 percent believed that there was neither truth nor justice; 3.2 percent believed that no human rights violations had taken place under the previous regime; and 9.3 percent had no opinion. As for the Rettig Report, 79.1 percent claimed to know of it or to have heard of it and 20.9 percent had not heard of it. Yet only 6.2 percent believed that the report resolved the human rights problem; 60.1 percent considered it to be a step toward resolution; and 29.6 percent said that it did not resolve the problem. Regarding the problem of political prisoners, 10.6 percent said that it had been resolved; 71.6 percent said that it had not been resolved; 6.2 percent said that no such problem existed; and 11.1 percent said that they did not know whether the report had resolved the problem.

Concerning the public debate about the future of the human rights issue, 13 percent of the respondents said that it is necessary to get past the human rights problem; 17.9 percent preferred to clarify the truth and then to declare an amnesty; 60 percent were in favor of clarifying the truth and punishing the guilty; and 8.3 percent did not respond. Evaluations of the Judiciary were as follows: 47.8 percent said that the existing courts would provide neither truth nor justice; 29.2 percent said that the courts had guaranteed both truth and justice; 6.6 percent said that no human rights problems were pending; and 16 percent did not respond. With respect to the functioning of the justice system, 14.2 percent considered it acceptable and 30.8 percent attributed its problems to a lack of resources, but 50.3 percent indicated that the system of justice always favors the powerful.[10] It was precisely this negative evaluation of the Judiciary, reflected in all the surveys, that prompted the government following publication of the Rettig Report to concentrate on judicial reform, essentially attacking the problem at its weakest link.

To this assessment of public opinion it is necessary to add the criticisms of the government's policy lodged by human rights organizations (Fruhling and Orellana, 1991; Bravo, 1992). These groups decried the insufficiency of measures taken in the area of truth, particularly the Amnesty Law and restriction of the problem to cases involving disappeared and assassinated people. In the area of justice, they denounced the persistence of impunity due to the absence of trials and punishments. Similarly, they pointed to the continued legal obstacles in the way of reparations as well as to their limited scope. It is striking to note, however, that the radical positions expressed in public opinion and the frustrated expectations of both the general public and the human rights organizations have not been accompanied by actions, mobilizations, or pressures of similar intensity. It would seem that frustration coexists with an indestructible ethical reserve that is not converted into political capital or any practical political orientation.

Hence we are led to conclude that not much more official action will be taken in the human rights area. Even though legal investigations will continue to throw light on events that occurred under the military regime, human rights aspirations will remain unsatisfied. In turn, the human rights issue itself will likely lose significance, even though neither the officials nor the social actors involved in this issue believe that the problems have been overcome. Yet so long as the issue remains unresolved, it will continue to be a constant feature of public debate and consciousness, surfacing in different ways and in different circumstances, often under the guise of contexts that at first glance would appear to have little connection to human rights.

A situation that commenced in 1991 and unfolded in 1993 demonstrates the risks posed by issues left pending by the authoritarian regime and not confronted effectively by the democratic government. Recall that in August 1991, specifically as a result of the Rettig Report and the military reactions to it—which had led to a political impasse—the government declared that the transition had ended and that the problems of the future and of democratic consolidation would now be given priority. Then, in May 1993, taking advantage of a European trip by the president, the army carried out a maneuver known as the *boinazo* (during which it paraded in the street wearing special campaign uniforms) that was explicitly intended to demonstrate the military's discontent with the growing number of high officials and other officers who were being named in trials dealing with human rights violations. A basic theme of the incomplete transition thus resurfaced in a conflictive setting that obliged the government to acknowledge that incompleteness.

In addition to recognizing that its 1991 declaration had been a political error, the government responded by initiating a series of meetings with key figures in military, political, judicial, and human rights circles, in the hopes of reaching a definitive resolution to the human rights problem before the end of Aylwin's term in March 1994. Among the solutions that were proposed but rejected by the government were the Ley de Punto Final, the abrogation or reinterpretation of the Amnesty Law, and the setting of deadlines for trials. In the absence of consensus, the president chose to submit legislation to Parliament calling for an acceleration of trials, the creation of special ministers of the judicial branch to accomplish this end, and guarantees of secrecy for individuals who provided information on the whereabouts of people who had disappeared from police custody. The Christian Democrats and some sectors of the right supported the project; however, it failed to satisfy the military and was rejected by human rights organizations, which saw it as leading to impunity and as caving in to military pressure. In what many considered to be the first serious schism at the heart of the governing coalition, both the Socialist Party and the Party for Democracy opposed the project. Modifications introduced in the Chamber of Deputies, especially those limiting secrecy for informants, led the president to withdraw the legislation, convinced that there was insufficient consensus in the country to resolve such a deeply rooted problem.

Meanwhile, as noted earlier, the courts continued to respond erratically to pending human rights cases—in some instances, placing them under the jurisdiction of ordinary courts; in others, assigning them to military courts; in still others, furthering investigations or falling back on the Amnesty Law. With regard to the justice principle, then, since the end of the first government of the Concertación the country has increasingly witnessed a diminished involvement of elected officials and a "privatization of the human rights issue" (Bengoa, 1994).

Recent experience thus confirms the three basic affirmations set forth in this chapter concerning the Chilean case as an illustration of dilemmas shared by many postauthoritarian societies. First, the human rights issue represents part of a situation of transition rendered incomplete by the continued presence of authoritarian enclaves, which in turn need to be treated with a comprehensive strategy. Second, despite progress toward democratic consolidation in Chile, there has been no effective strategy to complete the transition. Third, despite the climate of democratic coexistence created by partial advances in dealing with the human rights issue, there has been no coherent human rights strategy. The result is the failure to resolve the human rights issue or to prevent the political complications outlined earlier.

CONCLUSION: HUMAN RIGHTS IN DEMOCRATIC CONSOLIDATION

Our fourth and final topic concerns the prospects for the human rights issue in processes of democratic consolidation. As noted, this issue was defined in terms of the specific problem of what to do about violations that occurred under preceding military regimes. In this sense, the principle of *nunca más* (never again) was defined in practical terms as a symbolic and institutional exorcism of the past. Since the problem was cast in absolute terms, solutions could be only partial and insufficient. Nevertheless, as the Chilean case illustrates, this insufficiency has not impeded the progress of democratic transition and consolidation, despite the bitterness with which those most concerned with human rights have responded to the postauthoritarian regime. Of course, no one knows what the consequences of a more radical human rights policy would have been for the general success of democratization in Chile.

In any case, a more comprehensive and definitive solution would have to involve political parties, the government, Parliament, human rights organizations, and victims of violations. In particular, it would be necessary to reopen public debate involving all these different actors with a shared interest in human rights issues. If such debate does not occur, there is a risk that the conflict would be privatized, thereby favoring the status quo of impunity. And as already discussed, the problems engendered by this option would be significant indeed.

In this context, it is interesting to compare the Chilean situation with two other cases of postauthoritarian regimes in which more general but less satisfactory solutions were attempted. In Argentina, the first decisions taken by the Alfonsín democratic government and the judiciary were very radical. The top leaders of the military regime were imprisoned, and a host of trials were held in which military officials were accused of crimes and called upon to testify. As Carlos Acuña and Catalina Smulovitz discuss in Chapter 2 of this volume, the results included a serious backlash from the military and subsequent enactment of the law of "Punto Final," which sought to close the book on the human rights issue. Years later, a democratically elected president freed the imprisoned military leaders. In Uruguay, the amnesty negotiated with the military was challenged by the population, which forced a plebiscite that upheld the amnesty. Here, the solution—

whether one judges it positively or negatively—was legitimated by the people's will as expressed in the plebiscite. The lesson of both experiences is that there are serious risks for the principle of justice if a comprehensive solution to the human rights problem is attempted. As the Chilean case shows, however, partial and gradual solutions are also ineffective. Herein lies the tragic paradox facing much of Latin America in the postauthoritarian period.

In democratic consolidation, the issue of *nunca más* takes on prospective connotations, encompassing not only the avoidance of authoritarian regressions but also the desire to improve life according to the ethical principles embodied in the concept of human rights. The dilemma faced during democratic consolidation is whether to seek justice for past violations of human rights or, given the difficulties inherent in pursuing justice under such circumstances, to concentrate instead on preventing violations in the future. Yet regardless of how the dilemma is resolved, prevention of further violations requires reformation of the two institutions that made human rights violations possible under dictatorships or authoritarian regimes: the military and the Judiciary. In other words, what must be achieved is a drastic revision and reformulation of the coercive dimension of the state. These reforms are located in the conjunction of the *nunca más* of the past and the *nunca más* of the future, inasmuch as the latter precludes a repetition of the former.

Another question worth considering is whether it is possible to reformulate the human rights problem beyond the definition—made necessary under military regimes—of the "right to life" in terms of survival and physical integrity. This question arises from the construct noted at the outset of the chapter: Human rights are fundamentally a cultural projection of the "right to life," which in turn entails the right to a "good" or "livable" life. This reformulation would imply at least three dimensions.

First, human rights must be extended to the entire population. Here, questions regarding education, work, poverty, inequality, and access to justice begin to play a primary role in the transcendence of barriers to the extension of human rights to the entire population. In this case, social democratization and equitable development complement political democracy in the ideology of human rights (CEPAL, 1992).

Second, the fundamental challenge is no longer to ensure the minimal conditions consistent with the right to life for all citizens. Instead, it is to transform those conditions. Today, the issue of human rights is posed not only in terms of avoiding their violation or ensuring their fulfillment but also in terms of a set of rights consisting of multiple dimensions. The right to an education is no longer the right to just any education, and the same applies with regard to work and other aspects of human rights. Of relevance here is not just social and political democratization but a redefinition of modernity, conceived as an affirmation and expansion of individual and collective subjectivity (Touraine, 1992; Garretón, 1992a).

Finally, beyond the extension and deepening of quality, there is a human rights issue concerning discrimination. In this case the problem is not the extension of rights applicable to all but the generation, preservation, and development of rights that exist by virtue of membership in a social category (e.g., the rights of children, the elderly, women, ethnic minorities, and so on). But this conceptualization is based on particularity and difference, thus inverting the theory and ideology of human rights that is founded on the inalienable nature of the "human being." Would these rights, then, be human rights for some and not for others—essentially, human rights that are "dispensable" for the social categories not included? Any response to this question implies a fundamental revision of the theory and practice of human rights (Aylwin, 1992).

In referring to the quality of human rights and to rights associated with social categories, we must clarify the fact that we are dealing not with old discriminations, and thus with the practical extension or universalization of existing categories of rights, but rather with the emergence of a new definition of human rights (Garretón, 1992b). If the issue has to do with discrimination, the appropriate response would be to extend human rights to discriminated sectors, and the formulas and mechanisms for doing so are part of the patrimony and the collective memory of society and discriminated subjects. But the focus is different if our concern is with new human rights. Then the issue becomes the type of society that permits the specification and promotion of rights that come from collective identities, from the fact of belonging to a sociocultural category—indeed, from the simple fact of being human.

The various utopias known to us at this point in history have aspired to fashion societies in which rights arising from equalities and liberties were guaranteed. Today all of these utopias are in crisis. But, none of them provided blueprints of societies that ensured the fulfillment of these new rights, which are not reducible to equality and liberty. In such circumstances, rather than to think about models of society in which these rights would be made effective, we must think about principles and mechanisms that would allow their defense and development. These principles include positive discrimination in favor of social categories subject to these rights, transfer of power to social actors themselves so that they can specify and promote these rights while strengthening mechanisms of representation, and an active role for the state in proclaiming and protecting these rights. All of which brings us closer to a reformulation of the relationship between human rights and democracy, and to a new dimension of democratization processes in postauthoritarian societies.

Notes

Portions of this chapter were prepared for UNESCO, Division of Human Rights, Democracy and Peace, January 1995. The *Journal of Latin American Studies* 26 (1994) published an earlier, shorter version by permission. The author thanks Malva Espinosa for her collaboration and the Center for Analysis of Public Policies at the University of Chile for its support.

1. See Vicaría de la Solidaridad (1978) for a conceptualization of this point.

2. This coalition platform is outlined in Concertación de Partidos por la Democracia (1989).

3. An important use of the term *reconciliation* can be found in the Bishops' documents and in the Rettig Report.

4. This issue is treated explicitly in the "Programa de Gobierno" of the Concertación de Partidos por la Democracia (1989).

5. See Ministerio Secretaría General de Gobierno (1991). The proposal for a response from the country to the report was made in the president's presentation speech on March 4, 1991.

6. The National Office for the Return estimates that 150,000 exiles remained abroad as of the end of 1994 (Revista Ya, 1994).

7. The FASIC (Federation of Chilean Investigative Lawyers) team of lawyers has provided counsel in 201 cases involving 618 victims, including the well-known cases of Father Joan Alsina, Juan Meneses Reyes and Ricardo Lagos Salinas before the Comisión Interamericana de Derechos Humanos, as well as that of General Carlos Prats and his wife, who were killed in 1974.

8. This ruling was issued by Judge Humberto Nogueira in the Third Court of Appeal on September 26, 1994, in the cases of Lumi Videla, killed in 1974, and Bárbara Uribe and Edwin van Jurik, who disappeared. These cases are reported in *El Mercurio* (September 14, 1994, and September 23, 1994) and in *Revista Ercilla* (July 15, 1994). The juridical debate is reported in *El Mercurio* (September 16 and 20, 1994).

9. Two uncertain and potentially contradictory factors will likely determine whether the Supreme Court revises its judgments on this matter. On the one hand, some new judges have been appointed to the Supreme Court and can be expected to feel less constrained by previous decisions of the Court. On the other hand, the judges draw lots to determine which of them will be in charge of hearing specific cases.

10. These data were collected in a survey carried out by the author together with T. Moulian and I. Agurto, as part of a project entitled "Evolución de demandas y políticas sociales en un contexto de democratización." They can be found in Volumes 6 and 7 of the final report for that project.

References

Aylwin, Jose (ed.). (1992). *Derechos humanos: Desafíos para un nuevo contexto*. Santiago: Comisión Chilena de Derechos Humanos.

Bengoa, José. (1994). "Reconciliación e impunidad: Los derechos humanos en la transición democrática." Mimeo. Santiago (June).

Bravo, German. (1992). *Informe del proyecto evolución de demandas y políticas sociales en un contexto de democratización,* vol. 3. Santiago: FLACSO.

CEPAL. (1992). "Equidad y transformación productiva: Un enfoque integrado" (Santiago).

Concertación de Partidos por la Democracia. (1989). "Programa de Gobierno" (Santiago).

Fruhling, Hugo, and Patricio Orellana. (1991). "Organizaciones no gubernamentales de derechos humanos bajo regímenes autoritarios y en la transición democrática: El caso chileno desde una perspectiva comparada." In H. Fruhling (ed.), *Derechos humanos y democracia*. Santiago: Instituto Interamericano de Derechos Humanos.

Fundación de Ayuda Social de las Iglesias Cristianas. (1994). "Balance de la situación de derechos humanos en 1993: Vision general de lo realizado en el período del Presidente Aylwin." Mimeo. Santiago (January).

Garretón, Manuel Antonio. (1989). *La posibilidad democrática en Chile.* Santiago: FLACSO.

————. (1991a). "La democratización política en América Latina y la crisis de paradigmas." *Leviatan,* nos. 43–44 (Madrid).

————. (1991b). "La redemocratización política en Chile: Transición, inauguración y evolución." *Estudios Públicos,* no. 42.

————. (1992a). "América Latina: Cultura y sociedad en el fin de siglo." *Revista Tablero.* Bogotá (August).

————. (1992b). "Nuevos derechos o viejas discriminaciones." In José Aylwin (ed.), *Derechos humanos: Desafíos para un nuevo contexto.* Santiago: Comisión Chilena de Derechos Humanos.

Garretón, Manuel Antonio, M. Lagos, and R. Méndez. (1992). "Orientaciones y evaluaciones de la democracia en la sociedad chilena, 1991–1992." Santiago: Participa.

Ministerio Secretaría General de Gobierno. (1991). *Informe de la Comisión Nacional de Verdad y Reconciliación,* 3 vols. Santiago: Secretaría de Comunicación y Cultura (February).

Revista Ya. (1994). *El Mercurio* (November 29, 1994). Santiago.

Touraine, Allain. (1992). *Critique de la modernité.* Paris: Fayard.

Vicaría de la Solidaridad. (1978). "En torno a la problemática actual de los derechos humanos: Derechos humanos y crisis social." *Estudios,* no. 1. Santiago (May).

Viera Gallo, J. A., and D. Sánchez. (1988). "Reconciliación y violación a los derechos humanos." *Estudios Sociales,* no. 56.

PART TWO

The International Scene: Networks and Discourses

4

The Emergence, Evolution, and Effectiveness of the Latin American Human Rights Network

KATHRYN SIKKINK

International factors are key to an understanding of domestic human rights practices in Latin America. Since the 1970s, human rights groups in repressive countries have linked up with a variety of international actors—international nongovernmental organizations, international and regional organizations, and private foundations—to protest violations and pressure for change. We cannot understand the nature, effectiveness, and limitations of human rights work in Latin America without exploring the connections between these international groups and domestic human rights organizations (Mignone, 1991: 127). Accordingly, this chapter will address the emergence and evolution of the international human rights network in Latin America, its effectiveness, and its impact on the transformation of sovereignty in the region.

The Latin American human rights network emerged in the 1970s to respond to specific types of human rights abuses, for which the situation of Chile under Pinochet could be seen as the prototype: massive violations of basic rights of the person by an authoritarian military dictatorship. With recent changes in the international and domestic political situation, the Latin American human rights network has now entered a period of transition as it adapts to the changing nature of human rights violations in Latin America in the 1990s.

This chapter focuses on those international actions designed to have a positive influence on human rights practices. Obviously, international activities can also exacerbate human rights violations. Indeed, a significant body of literature traces increased abuses to such international activities as training in national security ideology; police training programs, antidrug campaigns, International Monetary Fund (IMF) conditionalities, covert action; and low-intensity conflict (Klare and Arnson, 1979; Frenkel and O'Donnell, 1979; Crahan, 1982; Stepan, 1986; Miles, 1986; Washington Office on Latin America, 1991). What has contributed most to the emergence of military rule and human rights abuses in Latin America are international actions that strengthen the military and the police, increase their resources and autonomy vis-à-vis civil society and other parts of the state, and inculcate ideologies that stress the special role of the military in protecting the nation from internal security threats. The following discussion, however, will address only those international actions explicitly directed toward improving human rights practices.

The manner in which states and other international actors respond to human rights violations has changed significantly over the past two decades. The contrast between the international responses to the 1973 military coup in Uruguay and to the presidential coup in Peru in 1992 illuminates the expansion of the human rights movement and network during the intervening years. In some respects the coups were quite similar: Both were *auto-golpes,* in which the elected president, with the support of the military, undermined the constitutional order, closed Congress, censored the press, and arrested members of the political opposition. Moreover, both countries faced an armed guerrilla movement. Yet the initial international response to the Uruguayan coup was extremely muted; international actors took more than five years to develop the same kinds of pressures that were applied immediately in the case of Peru.

Although approximately half the total number of political prisoners in Uruguay were taken into custody between 1972–1974 (Servicio Paz y Justicia, Uruguay, 1989), international attention to Uruguayan human rights abuses was virtually absent until 1976, when Amnesty International initiated a campaign of publicity about human rights abuses in that country. The Organization of American States (OAS) waited until 1978 (five years after the coup) to condemn these violations and the U.S. Congress delayed hearings on the human rights situation in Uruguay until 1976. One year later, Congress suspended military aid, against the will of the president. Then, in 1981, the European Parliament passed a strong resolution, urging European states to suspend arms sales to Uruguay.

In Peru, the situation was quite different. One week after the coup, the OAS foreign ministers met, condemned the coup, and sent a fact-finding mission to Lima. The U.S. Executive cut all but humanitarian aid immediately after the coup. Spain and Germany also suspended economic aid, and Japan withdrew assistance a month later. Nongovernmental human rights organizations issued reports and sent missions to Peru. The international response was rapid, clear, and forceful. There are indications that this international response contributed to the release of some prisoners taken in the early days of the coup. Similarly, pressure from abroad induced President Alberto Fujimori to accelerate his original timetable for convening a constituent assembly, and prestigious members of the Peruvian economic team resigned when they were told by foreign governments and international institutions that new funds would be scarce until Peru returned to democracy.

How can we explain the very different international response to these two comparable civilian-led coups in Latin America? The end of the cold war changed the political context within which the international response took place, but it cannot explain fully the disparity. Human rights policy towards Peru, even in the post–cold war era, was not without costs, especially given the priority that the United States and other countries placed on the war on drugs. Between the Uruguayan coup of 1973 and the Peruvian coup of 1992, an international human rights issue network had emerged and grown. In the new post–cold war context, this issue network was able to organize rapid actions in favor of democracy in Peru.

CONCEPTUAL CLARIFICATION

An array of international organizations play an active role in the field of human rights. This chapter focuses on the most influential of these actors, including intergovernmental organizations, international and domestic nongovernmental organizations (NGOs), foundations, and churches.[1] These international and regional actors are in turn linked to domestic human rights organizations in Latin American countries, which have served as a source of information and inspiration for organizations and individuals in the international network.[2] In practice these organizations are so interconnected that it is difficult to separate the work of external and internal actors.

I refer to these organizations as an *international issue network*. The concept of a network is useful in this context because it captures the informal, nonhierarchical links among groups, and because the theoretical literature on networks in sociology offers some insights that help us understand the nature of linkages among organizations (Aldrich and Whetten, 1981; Jonsson, 1986; Ness and Brechin, 1988; Kamarotos, 1990). But the concept is not entirely unproblematic. Some groups refer explicitly to networks or *redes* to describe the connections among human rights organizations. Others prefer to think of themselves as part of a movement, believing that the concept of a network suggests more coherence or coordination than actually exists among human rights groups.[3]

The concept of a network does not imply high levels of coordination among groups. Rather, to be considered a network, groups must share values and participate in a dense flow of information and services.[4] The flow of information among human rights organizations reveals an extremely dense web of interconnections among these groups. In most cases, this flow of information takes place informally through the exchange of reports, telephone calls, and attendance at common conferences and meetings. In other instances, the connections are formalized, as when NGOs having official consultative status with intergovernmental organizations present reports to those organizations. In addition, the members of the network share allegiance or loyalty to similar values and principles, which in the human rights case are embodied in international human rights law. Another type of interconnection among these organizations concerns the flow of funds and services. This type is especially true of relations among foundations and NGOs, but some NGOs may also provide services such as training for other NGOs in the network.

The definition of a social movement, with its emphasis on bottom-up citizen protest, does not capture the wide range of actors involved in the international human rights network. Although the social movement literature has concentrated on social movements within countries, it occasionally refers to the international linkages among social movements (Alger and Mendlovitz, 1987; Falk, 1987). A more useful characterization of the groups involved with human rights in Latin America might recognize that they constitute both a movement and a network. The groups of international and domestic NGOs that work on human rights fit the definition of a social movement, but these organizations are also embedded in a broader framework of organizations that could be referred to as a network. For the purposes of exchanging information, they function as a network. In the context of many human rights organizations, however, their identities, their political actions, and their strategies more closely fit the image of a social movement.

THE EMERGENCE AND EVOLUTION
OF THE HUMAN RIGHTS NETWORK

The human rights movement has undergone tremendous changes in the last twenty years in terms of its size, the issues on which it works, and the manner in which it conducts its work. These changes are the result of three factors: the movement's response to new situations of human rights abuses and to a new international context, its evaluation of the effectiveness of its earlier work, and its reaction to the constant dialogue that the human rights movement maintains with the governments and people of each country.[5] In addition to these changes, important continuities can be found among the people who work in the movement and the ideals that motivate them.

We can distinguish three historical periods in the development of the human rights network in Latin America. The first, dating roughly from 1973 to 1981, was the period during which the human rights movement emerged. At this time, many of the key human rights organizations, both international and domestic, were set up or expanded, formed connections among groups, and developed the basic methodology of their work. The second period, dating roughly from 1981 to 1990, witnessed the consolidation of the human rights network. Many new groups formed during these years, and existing human rights organizations expanded their funding base and membership while experiencing some of their most important successes, as many of the key countries in Latin America that had been the focus of their early efforts made the transition to more democratic governments. The third period, from 1990 to the present, is one of refocusing and retrenchment for the Latin American human rights movement, as it struggles to respond to new forms of human rights violations in a global context in which attention is focused elsewhere.[6] Each of these historical stages will be examined, in terms of the nature of the movement, the target countries that were the focus of its work, and the evolution of the characteristic human rights themes and tactics used by the movement during each period.

Stage 1: The Emergence of the Human Rights Movement (1973–1981)

Human rights as a central foreign policy issue, and human rights groups as an important type of social movement, are relatively recent phenomena. Prior to 1973, most human rights organizations did not yet exist or were relatively small. Only eight years later, a wide range of organizations and policy options were capable of generating a forceful international response to human rights violations. International human rights pressures were often applied inconsistently, however.

The 1973 coup in Chile was a watershed event in the creation of the Latin American human rights network. As one human rights activist put it "Human rights was not in my vocabulary. Human rights entered my vocabulary on September 11, 1973 [the day of the Chilean coup], when it was suddenly denied to one-third of the Chilean population."[7] Membership in existing human rights organizations such as Amnesty International (in both Europe and the United States) grew in response to the Chilean coup, and new organizations were created, including the Washington Office on Latin America and the Council on Hemispheric Affairs. Chilean organizations that formed to confront government repression, especially the Committee for Peace (subsequently known as the *Vicaria de Solidaridad*), became models for human rights groups throughout Latin America as well as sources of information and inspiration for human rights activists in the United States and Europe. U.S. and European groups also served as links between human rights groups in Chile and intergovernmental human rights groups.[8]

The emerging network of the 1970s built upon international legal norms created in an earlier period. The touchstones for international human rights efforts were the Universal Declaration of Human Rights, the Covenant on Civil and Political Rights, and the Covenant on Economic, Social, and Cultural Rights. These in turn were the product of an earlier generation's concerns with human rights that had emerged out of the horror of the Holocaust. Latin America was an important player in the post–World War II debate over human rights. Latin American states championed the inclusion of human rights language in the United Nations charter and passed their own American Declaration of Human Rights even before the UN Declaration had been signed. This set of legal norms gave the human rights network of the 1970s a solid legal and institutional basis.

Although these international human rights norms already existed before the 1970s, they were not implemented in practice. Human rights did not constitute an important foreign policy category, nor was the term used frequently by social movements to frame their concerns or demands. What happened in the 1970s was essentially the "creation" of the human rights issue as an important and shared category to express the concerns of groups in both the south and the north—a category that found an echo in policy circles in the United States and in Europe.

The issue of human rights provided a meeting place for diverse groups that found it to be a useful framework for their concerns as well as a common ground on which to work. The early human rights network focused its efforts on a range of rights narrower than that included in the human right documents of the UN—especially on the so-called rights of the person, including the freedom from execution, torture, and arbitrary imprisonment. The early human rights NGOs helped set the tone. Amnesty International, founded in 1961, has a narrow mandate to concentrate its efforts on defending prisoners of conscience, opposing torture and the death penalty, and advocating the right of any accused person to a fair trial. The focus on basic rights of the person found a parallel in the liberal ideological tradition of the Western countries, where the human rights movement had the majority of its members. But this focus was also consonant with the human rights problems in the main target countries of the early movement. Given such cases as those of Chile, Uruguay, Argentina, and Brazil, it seemed imperative to address the problems of execution, torture, disappearance, and political imprisonment committed on such a large scale by the military regimes in these countries.

Most of the key human rights organizations were established during this period of emergence of the human rights network. Amnesty International already existed, but in the 1970s the Washington Office on Latin America, the Lawyers Committee for International Human Rights, and many other groups were set up in the United States and Europe. In Latin America, SERPAJ and many of the pioneering groups in Argentina and Chile were established. By the end of the period, with the founding of Americas Watch in 1981 and of the Inter-American Institute for Human Rights in 1980, many of the key institutional actors were in place, thus allowing the network to start functioning. In addition, new human rights legislation in the United States, changes at the OAS/IACHR and the UN, and support of the progressive church in Europe and many Latin American countries provided channels for the movement to begin to have an effect.

During this period, the human rights movement developed its basic strategies and tactics. The bulk of network activity revolved around information and denunciation, which involved gathering, publishing, and disseminating information about human rights violations and calling upon governments to criticize and isolate the worst violators. Groups in the human rights movement provided both facts and testimony—direct stories of people whose lives had been affected. Most important, activists interpreted facts and testimony in such a way as to make political action possible.[9] Activist groups framed issues in clear-cut terms and referred to notions of right and wrong because their purpose was to stimulate people to take action. Without clear messages, powerful testimony, and appeals to shared principles, NGOs would not have been able to capture the imagination and energy of so many people.

One problem during this early period of the human rights network was that information tended to flow largely in one direction: from south to north. Specifically, human rights organizations in Latin America sent reports and information to intergovernmental organizations and nongovernmental organizations located in the north. This arrangement reflected the crisis mindset that often characterized early network activity, for the urgent need to document massacres or to free a particular person from prison inevitably meant that the priority was to get information into the hands of an individual who could do something about it. In short, it was usually a matter of getting information out of a repressive country. Yet this one-way flow of information often left strategic and agenda-setting activities mainly in the hands of the "information receivers" in the United States and Europe.

Of course, providing information would not be an effective strategy for changing human rights practices unless this information were used to engage more powerful actors to pressure repressive governments. The primary strategy that human rights organizations developed during this period was to provide information designed to convince governments and international organizations to use other policy tools, such as aid cutoffs, to try to limit human rights abuses. Elsewhere, this practice has been referred to as "leveraging" (Keck and Sikkink, 1992). By getting their information published in the media, NGOs placed added pressure on governments to raise human rights issues in their talks with repressive governments.

Stage 2: Consolidation of the Human Rights Network (1981–1990)

This second period was characterized by increased numbers of human rights organizations, the growth of existing groups, and the evolution of targets, themes, and tactics within the human rights network. Indeed, the regional and international context within which the network operated had changed. The Reagan and Thatcher administrations created a political atmosphere in the north much less conducive to the theme of human rights. And regionally, governments in Latin America were suffering their worst economic crisis since the Great Depression, with many undergoing a process of transition from authoritarian to electoral regimes. The network had to confront the difficulties of working on human rights situations in the context of political transition. By the end of the decade, some of the main targets of the early human rights network—Argentina, Uruguay, Chile, Brazil, and Paraguay—had returned to democratic regimes, whereas in a handful of other cases, such as Guatemala, El Salvador, and Honduras, the existence of formally elected civilian governments made it more difficult for the network to draw attention to the ongoing violations of basic rights.

Despite these apparent difficulties, this period was one of growth and consolidation for the Latin America human rights network. Contrary to the expectation that human rights policy would disappear when Carter left office, the Reagan administration paradoxically stimulated human rights efforts: The cold war vision of Reagan and UN Ambassador Kirkpatrick, and their support for repressive, right-wing governments, brought a new constituency to the human rights movement. By offering a consistent policy of opposing human rights abuses whatever the ideological coloration of the government involved, in stark contrast to the Reagan administration's single-minded anticommunism, the human rights network gained a higher profile and expanded its funds and supporters.

Nongovernmental human rights organizations, the most important part of the human rights network, grew dramatically in terms of both absolute numbers and size (including membership and coverage). From 1980 to 1990, the total number of international human rights NGOs doubled.[10] The combined staffs of the three largest NGOs in the United States doing international human rights work in the 1990s—Amnesty International/USA, the Watch Committees, and the Lawyers Committee for Human Rights—grew from approximately 25 in 1981 to over 200 in 1992, while their combined budgets went from less than $4 million in 1981 to almost $40 million in 1992.[11]

These groups expanded their coverage of the world as well. The fastest growing of the U.S.-based human rights organizations, Human Rights Watch (of which Americas Watch is one branch), evolved from the small Helsinki Watch organization established in 1978 to a large umbrella organization for five regional Watch committees covering the entire globe. The organizations that experienced the greatest growth in the United States were precisely those with greater global coverage—that is, the ones that worked on Latin America as well as on other parts of the world and strived to criticize human rights violations wherever they occurred.

The number of Latin American human rights organizations also expanded dramatically. A 1981 directory of organizations in the developing world concerned with human rights and social justice listed 220 such organizations in Latin America, compared to 145 in Asia and 123 in Africa and the Middle East (Human Rights Internet, 1981). And an updated directory, published in 1990, lists over 550 human rights groups in Latin America. Of all the countries of Latin America and the Caribbean, only Grenada does not have a domestic human rights organization (Human Rights Internet, 1990). Some countries such as Brazil, Mexico, and Peru have 50 to 60 domestic human rights organizations. And more than 200 groups outside the region specifically work on human rights in Latin America, Central America, and the Caribbean, whereas 140 international organizations were identified as having a concern with human rights in Latin America.[12]

The changing political situation in the region led the Latin American human rights network to adopt new themes and tactics and thus to begin to alter the nature of its work. In a number of countries, the human rights movement became an important component of the coalition calling for transition to democracy, and the human rights agenda formed a part of the demands of the political opposition. Whereas previously the movement had focused on documenting and denouncing abuses by military governments, it now called on emerging democratic regimes to hold accountable the perpetrators of past human rights abuses.

Most human rights groups in the region adopted a legal strategy focused on advocating trials for those responsible for repression.[13] The strategy of legal accountability enabled the human rights movement to be consistent with its members" shared values, which were embodied in international human rights law, and to provide a united lobby to pressure governments. The decision of the Alfonsin government to try the commanders in chief of the Argentine junta briefly encouraged confidence that more far-reaching accountability was possible in Argentina and elsewhere in the region. By the end of the decade, however, it had become clear that legal accountability was extremely difficult to implement in all but exceptional cases. This realization led to a new concern within the network toward the end of the period—a concern over the problem of impunity. What, indeed, were the implications of the failure to punish perpetrators of human rights abuses?

This period was also one in which the human rights movement increased its support from public and private foundations. Some membership organizations, such as Amnesty International, have raised the bulk of their funding from individual donations and through direct mail appeals, but most human rights organizations have sustained their work on money from private and public foundations. Perhaps the most understudied aspect of the growth of the human rights issue network is the support that nongovernmental groups have received from a handful of key foundations and funders.

The Ford Foundation was the leader among large U.S. private foundations in initiating an international human rights program.[14] Long a supporter of academic research in Latin America, Ford increasingly found its academic grantees under attack from repressive regimes determined to silence any protests. In an attempt to protect the grantees and to maintain academic freedom, the foundation helped them leave their countries and work abroad; it also set up independent research centers to continue research within repressive countries (Puryear, 1982). After approving these pilot human rights programs, Ford decided to make international human rights one of its program priorities in 1978–1979. Since that time, it has maintained a substantial human rights grants program, continuing its support of academic institutions but also venturing to fund nongovernmental human rights organizations in the United States, Latin America, and elsewhere. Of the NGOs that Ford funded, the Vicaria de Solidaridad in Chile was seen as the "flagship" organization, a model of NGO activism. Ford also funded groups such as the Abuelas de la Plaza de Mayo and Centro de Estudios Legales y Sociales (CELS) in Argentina. In addition, virtually all of the large human rights NGOs in the United States have received money from Ford.

Other foundations, as well as government funding agencies in Europe and the United States, have also initiated programs funding human rights. By the early 1990s, a group of fifteen to twenty major U.S. private foundations were making regular grants for human rights work, while another twenty foundations gave occasional support for human rights. Another extremely important source of funding for Third World human rights groups has been grants from government agencies such as the international development agencies of Sweden, Canada, the Netherlands, and the United States. Both Sweden and Norway now have special agencies designed to fund NGO human rights work, and the political party foundations in Germany have also contributed to human rights organizations in Latin America. International church organizations, such as the World Council of Churches, have also provided crucial funding for human rights work.[15]

During this period, NGOs began to work more effectively with regional and international human rights organizations. Latin American NGOs started to become more interested in and savvy about the potential role for NGOs at UN and OAS human rights meetings (Palacio, 1992). Much of the information received by the United Nations Human Rights Commission outside of actual sessions comes from NGOs (International Service for Human Rights, 1992). Nongovernmental organizations and foundations have also carved out an important role for themselves in connection with the work of the Inter-American Court of Human Rights. Indeed, NGOs played a crucial role in three significant recent cases of disappearances in Honduras heard before the Inter-American Court. The initial complaints were filed by a Honduran human rights organization, and the legal team assembled to represent the complainants included lawyers associated with Americas Watch and the International Human Rights Law Group. These lawyers not only offered their services *pro bono* but also received important institutional support from their organizations. Since neither the court nor the commission provided funding for travel by witnesses or lawyers to attend hearings, funds had to be raised to pay for these costs (Mendez and Vivanco, 1990). Ford was among the foundations that supported that effort. Although it is somewhat troubling that a regional court could not litigate an important case like this without major support from foundations and nongovernmental organizations, such funding certainly speaks to the increasingly interconnected nature of intergovernmental and nongovernmental human rights efforts.

Stage 3: Refocusing and Retrenchment of the International Human Rights Network in Latin America (1990–Present)

Today the human rights movement in Latin America is confronting a period of transition and challenge. In part, the challenge is a product of success and of changing international circumstances. Because the movement has contributed to blocking the worst violations of human rights in many countries, it is perceived as less necessary than before. Moreover, many of its initial demands have been incorporated into government policy and in the work of international organizations, which now move independently to condemn human rights abuses in a manner that would have been unimaginable twenty years ago.

The other part of the challenge facing the network is the need to continually adapt its definitions and strategies to the changing global and regional context.

Most of the human rights situations in the hemisphere are no longer gross violations of human rights by a military dictatorship but, rather, the more difficult and complex problems of human rights violations under various types of elected regimes. Haiti and Peru still command attention, but world concern with human rights has largely turned to other regions and problems. In this new context, the Latin American human rights movement has been undergoing a period of refocusing and retrenchment.

Some organizations have responded to the new context by closing their doors. The most symbolic of such actions was the Chilean Catholic Church's decision to shut down the Vicaría de Solidaridad, perhaps the most renowned human rights organization in Latin America, at the end of 1992. In its place, the church is opening a new office to work on issues of poverty in Chile.

Some institutions in the network, such as the Inter-American Commission on Human Rights, have been partially neutralized within the new context. Most analysts agree that the high point of the commission's work was the Argentina report presented in 1980 to the OAS General Assembly. The member-governments of the OAS were able to allow criticism of the most blatant practices of military regimes. With the return to electoral forms of government throughout the region, however, some OAS members have strenuously objected to attempts by the commission to investigate continuing human rights violations. Many OAS members associate human rights violations with authoritarian regimes and thus argue that, by definition, the commission is overstepping its mandate by investigating the human rights practices of elected governments.

Countries that once held themselves up as champions of human rights are now on the receiving end of the commission's inquiries and resolutions. For example, the commission found admissible for the first time in 1989 a case against Mexico related to irregularities of the electoral process. The Mexican government, which prided itself as a defender of human rights in Chile and El Salvador, vehemently protested that the decision of a domestic electoral body "is not and cannot be subject to international jurisdiction," adding that, should a state submit itself to such jurisdiction, it "would cease to be sovereign" (Organization of American States, 1990: 103–105).

The Inter-American Commission needs to make the transition that the European Human Rights Commission has made. Although the latter's early fame also rested on its investigations of human rights abuses in Greece under the military junta, it now spends its time investigating the human rights practices of democratic states. But, the Inter-American Commission, severely underfunded and understaffed, facing a constantly mounting workload, under pressure from governments resentful of its work, and lacking strong champions, has thus far not been capable of making this transition.

Likewise in the foundation community, the changing international context has led to difficulties. The human rights program at the Ford Foundation, for example, was set up in response to the human rights violations by military dictatorships in Latin America. In these "black and white situations," where the good guys were distinct from the bad, it was easier for the regional staff to generate support for human rights projects within the foundation. But as they became involved with human rights activities in other countries such as Peru and Colombia, where high levels of violence existed under formally democratic governments and lines of responsibility were not always clear, the foundation staff sometimes found that funding decisions were more difficult to make.[16]

One dilemma currently facing the human rights movement is that it may have become too dependent on foundation funding. Indeed, excessive reliance on international funding can discourage the search for domestic sources of finance and distort policy priorities. By the same token, international funding decisions can decisively determine which groups will prosper and grow and which will wilt away. Foundations may now be shifting resources out of human rights work in Latin America to other regions, as well as to other issues such as the environment.[17] For instance, human rights groups in the Southern Cone, which are no longer perceived as priorities in the funding community, have experienced a significant decrease in external funding over the past five years, and church funding for NGO human rights work on Latin America also appears to be declining. Dwindling funds have forced many human rights organizations in the Southern Cone to reduce their size and the range of their programs.

Nongovernmental human rights organizations have responded to this changing human rights situation by addressing new targets and developing new themes and tactics. New themes that have taken on importance in the human rights movement of the 1990s include issues of impunity; rights violations committed both by governments and by insurgents in situations of armed conflict; problems of endemic human rights violations under electoral systems; and rights violations of especially vulnerable groups, such as women, children, homosexuals, and indigenous peoples.

The Watch Committees have led the way by deciding to focus on the application of the Geneva Convention (i.e., the laws of war) as well as on that of the UN Declaration and Covenants on Human Rights. Because the protection of human rights is primarily the responsibility of governments, human rights organizations tend to direct their criticisms to the practices of governments. In doing so, however, they are left with little to say in the context of civil wars in which abuses are committed by guerrilla organizations, as in the cases of Sendero Luminoso or the contras in Nicaragua. They are also left open to the opportunistic challenges of governments claiming that human rights organizations "never talked about the other side." This was a particularly effective rhetorical device used by the Argentine military to condemn human rights organizations during the military dictatorship. The Inter-American Commission on Human Rights, in its report on Argentina, felt compelled to directly respond to the question "Why doesn't the Commission investigate terrorist acts? In other words, why is it that the commission concerns itself exclusively with actions attributable to governments?" In response, the Commission contended that

> the simple and legally precise answer to the first question is that the sovereign states of the OAS have not chosen to give the Commission jurisdiction to investigate terrorism and subversion. . . . Even the most cursory review of these norms reveals that the task of the Commission—as, in general, that of all other intergovernmental bodies set up for the protection of human rights—is to investigate only those actions imputable to governments. (Organization of American States, 1980)

Although this answer is straightforward and compelling, Americas Watch has discovered that the decision to monitor the application of the Geneva Convention allows them greater latitude in investigating the range of new forms of human rights abuses, especially those that occur in situations of civil war or armed conflict. The members of Amnesty International have also recently approved a change in their mandate that allows them to condemn human rights violations perpetrated by insurgents as well as by governments in the context of armed conflict (Amnesty International, 1991b).

In Latin America, examples of the trend toward investigating and denouncing "endemic" human rights violations under formally elected governments include work on human rights in Mexico, Brazil, and Colombia. The human rights movement turned its attention to Mexico in the late 1980s and became especially active in the 1990s in denouncing the problems of executions, routine use of torture, violence related to land disputes, and violations of press freedom (Americas Watch, 1990; Amnesty International, 1991a). In Brazil, too, there is a new awareness of endemic human rights abuses, including vigilante executions, poor prison conditions, and violence related to land disputes (Americas Watch, 1989, 1992). As demonstrated by Jennifer Schirmer (in Chapter 5 of this volume) and Teresa P.R. Caldeira (in Chapter 11), these issues are often more difficult for the movement to work on because responsibility is harder to locate and there may be limited sympathy or even opposition from domestic groups.

The human rights movement is refocusing its work on new groups. During the period of its emergence, the movement was concerned primarily with victims of political repression. These were often political leaders, students, and union leaders, and more likely to be male and middle class than otherwise. Today, however, the human rights movement is increasingly turning its attention to new groups such as women, street children, homosexuals, and indigenous peoples. The International Council of Amnesty International recently voted to consider for adoption as prisoners of conscience those persons who are imprisoned solely because of their homosexuality (Amnesty International, 1991a). Similarly, Americas Watch has developed a new program dedicated to the defense of women's rights, and groups in Argentina and Brazil have turned their attention to the rights of children and adolescents.

The human rights movement has also adopted new strategies and tactics. Some groups are now making an active attempt to reverse the flow of information and to include a wider range of actors in the process of strategizing and agenda setting. For example, the Washington Office on Latin America disseminates a newsletter and information packets in Spanish to inform human rights groups in Latin America of developments in Washington that could affect their countries. The Inter-American Institute for Human Rights, based in Costa Rica, has been offering classes and training sessions for human rights leaders and activists since it was established in 1980. The International Human Rights Internship Program, in addition to arranging for internships and training opportunities for human rights activists in both the north and the south, informally tries to help supply information to Third World organizations about sources of funding. And, finally, the Watch Committees cultivate intense relations with key nongovernmental organizations in target countries, sometimes serving as conduits for funds to Third World NGOs.

The human rights movement continues to rely primarily on the tactics of documentation and denunciation. In countries where gross violations of the basic rights of the person have increased or continue unabated, such as Peru or Haiti, this strategy is likely to remain effective. But in the new international context, the network is placing increasing emphasis on influencing public opinion as well as governments. In the context of dictatorships, it was usually impossible for human rights organizations to reach the public through domestic media; but the return of elected governments with relatively free press has enabled both international and domestic human rights organizations to reach out directly in their efforts to influence public opinion.[18]

Once the process of transition to democracy has been completed, local human rights organizations may find it harder to attract funding for their ongoing work; but they may also lose contact with the international network as the human rights situations in their countries are perceived to be less important or less dramatic than before. One participant in a recent retreat for NGO activists expressed the resulting sense of isolation as follows: "In the transition period, all these international groups drew back. . . . Then we lost touch with those organizations. That's terrible for us because there is a kind of central decision that when a country starts a new process, there is no longer any need for international action and support" (Steiner, 1991: 51).

In this situation, human rights organizations may find it necessary to carve out new roles for themselves in the post-transition period, yet there are few models detailing how to accomplish this shift. After the return to democracy in Greece, for example, domestic human rights organizations were simply dissolved and the international and domestic human rights movement around Greece could not be sustained. Yet, as all of the contributions to this volume suggest, there continue to be enormous obstacles to the full realization of human rights for everyone living in Latin American democracies. National, regional, and interregional human rights organizations can play an important role in meeting the challenges brought to the fore by the consolidation of democracy, but doing so will require flexibility and an openness to grappling with new issues and to adopting novel organizational forms. The possible directions for human rights organizations include the following:

1. a move toward becoming more traditional civil liberties organizations, using domestic law and courts to fight against infringement of basic civil and political rights;
2. expansion of their mandates to encompass a wider range of rights, including economic, social, and cultural rights, as well as the rights of previously neglected groups, such as indigenous groups, women, and children; and
3. devotion of more energy to human rights education or training in schools, the Judiciary, the military, and the police.

EFFECTIVENESS OF INTERNATIONAL MEASURES

We know very little about the effectiveness of human rights pressures exerted by the international network as a whole, although there are some studies of the impact of different parts of the network (e.g., Smith, 1986; Kamarotos, 1990). The first task is to define what we mean by a successful or effective human rights movement. Above all, a successful human rights movement is one that has an immediate impact on the victims of human rights violations—that is, by saving lives, stopping torture, helping to get political prisoners released from prison, limiting police abuse, and so on. This human aspect must be taken into account in any discussion of success; it can be called the short-term impact of human rights work. However, with all measures of effectiveness in the human rights realm, such effectiveness is extremely difficult to prove or document.

But we cannot limit our definition of success only to the direct impact on victims of repression. As important as it is to help such victims in the short term, human rights work also has broader, medium-term objectives (Hoffman, 1981). In particular, we can consider a human rights movement to be effective if it helps to

1. strengthen regional and international human rights organizations;
2. destabilize and delegitimize authoritarian governments, and contribute to redemocratization;
3. influence linkages between the democratic opposition in Latin America and political groups abroad; and
4. reinforce transnational ties between rights groups in Latin America and policymakers and NGOs elsewhere.[19]

In an even less visible and yet equally important sense, the human rights movement is effective when it helps transform the cultural and moral context, both globally and in target countries where violations are occurring. Here I refer to the potential long-term impact of the human rights movement, which is intimately connected to the evaluation of short- and long-term effects. For example, when Amnesty International issues an Urgent Action to alert its members to serious violations of rights that are occurring at that moment, its first concern is with short-term effectiveness: securing the release of a prisoner or preventing torture or disappearance. To the extent that this action also makes visible actions that were once hidden, it may also help to undermine a culture of impunity that perpetuates rights violations. Many human rights organizations are increasingly focusing on human rights education in the hopes of having the long-term cultural or moral impact that might serve as a deterrent to human rights abuses by future generations.

Several studies analyzing U.S. human rights policy (Stohl, Carleton, and Johnson, 1984; Escudé, 1991; Egeland, 1988) offer insights into the difficulties of demonstrating effectiveness, although there are few studies of the impact of the human rights movement itself. In addition, few studies explore the precise linkages between the implementation of policy and the changing human rights practices in specific countries. Establishing such a causal relation requires comparative case study research and a longer time frame than most existing studies can offer. A study using this approach to compare Guatemala and Argentina (Sikkink, 1991) concluded that U.S. policy was more effective in Argentina because it was implemented more forcefully. The study also found that NGOs working behind the scenes were often crucial to the development and effectiveness of U.S. human rights policy.

A comparative study of U.S. and Norwegian human rights policies (Egeland, 1988) concludes that small countries such as Norway can have more effective human rights policies than large countries. The study appears to equate effectiveness with the existence of coherent or consistent policies, however. Indeed, although Norway and a number of other small European countries undoubtedly have more coherent and consistent human rights policies than does the United States, it does not necessarily follow that this greater consistency is more effective in shaping human rights practices in target countries. In any event, virtually all of the existing studies of effectiveness focus only on the policies of a single country. What is missing is an understanding that the human rights policies of one country often form part of a more comprehensive effort by the broader human rights network. All parts of the network do not work in coordinated fashion, but their efforts often converge to produce a collective effect more significant than the efforts of any single part of the network. As difficult as it is to sort out the effectiveness of such a large and diffuse entity as a network, it is almost impossible to study the influence of any single actor in the network in isolation.

Although the research still needs to be completed, the following preliminary conclusions about the effectiveness of the human rights movement can be drawn from a project now under way. First, there are strong limits to the possibilities for effective international human rights actions. Even where human rights efforts are very actively engaged, they often must counteract other international pressures. For example, although dictatorships in Chile, Argentina, and Uruguay eventually were isolated politically as a result of the international response to their human rights practices, they were highly integrated into the global economy. The money funneled to human rights work in these countries pales in comparison to the large sums directed toward support of the economic projects of the military.[20]

International pressures do not work directly to change international human rights practices. Rather, they work indirectly by entering into the decisionmaking calculus of key political actors at crucial turning points. Some theorists of transition to democracy (O'Donnell and Schmitter, 1986) assert that transitions always begin as a direct or indirect result of important divisions within the authoritarian regime itself. It is exactly at this point of decisionmaking within the authoritarian regime, when civil society is still severely repressed and not yet able to mobilize actively, that international human rights efforts may help to shift the calculations of actors inside the regime, giving weight to arguments of "soft-liners" in favor of liberalization. For example, international human rights actions appeared to have the most impact in Argentina between 1978 and 1979 and in Uruguay between 1977 and 1980, when severe repression constrained domestic political actors. Following the plebiscite in Uruguay in 1981, and after the military had initiated dialogue with political parties in Argentina in 1979, external pressures became less central than they had been earlier.

This argument is reinforced by the two-level game negotiation theory proposed by Robert Putnam (1988: 427–460). Putnam argues that international pressure may enable government leaders to shift the balance of power in their domestic game in favor of implementing a policy that "they privately wish to do but felt powerless to do domestically." Although Putnam's model is used to describe negotiations between two states, the central insight applies to the more diffuse international pressures that the international human rights network places on repressive governments.

The argument about divisions inside authoritarian regimes is often misused by opponents of a human rights policy who contend that strong human rights pressures fortify the positions of the hard-liners and undermine soft-liners. But the contrary conclusion is suggested by evidence from Argentina and Uruguaya, where it was the existence of the most consistent and forceful pressures anywhere in Latin America, pressures that were denounced and criticized by the soft-liners, that eventually led to an improvement of the human rights situation. Since soft-liners can use international pressures to fortify their positions vis-à-vis hard-liners, more forceful pressures create more leverage in internal negotiations. But international pressures depend for their effectiveness on leaders' concerns about their international image. For example, in the case of Haiti during 1993–1994, when the military regime was relatively unconcerned about its international image and the economic pressures of boycott could be passed on to the civilian population, external pressure was less effective.

All other things being equal, the stronger the international pressure, the more effective it is. The larger the number of actors exerting pressure and the wider the range of policy options employed, the more likely there is to be an impact. In particular, the combination of political and economic pressures is more effective than political pressures used separately.

Yet there is no direct correlation between the severity of human rights abuses and the degree of international response. The response is most forceful where the issue network is strongest, and where the national security concerns of major powers are the weakest (Sikkink, 1991). Since domestic human rights NGOs are key links in the network, paradoxically the network may not function well in many countries where it is most needed. The most repressive governments may simply eliminate those domestic NGOs that are crucial to the functioning of the network. For example, Guatemala has one of the most severe and prolonged patterns of repression in the hemisphere, yet the international response to that country has been inadequate. Cambodia is another case from a different region where extremely severe human rights abuses have elicited only a feeble response from the international community.

These cases are often interpreted as examples of the profound inconsistency of human rights policies in which the national security interests of superpowers are at stake. This was certainly true in two additional instances: U.S. counterinsurgency policy in Central America undermined its human rights concerns there, and Soviet-Argentine trade led the USSR to help block UN action on Argentine human rights violations (Guest, 1990). Yet this inconsistency is also rooted in the voluntary and fragile nature of the human rights network and in the difficulty faced by NGOs that are working in countries where governments severely violate the rights of their citizens (Weissbrodt, 1988). Since the human rights network has been strongest in Latin America, the most forceful human rights policies have been directed at violations in that region. In those Latin American countries with the most severe repression, however, the offending governments may eliminate these groups before they get off the ground. And where these groups are absent, international human rights work is hampered. International human rights groups can partly overcome this problem as they become more professional and thus are better able to support larger research staffs, but the inherent difficulties associated with a voluntary and understaffed network will likely persist.

Finally, we should note that many of the network's most important contributions are of a long-term rather than short-term nature. One particularly significant and yet potentially problematic long-term effect of the human rights movement has been its impact on the understandings and practices of sovereignty in the world. It is to this issue that we now turn.

SOVEREIGNTY AND HUMAN RIGHTS

The debate over human rights is embedded in a more fundamental debate over the changing nature of sovereignty in the modern world. State sovereignty is often seen as a series of claims about the nature and scope of state authority, implying a double claim of autonomy in foreign affairs and exclusive competence over internal affairs. Under this second claim, the state asserts absolute authority to make and enforce laws within its domestic jurisdiction (Haanstad, 1984). But sovereignty is more than a series of claims about authority. Claims about sovereignty are forceful because they represent *shared* understandings and expectations that are constantly reinforced through the practices of states (Wendt, 1992) and of nonstate actors.

The legal corollary to this concept of sovereignty is the doctrine of nonintervention. Sovereignty and nonintervention have taken on added significance in the Latin American context as a legal and rhetorical defense against a long history of U.S. intervention. Although the classic doctrine of nonintervention prohibited only the use of military force, the term has been expanded to refer to other means of political and economic intervention as well (Pinto, 1989).

Until World War II, the treatment of subjects remained within the discretion of the state; no important legal doctrine challenged the supremacy of the state's absolute authority within its borders. Internal sovereignty exhibited a fundamental moral flaw, however: If the state itself posed the primary threat to the well-being of citizens, the citizens would have nowhere to turn for recourse or protection. The expansion of human rights law and policy in the postwar period represented a conscious attempt to modify the shared understandings and practices of sovereignty. The doctrine of internationally protected human rights offers one of the most powerful critiques of sovereignty as currently constituted, and the practices of human rights law and human rights foreign policies provide concrete examples of shifting understandings of the limits of sovereignty. Indeed, the practices of the issue network are gradually eroding classical sovereignty and reconstituting the relationship among the state, its citizens, and international actors.

In the Inter-American system, there has been a profound tension between the norm of nonintervention and the international defense of human rights and democracy (Pastor, 1992). Although the preamble to the OAS charter states the necessity of democratic institutions and human rights, Article 15 of the charter bars any state from interfering directly or "indirectly for any reason whatever, in the internal or external affairs of any other state." Yet, by definition, a citizen's claim to internationally guaranteed human rights challenges the claim of internal sovereignty, since it implies that the state no longer has absolute authority over the treatment of its citizens.

Many Latin American policymakers have argued that human rights policy is a fundamental intervention in the internal affairs of states. Even under a narrow positivist definition of the sources of international law, however, this position is increasingly difficult to sustain. Europe and the Americas, in particular, have witnessed the development of a substantial body of treaty law that legitimates international concern and action regarding the internal human rights practices of states. For example, by the early 1990s most Latin American countries had ratified the UN Covenant for Civil and Political Rights, and a smaller but still significant number had ratified the Optional Protocol of the Covenant. In addition, as of 1995 most countries in the hemisphere have ratified the American Convention on Human Rights, and many have recognized the compulsory jurisdiction of the Inter-American Court of Human Rights. This history of the formation of human rights treaty law, legislation that has intensified dramatically in the last fifteen years, undermines the argument that human rights policies violate sovereignty.[21]

The human rights policies normally employed by the Latin American international human rights network fall well within the range of acceptable international responses. Only with difficulty can the most common policy tools—the provision of information, and the cutoff of military and economic aid—be construed as an intervention in internal affairs. The decision to grant aid is well within the discretion of the aid-granting state. Because all decisions about military and economic aid represent some form of intervention, one could argue that it is no more interventionist to deny aid than to grant it.

The dangers of illegal intervention are less likely to arise in multilateral approaches to human rights than in bilateral policy. In this sense, the trend toward the weakening and undermining of the Inter-American Commission of Human Rights reflects a particularly short-sighted policy on the part of governments in the region. Other developments in the Inter-American system, however, are more encouraging. At the OAS General Assembly meeting in Santiago in 1991, all thirty-four member-states declared "their firm political commitment to the promotion and protection of human rights and representative democracy" and instructed the secretary-general to convoke a meeting of the Permanent Council "in the case of any event giving rise to the sudden or irregular interruption of a democratic government." This Declaration of Santiago provided the legal and procedural basis for the rapid regional response to military coups in both Haiti and Peru (Pastor, 1992). Although regional pressures did not produce immediate success in either of these cases, we can reasonably conclude that forceful regional responses, within the bounds of clear legal guidelines, would limit the misuse of human rights rhetoric to justify illegal bilateral interventions that serve narrow national interests.

CONCLUSIONS

A Latin American human rights network emerged in the past two decades as a response to the increasing level of gross violations of human rights throughout the hemisphere in the 1970s. In particular, the coups in Chile and Uruguay in 1973, the coup in Argentina in 1976, and the upsurge of repression in Brazil in the late 1970s were key turning points for the formation of the human rights network. The groups formed in these countries were inspirations and sources of information, strategies, and tactics for organizations throughout the hemisphere. Indeed, a process of "learning" took place as certain forms of human rights organizing became widespread. This process was given impetus by the concomitant emergence and growth of the human rights movement in the United States and Europe.

With the transition to formal electoral regimes in many countries in the region, the human rights movement has entered a new era. International attention now focuses on human rights violations elsewhere, funding sources have dried up, groups have experienced a loss of domestic support as their members channel their energies into other political work, and intergovernmental organizations have found it much more difficult to work on human rights violations committed by formally elected governments.

Governments, too, have learned lessons from the human rights movement; now they know not only how to manipulate the discourse of human rights but also how to present their cases convincingly to foreign governments and intergovernmental organizations, and how to co-opt and marginalize the human rights movement. This outcome is in part an indication of the movement's success and in part a result of the very definitions and strategies that proved instrumental in responding to situations of human rights abuse. In the future, new definitions and new strategies will be necessary as the movement responds to the changing international and domestic context.

The human rights network has certainly contributed to new practices that have modified sovereignty. On the positive side, these practices have created a series of protections and possibilities for victims of human rights abuses around the world. But the network needs to be vigilant in its efforts to prevent cynical misuse of the new practices for purposes that are not justifiable under international human rights law. In other words, it must monitor not only human rights abuses, but also the misuse of human rights rhetoric and tools for other purposes. The network can best achieve this end by highlighting the gap between rhetoric and practice in those countries espousing human rights.

The human rights network in Latin America is not the only example of an international issue network. Similar forms of international organizing have also arisen in such areas as the environment, indigenous rights, and women's issues (Brysk, 1992; Keck and Sikkink, 1992). The international human rights network, however, is one of the oldest and most institutionalized of the emerging international issue networks. Indeed, other movements have borrowed and learned from this network. The capacity of the international human rights network to transform itself in the current period will long serve as an example of the adaptability, durability, and ongoing effectiveness of this new form of international actor.

Notes

I am indebted to Elizabeth Jelin, Juan Mendez, Emilio Mignone, Margaret Crahan, and Michael Shifter for their thoughtful comments on an earlier version of this chapter; to David Weissbrodt and Douglas Johnson for their insightful discussions with me; to Kristina Thalhammer for her research assistance; and to the Social Science Research Council and the McKnight–Land Grant Professorship of the University of Minnesota for their financial support.

1. The most important organizations in the international human rights network as it relates to Latin America include the United Nations Human Rights Commission, the Inter-American Commission on Human Rights, Amnesty International, Americas Watch, the various organs of the Catholic Church involved in human rights work, the Ford Foundation, and a variety of European public and private funding agencies. The key Latin American regional organizations include the Inter-American Institute for Human Rights, Servicio de Paz y Justicia (SERPAJ), Federacion de Familiares (FEDEFAM), and Latinamerican Institute for Alternative Legal Services (ILSA).

2. There is a vast and growing literature consisting of case studies of such movements in different countries. The works cited in this chapter are limited to those addressing the international human rights network.

3. Juan Mendez, director of Americas Watch, made this point in reference to an earlier version of the chapter.

4. Organization theory examines relations among organizations from a variety of perspectives. For example, Mitchell (1973: 23) refers to three types of relations content: "(1) communicative content, or the passing of information from one organization to another; (2) exchange content, or the goods and services flowing between organizations; and (3) normative content, or the expectations [that] organizations have of one another because of some social characteristic or attribute." Communicative and normative content are most relevant to the human rights network.

5. Juan Mendez made this point in his comments on an earlier version of the chapter.

6. The periodization outlined here applies to Latin America as a region, but it may not fit the experience of particular countries. For example, the human rights movement in Peru and Colombia did not emerge in the 1970s but, rather, began to form as late as the middle to late 1980s.

7. This quote was taken from an interview with Joseph Eldridge, held on March 18, 1992, in Washington, D.C. In addition, Hoeffel and Kornbluh (1983: 27–39) discuss the importance of the Chilean coup to the growth of the human rights movement in the United States.

8. As Thomas Quigley noted during an interview on March 18, 1992, in Washington, D.C., the human rights office of the National Council of Churches (NCC) and the human rights division of the U.S. Catholic Conference (USCC) filed cases for the Chilean Committee for Peace with the Inter-American Commission on Human Rights (IACHR) and the UN Human Rights Commission.

9. This point was developed by Margaret Keck and is elaborated in Keck and Sikkink, 1992.

10. I reached this conclusion using a relatively restricted definition of human rights (i.e., one encompassing the basic rights of the person, and civil and political rights) to code organizations listed in the 1980 and 1990 editions of the *Yearbook of International Organizations.* In the process I was able to distinguish between human rights organizations and the much larger number of development organizations.

11. These figures are based on information given in interviews with staff from the three organizations listed.

12. The definition of human rights used by these directories is broader than that employed in many discussions about human rights groups in Latin America. The directory lists groups that focus on civil, political, economic, social, and cultural rights, including

organizations concerned with indigenous peoples' rights, women's rights, labor rights, and the rights of children and refugees; bar associations and groups that offer legal services; religiously based justice and peace groups; and organizations concerned with development as a human right (Human Rights Internet, 1990: 10–11). Accordingly, the latest directory lists twenty-five human rights groups in Argentina, whereas most discussions about the human rights movement in Argentina focus on eight or nine core groups. Likewise, the directory lists forty-one human rights groups in Chile, but only about seven of these played on active role during the Pinochet regime (Mignone, 1991; Orellana and Hutchinson, 1991; Brysk, 1990). Nevertheless, the comparison of the 1981 and 1990 figures gives an idea of the dramatic growth in the Latin American human rights network and of the wide range of groups working on diverse human rights issues throughout the region.

13. Carlos H. Acuña and Catalina Smulovitz (in Chapter 2) and Manuel Antonio Garretón (in Chapter 3) analyze this issue in detail.

14. This analysis of the development of Ford's human rights policy is drawn from discussions with Christopher Welna, from interviews in New York with Peter Bell (March 20, 1992) and William Carmichael (May 11, 1992), and from an interview with Michael Shifter in Santiago, Chile (November 2, 1992).

15. The World Council of Churches provided crucial support for many human rights organizations in Latin America. Individual religious organizations also gave significant financial support, especially in the early period. Brian Smith (1986: 291) estimates that, between 1976 and 1979, Protestant churches alone contributed around $8 million to the Vicaria de Solidaridad, whose work also received substantial support from the Catholic Church and from foreign governments.

16. Interview with Jeffrey Puryear, New York, March 19, 1992.

17. Interview with Charles Reilly, Inter-American Foundation, Washington, D.C., March 17, 1992.

18. Juan Mendez stressed this point in comments made during the October 1992 workshop that gave rise to the present volume.

19. These ideas about how to define the "success" of a human rights movement were based in part on comments made by Marcelo Cavarozzi, Catalina Smulovitz, and Carlos Acuña in response to a previous discussion of the human rights issue. Of course, the medium-term impact of the movement may be even more difficult to measure than its short-term impact.

20. This point, in the specific context of Argentina, was made by Carlos Escudé, (1991). It was reinforced by comments recorded in interviews with the ministers of economics of Argentina and Uruguay during the military regime. Both officials (Alejandro Vegh Villegas, interviewed on August 29, 1991, in Washington, D.C., and José Martinez de Hoz, interviewed on August 6, 1990, in Buenos Aires) stressed the smooth relations that these countries had with international financial organizations even at the height of international human rights pressures.

21. A worrisome question in this regard is whether the erosion of sovereignty presaged by human rights policy could also have negative side effects by legitimizing wider-ranging interventions in the affairs of Latin America countries, such as the invasion of Panama or the funding of the contras in Nicaragua. Neither of these actions was justifiable under international human rights law; yet in both cases human rights rhetoric was sometimes used to justify the interventions.

References

Aldrich, Howard, and David A. Whetten. (1981). "Organizations-sets, Action-sets, and Networks: Making the Most of Simplicity." In Paul Nystrom and W. Starbuck (eds.), *Handbook of Organizational Design.* New York: Oxford University Press.

Alger, Chadwick, and Saul Mendlovitz. (1987). "Grass-roots Initiatives: The Challenges of Linkages." In Saul Mendlovitz and R.B.J. Walker (eds.), *Towards a Just World Peace: Perspectives from Social Movements.* London: Butterworths.

————. (1990). *Human Rights in Mexico: A Policy of Impunity.* New York: Human Rights Watch.

Americas Watch. (1989). *Prison Conditions in Brazil.* New York: Human Rights Watch.

————. (1992). *The Struggle for Land in Brazil: Rural Violence Continues.* New York: Human Rights Watch.

Amnesty International. (1991). *Mexico: Torture with Impunity.* New York: Amnesty International USA.

————. (1991b). "20th International Council Meeting: Report and Decisions." Yokohama, Japan (August 31–September 7).

Brysk, Alison. (1990). "The Political Impact of Argentina's Human Rights Movement: Social Movements, Transition and Democratization." Ph.D. dissertation, Stanford University.

————. (1992). "Acting Globally: International Relations and Indian Rights in Latin America." Paper prepared for the Seventeenth International Congress of the Latin American Studies Association, Los Angeles.

Crahan, Margaret E. (ed.). (1982). *Human Rights and Basic Needs in the Americas.* Washington, D.C.: Georgetown University Press.

Egeland, Jan. (1988). *Impotent Superpower—Potent Small State: Potentials and Limitations of Human Rights Objectives in the Foreign Policies of the United States and Norway.* Oslo: Norwegian University Press.

Escudé, Carlos. (1991). "Argentina: The Costs of Contradiction." In Abraham F. Lowenthal (ed.), *Exporting Democracy: The United States and Latin America: Case Studies.* Baltimore: Johns Hopkins University Press.

Falk, Richard. (1987). "The Global Promise of Social Movements: Explorations at the Edge of Time." In Saul Mendlovitz and R.B.J. Walker (eds.), *Towards a Just World Peace: Perspectives from Social Movements.* London: Butterworths.

Frenkel, Roberto, and Guillermo O'Donnell. (1979). "The Stabilization Programs of the International Monetary Fund and Their Internal Impacts." In Richard R. Fagen (ed.), *Capitalism and the State in U.S.–Latin American Relations.* Stanford: Stanford University Press.

Guest, Iain. (1990). *Behind the Disappearances: Argentina's Dirty War Against Human Rights and the United Nations.* Philadelphia: University of Pennsylvania Press.

Haanstad, Nancy Newcomb. (1984). "Compulsory Jurisdiction over Human Rights and Domestic Jurisdiction." Ph.D. dissertation, University of Utah.

Hoeffel, Paul Heath, and Peter Kornbluth. (1983). "The War at Home: Chile's Legacy in the United States." *NACLA Report on the Americas* 17 (September-October).

Hoffman, Stanley. (1981). *Duties Beyond Borders.* Syracuse, N.Y.: Syracuse University Press.

Human Rights Internet. (1981). In Laurie S. Wiseberg and Harry M. Scoble (eds.), *Human Rights Directory: Latin America, Africa, and Asia.* Washington, D.C.: Human Rights Internet.

————. (1990). "Human Rights Directory: Latin America and the Caribbean." *Human Rights Internet Reporter* 13, nos. 2–3 (January).

International Service for Human Rights. (1992). *Human Rights Monitor* 16 (April).

Jonsson, Chirster. (1986). "Interorganizational Theory and International Organization." *International Studies Quarterly* 30: 39–57.

Kamarotos, Alexander S. (1990). "A View into NGO Networks in Human Rights Activities: NGO Action with Special Reference to the UN Commission on Human Rights and Its Sub-Commission." Paper presented at the International Political Science Association (IPSA) Convention, Washington, D.C. (April 10–14).

Keck, Margaret, and Kathryn Sikkink. (1992). "Transnational Issue Networks in Human Rights and the Environment." Paper presented at the Latin American Studies Association Congress, Los Angeles (September 21–23).

Klare, Michael T., and Cynthia Arnson. (1979). "Exporting Repression: U.S. Support for Authoritarianism in Latin America." In Richard Fagen (ed.), *Capitalism and the State in U.S.–Latin American Relations. Stanford: Stanford University Press.*

Méndez, Juan E., and José Miguel Vivanco. (1990). "Disappearances and the Inter-American Court: Reflections on a Litigation Experience." *Hamline Law Review* 13, no. 3 (Summer).

Mignone, Emilio F. (1991). *Derechos humanos y sociedad: El caso Argentino.* Buenos Aires: Centro de Estudios Legales y Sociales y Ediciones del Pensamiento Nacional.

Miles, Sarah. (1986). "The Real War: Low Intensity Conflict in Central America." *NACLA Report on the Americas* 20 (April-May).

Mitchell, J. Clyde. (1973). "Networks, Norms, and Institutions." In Jeremy Boissevain and J. Clyde Mitchell (eds.), *Network Analysis.* The Hague: Mouton.

Ness, Gayle, and Steven R. Brechin. (1988). "Bridging the Gap: International Organizations as Organizations." *International Organization* 42 (Spring): 245–273.

O'Donnell, Guillermo, and Philippe Schmitter. (1986). *Transitions from Authoritarian Rule: Tentative Conclusions About Uncertain Democracies.* Baltimore: Johns Hopkins University Press.

Orellana, Patricio, and Elizabeth Quay Hutchinson. (1991). *El movimiento de derechos humanos en Chile 1973–1990.* Santiago: Centro de Estudios Politicos Latinamericanos Simón Bolívar.

Organization of American States. (1980). *Report on the Situation of Human Rights in Argentina,* submitted by the Inter-American Commission on Human Rights. Washington: General Secretariat of the OAS.

————. (1990). *Annual Report of the Inter-American Commission on Human Rights 1989–1990.* Washington, D.C.: General Secretariat of the OAS.

Palacio, Germán. (1992). "Derechos humanos y trabajo internacional: A propósito de la Subcomisión de las Naciones Unidas para la Prevención de la Discriminación de las Minorías." *El Otro Derecho* 10 (March): 139–158.

Pastor, Robert. (1992). "Redefining Sovereignty to Realize a Hemispheric Democratic Community." Paper presented at the annual meeting of the American Political Science Association, Chicago (September 3–6).

Pinto, Mónica. (1989). "No intervención y derechos humanos," *Revista Jurídica de Buenos Aires* 2–3.

Puryear, Jeffrey. (1982). "Higher Education, Development Assistance and Repressive Regimes." *Studies in Comparative and International Development* 17, no. 2.

Putnam, Robert. (1988). "Diplomacy and Domestic Politics: The Logic of Two-Level Games." *International Organization* 43, no. 3 (Summer).

Servicio Paz y Justicia, Uruguay. (1989). *Uruguay: Nunca Más—Informe sobre la violación a los derechos humanos (1972–1985).* Montevideo: Serpaj.

Sikkink, Kathryn. (1991). "The Effectiveness of U.S. Human Rights Policy: Argentina, Guatemala, and Uruguay." Paper prepared for the International Political Science Association, Buenos Aires (July 21–24).

Smith, Brian H. (1986). "Old Allies, New Enemies: The Catholic Church as Opposition to Military Rule in Chile, 1973–1979." In J. Samuel Valenzuela and Arturo Valenzuela (eds.), *Military Rule in Chile: Dictatorship and Opposition.* Baltimore: Johns Hopkins University Press.

Steiner, Henry J. (ed.). (1991). *Diverse Partners: Non-Governmental Organization in the Human Rights Movement.* Boston: Harvard University Law School Human Rights Program and Human Rights Internet.

Stepan, Alfred. (1986). "The New Professionalism of Internal War and Military Role Expansion." In Abraham Lowenthal (ed.), *Armies and Politics in Latin America.* New York: Holmes and Meier.

Stohl, Michael, David Carleton, and Steven E. Johnson. (1984). "Human Rights and U.S. Foreign Assistance from Nixon to Carter." *Journal of Peace Research* 21, no. 2.

Washington Office on Latin America. (1991). *Clear and Present Dangers: The U.S. Military and the War on Drugs in the Andes.* Washington, D.C.: WOLA.

Weissbrodt, David. (1988). "The Role of International Organizations in the Implementation of Human Rights and Humanitarian Law in Situations of Armed Conflict." *Vanderbilt Journal of Transnational Law* 21: 355–358.

Wendt, Alexander. (1992). "Anarchy Is What States Make of It: The Social Construction of Power Politics." *International Organization* 46, no. 2 (Spring).

Willetts, Peter (ed.). (1982). *Pressure Groups in the Global System: The Transnational Relations of Issue-Oriented Non-Governmental Organizations.* New York: St. Martin's Press.

◀ 5 ▶

The Looting of Democratic Discourse
by the Guatemalan Military:
Implications for Human Rights

JENNIFER SCHIRMER

The emergence of an international human rights network has transformed the discourse and politics of accountability of repressive states in the late twentieth century. In the late 1970s and throughout the 1980s, demands by human rights organizations for the universal respect for human life and democratic participation have influenced actions in many such states, particularly in Latin America. As issues of human rights, democracy, and political participation have become standard elements of international political discourse, traditionally authoritarian states have been compelled to redefine the rationale for their actions, create more democratic political structures, and open political activity to previously outlawed and repressed groups.

In Latin America, where human rights activism has played a critical role in shaping recent political discourse, most countries have established democratic structures and achieved a significant measure of political opening. Although these changes are welcomed by human rights organizations everywhere, there are reasons to be cautious about accepting all *aperturas* at face value. At the same time that rights are being acknowledged in much of Latin America, they are being challenged in new and creative ways by the forces of domestic national security states. Hence, notwithstanding the important advances obtained through the networking of the international human rights community, newly democratizing states in the region pose renewed challenges to that community, and to the advancement of human rights, during the 1990s and beyond. This chapter suggests, however, that such challenges cannot be met by using the traditional universal claims and language of the human rights community. Indeed, the continued reliance on a decontextualized language regarding democracy and human rights allows the meaning of rights to be obscured and leaves open the possibility that democratic discourse will be looted by national security states.

The debate between those who argue for a universal language of human rights and those who seek to base human rights on cultural relativism is rendered insignificant when confronted by a repressive regime that utilizes a human rights language. Neither side in the current debate is sufficiently grounded to confront the subtleties, ironies, and contradictions that emerge when the discourse of human rights is appropriated by states engaged in continuing rights violations. My concern in this chapter is with the way rights are perceived, manipulated, and redefined by powerful actors who have apparently accepted human rights discourse but who at the same time utilize that language to further their own political and military objectives—objectives that redefine rights through the prism of national security. By focusing on the Guatemalan military, the chapter provides a case study that illustrates a potentially broader phenomenon under contemporary conditions—one that inevitably affects the viability of strategies for promoting respect for human rights.

THE CASE OF THE GUATEMALAN MILITARY:
HISTORICAL BACKGROUND

As expressed by a retired Guatemalan colonel–political scientist, since 1966 the Guatemalan army has functioned as a political force by "giving orders."[1] It has grown "accustomed to making political decisions within a special framework directed by the concept of national security. . . . From this, no government could escape, especially the [one or two] civilian ones." In 1981, however, after years of fighting a counterinsurgent war, the army had a political awakening: Its own survival depended on civilian elections based on a form of conditional opening and civilian-military co-governance in Guatemala. With the March 1982 military coup, the army initiated a project that began with massacres and ended, by 1985, with civilian presidential elections. The initial campaigns focused on the violent destruction of the social fabric at the local level; in eighteen months, 446 villages were razed, entailing the massacre of 50,000 to 75,000 people and the forced displacement of more than a quarter of the rural indigenous population. Permanent counterinsurgency structures were also established during this period.

Beginning in 1982, the Guatemalan military put in place a unique form of constitutionalist state, fashioning a process of political transition that consolidated the existing military structure institutionally while utilizing the vocabulary of democracy and human rights. Having generated an alternative way to conduct a war to gain the "hearts and minds" of each inhabitant through the creation of such institutions as "Civil Patrols" and "Poles of Development," the army by the late 1980s was postulating a post–cold war substitute for the doctrine of low-intensity conflict pursued throughout much of the previous decade. As outlined in General Hector Gramajo's 1989 Thesis of National Stability, this strategy acknowledges the Constitution while delegating the role of guardian of national interests to the army; the mission of the latter, in turn, is to preserve "equilibrium" when the state is endangered by "opponents of the state" or by a power vacuum created by inept civilian politicians. Implementation of this strategy has enabled the Guatemalan military to act on the basis of a new constitutional, legal, and democratic calculus, even though it remains one of the worst violators of human rights in the region.

Two factors account for the doctrinal and discursive shifts in military thinking that began after 1982. First, the military needed to transform its strategy in order to save the army as an institution—and, by extension, the state itself—from a potentially successful insurgency. Indeed, many in the military feared that the army itself risked fragmentation and institutional ruin if it were to lose the counterinsurgency war. Second, and in conjunction with the need to defeat domestic insurgents, the military understood the need to improve its image abroad. In the words of the legal architect of the military plan, a colonel-lawyer, the new framework sought

to guarantee respect before the international community. It is [thus] at once an internal and external juridical regime with one of the objectives to make the international community aware and secure that Guatemala is fulfilling international agreements, and so that one cannot say that there is a *de facto* but a *de jure* regime in Guatemala. . . . One must run down the constitutional corridors, isn't that so? (1986 interview by author)

Given both internal and external pressures to create a juridical-political regime, in 1981 the military elite pondered three options for effecting a transition from a *de facto* to a *de jure* regime. As one colonel–political scientist put it:

What were the possibilities? The first, of no change: [direct] military rule. The second possibility was to control the structure, combining it with the army so that while the authoritarian structure of the army is relieved, the army is given the flexibility to use it [whenever deemed necessary]. The third possibility was to make these structures totally civilian and leave them only to the civilians to run. (1986 interview by author)

The army, this colonel continued, realized that it could never finally defeat the insurgency militarily; and in order to maintain its historical dominance, it "damn well had to learn to conduct political wars."

Institutionalists within the Guatemalan military thus began to reformulate their ideology, rejecting the U.S.-imposed national security doctrine of the 1950s and creating instead a new vocabulary and strategy by which to assert their autonomy from both the United States and the domestic elite. The result was a shift away from the static, Vietnam-style model of "occupation" and the implementation of a more integrated, "more humanitarian" approach known as the "30/70% Beans and Bullets" program. As General Gramajo, one of the key architects of the policy, explained:

Rather than killing 100%, we provided food for 70% [of war refugees], while killing 30%. Before, the doctrine was [to kill] 100%. . . . We aren't going to return to the killing zones, we aren't going to return to that. This emphasis on killing 30%, you know, is not rational. It's not civilized. We know that. But you need to take into account that [at least] we are operating within our own country, while out in Iraq, [the United States] is using 100 vs. 0 per cent! (Schirmer, 1991)

The 30/70 formula is the army's calculation for a political repression that appears less violent and "more humanitarian," and operates within a democratic structure. Indeed, the Beans are to be provided only in relation to the Bullets in order to establish a democracy premised upon security concerns, a form of which is analyzed later in the chapter as "coercive consensus."

The Thesis of National Stability aimed to justify the practice of attacking and eliminating "opponents of the state" by attempting to erase the apparent contradiction between two competing worldviews: one based on counterinsurgency and the other predicated on democracy and human rights. Written before the demise of the Soviet Union, the Thesis reveals the army's acute awareness of international opinion in terms of the permissible methods of repression; it also emphasizes the need for countries to develop their own approaches to national security as an alternative to a U.S.-imposed national security doctrine. As explained by General García Samayoa, who served as defense minister in 1992–1993,

National Stability was established in order to achieve a stable platform for the State, such that the State will be able to develop its administrative policies. [This was achieved by] strengthening one of the institutions [the army] that provides consistency to government decision-making. . . . We [the army] must comply with our mission in providing a framework of security [against terrorist-delinquency] so that the country can develop integrally. (1991 interview by author)

A key element of the Thesis, "Military Fundamentalism," exhorts officers to prepare justifications for army actions, both internally toward its own troops and domestic elites, and externally toward Washington and Geneva. At the same time, the military rejects its historically subordinated role vis-à-vis an extreme right that, for the most part, sees no need to justify the use of the military for a "100 percent" solution to dissent and insurgency. As Gramajo has argued (Schirmer, 1991: 13), "We are no longer the redeemers for rightwing *latifundistas.* . . . We are not concubines, we are professionals!" Thus, the military project demands co-governance with civilian regimes, based on the 30 percent security and 70 percent development strategy. The project constitutes a mixed solution, a division of labor between a security apparatus kept intact to preserve military prerogatives and a civilian administration put forth to handle foreign affairs and, especially, the human rights problem. Security prerogatives are structured into the legal and political order. Ironically, as Gramajo explains, the existence of a civilian government

has allowed the army to carry out much broader and more intensified operations because the legitimacy of the government, in contrast to the illegitimacy of the previous military governments, doesn't allow the insurgency to mobilize public opinion [against us] internationally—something which proved to be an obstacle in fighting the guerrillas. (Interview quoted in Cruz Salazar, p. 3)

This "mixed solution" consists of a war on two fronts. On one front, the military continues guerrilla warfare legitimated within a constitutional framework. On the other, it fights a political war in the human rights arena. It is this latter arena about which the military is particularly sensitive. Especially galling to many military officials has been their "pariah status at international conferences." Yet the mixed solution provides legitimation, as the civilian president can address the United Nations, and can speak of "excellent relations" with the United States and Europe. A case in point was President Vinicio Cerezo's Active Neutrality policy, as expressed in the Esquipulas II Accords, which directed Central American governments to begin direct talks with the armed insurgencies. As one Guatemalan editorial stated: "The principal objective of President Cerezo's trip to Europe and the U.N. will be to improve the image of the country and seek support for his foreign policy of active neutrality . . . to gain credibility from the international community" (*La Hora* [September 26, 1986], p. 1).

Through this mixed solution, then, civilian presidents serve to absorb international pressures regarding continuing human rights violations as well as domestic social demands and protests on these and other issues. Yet rather than breaking with traditional forms of repression, this arrangement is designed to "reconstitute the equilibrium between coercion and consensus," as one Cerezo aide averred during a 1986 interview with the author.

The use of traditional constitutional and legislative structures, including the 1985 Constitution itself, to confront dangers to public order has led one Guatemalan lawyer to label the military project as a "counterinsurgent constitutionalism." Security is immersed within the law, justifying human rights violations as necessary and constitutionally mandated (Linares Morales, 1985). Shaped by a series of mutual concessions between the army and the dominant class, the 1985 Constitution included provisions approving all decree laws enacted by the military government between 1982 and 1986 to establish counterinsurgency structures and, just four days before the inauguration of Cerezo, the new civilian president, an amnesty for the army's past crimes. To better understand how rights become securitized and camouflaged in this context, we must analyze the manner in which security objectives have been embedded in the 1985 Constitution as well as the military's perception of rights and duties. Similarly, we must examine the military's language of myth making and politics of human rights.

THE MILITARY'S VIEW OF LAW

Although militaries have long resorted to constitutionalism as a means of seeking either domestic or international legitimacy, their perception of law is not so clearly understood. What is the perception of law that military regimes impose on their societies to create "proper legal orders"? Do they consider themselves above or within the law? How do they define human rights? How do they perceive the political opposition?

Juridical norms today, based on nineteenth- and twentieth-century natural law, usually are both imperative and attributive. They impose duties and confer power (Tapper, 1973: 249; Linares Morales, 1985), they define obligations and concede rights, and they are meant to be respected both by the governed and by the governors. The Guatemalan military's vision of rights, in contrast, is premised on a lawlike system of norms and injunctions that demands obedience to these norms. Commands may come in the form of obligations or duties, as one member of the 1982 Junta declared:

> The citizen does not have only rights, but also obligations. . . . Above all, he must comply with these obligations because everyone has the right to discuss, to speak, and thousands upon thousands of rights, but obligations, one doesn't make enough of *them.* (1988 interview by author)

Within this legal scheme, only one-half of the juridical norms of rights within a nineteenth-century image of rule of law are fulfilled. Ignored is the twentieth-century principle of consent (i.e., socially approved use of force as the distinguishing element of law), upon which the philosophy of human rights is based. Similarly, despite the preamble to the 1985 Constitution, which urges full respect for "human rights within a stable, permanent, and popular institutional order, where the governed and the governors act with absolute loyalty to the law," the military clearly views as separate the rules and rights for governors and those for the governed. No mention is made of the governors conceding rights, only of demanding obedience, of having the "rational power . . . to make [their] force felt." The sole equality within this perception of law is that of obligation: The governors are obliged to force compliance of the governed to protect public order; the governed are obliged to comply with this forced obedience. Within this Hobbesian universe of coerced consensus, human rights are defined as socially and legally bounded norms of conformity for security purposes. Human rights become securitized, as they are continuously subject to qualification or denial, and denied whenever they are deemed in conflict with state security interests.

ARMY OPERATIONS AS CONSTITUTIONAL MANDATE: "OPERATIVE LAWS"

General Gramajo has stated repeatedly that the capacity of the army—the institution that planned and executed the *apertura*—to dedicate itself to maintaining peace is mandated within the Constitution:

> We are continuing our [military] actions, our operative pressure, because the Constitution mandates this. . . . The army of Guatemala is participating actively in strengthening the democratic system [and] is pledged to maintain all military action as a basis for national stability. And we are pledged to maintain the constitutional order as a principal factor by which to achieve that national stability. (Gramajo, quoted in Ejercito de Guatemala, 1987: 16, 21)

What exactly does this "constitutional mandate" entail? How does the army think of law in relation to "military operations"? Denying any contradiction between fighting an insurgency while establishing a democracy, the army public relations chief explained that the military is "complying with the operative laws against the delinquent subversives, and against common delinquency" (1988 interview by author).[2] Law, in this instance, is operative, providing the army with legal entitlement to force compliance, even to the point of physical injury or death; hence law is part and parcel of the operations that provide security and peace.[3] The salience of law here is a function of what one can do with it, how it can be used to carry out "operations" against opponents, and how power can be consolidated in its name without releasing one iota of control. Previously, counterinsurgency operated outside the law because (1) there was no document with democratic legitimacy, so the military could act only on the basis of the Fundamental Statute of Government, promulgated by the ruling junta in April 1982; and (2) the lawless guerrillas created conditions in which the army, in its view, had no choice but to operate (however reluctantly) outside the law, violating human rights.

Thus, the military perception of the rule of law is based on the Hobbesian vision of a world in which law is important only when it is literally or even potentially disobeyed. Emphasis is on the law as sanction rather than as a system of rules. And rights are perceived as having no abstract or inherent quality attached to them: They do not inhere to an individual by virtue of being, but are provided to the individual by the state only conditionally (Damaška, 1986: 77, footnote 11).

Nor does the military separate the demand for rights from the potential consequences of the active use of those rights. Indeed, it understands that an authentic provision of rights would necessarily mean real change in the *status quo*. Determined to force compliance with the norms institutionalized by the prevailing order, the military cannot just will the governed to obey; the governed must also face the prospect of sanctions imposed through legalized political force.

THE MILITARY'S VIEW OF OPPONENTS AS FALLING OUTSIDE THE BOUNDARIES OF LAW

Operating "within the law" accomplishes a separation, at least rhetorically, between the legal coercion of the state and the space outside the law occupied by the enemy. For example, the document "Operación Ixil," the backbone of the "pacification campaigns" of scorched earth and massacre between 1982 and 1984, is clear about distinguishing between the legitimate and necessary violence of the state and lawless violence:

> The legitimate use of violence by the state is moral and necessary because it is inherent in the legal order and political power, without which Man could not live reasonably. Illegitimate violence is that violence exercised by individuals and groups of individuals on the margins of the state and [thus] of the law. (Cifuentes, 1982: 36)

This interpretation reinforces the idea that unjustifiable violence occurs only outside state structures and, conversely, that violence by the state to defend itself is mandated and thus justifiable. Defensive, preventive measures are collapsed into offensive ones; and the more effective the security apparatus is in defining the boundaries of "legal" action, the more reasonable it will appear in defining and isolating those who are unwilling to conform and, thus, are "outside the law."

In the end, a securitized legal framework makes it all the easier to identify and "eliminate" those whose politics are, by definition, in opposition to the state. Groups active in denouncing human rights abuses within Guatemala, such as CERJ, GAM, and CONAVIGUA,[4] are themselves denounced by the army as front groups financed by and speaking for the left political opposition and the guerrillas. According to the military, because these groups are led by "infiltrators" and "agitators" and are influenced by "international pressures," they are outside the boundaries of "lawful" dissent. Security operations against such groups are thus legitimated in the minds of officers—and, indeed, the groups have been systematically subjected to repressive actions. The assumption is that all denunciations of human rights violations are part of the international campaign against Guatemala.[5] Human rights groups are assumed to be puppets of "Marxist subversives." And as security risks acting outside the legal order, they are vulnerable to "elimination." In explaining, for example, why human rights groups such as CERJ or GAM were not invited to attend courses at the new civil-military Center of Strategic Studies for National Stability (ESTNA), General Gramajo dismissed them as "Marxist" and "lawless" and thus justly subject not only to exclusion but to repression as well.

According to the "operationalized" logic of counterinsurgent constitutionalism, these legal boundaries identify "the enemies of the state," who, by definition, fall outside the boundaries of law (with the military, by definition, within it), and simultaneously reinforce the idea that violence occurs only outside state structures. It is curious that the army believes itself capable of recognizing illegality, given that most of its commanders have neither legal training nor legal advisors to whom they turn for advice. Yet the military alone is deemed capable of recognizing illegal subversion and dissent. For the military, law is defined not by the realm of measurable juridical procedures and boundaries. Rather, law is placed squarely in the world of uncontemplated, imputed criminality of the remote future in which individuals are guilty of what they have not yet done and must be punished for what they might yet do (Shklar, 1964: 214). Such a preemptive strategy not only creates a paranoia in which everyone is suspect; it also provides officers with a basis for justifying their actions. Ultimately, this theory of punishment has more to do with provision of a legal facade for elimination tactics than with concern for establishing juridical boundaries and protecting human rights.

PSYCHOLOGICAL WARFARE AND DEMOCRATIC CAMOUFLAGE

Since 1982, the Guatemalan military has learned to utilize two kinds of language. The first is what might be called the "mythical language of camouflage." It hides its intentions, transforms history into nature, and fabricates an innocent world that denies the consequences of the military's other language, which might be called the "operational language of action and duty." The operational language, formulated with painstaking detail in Gramajo's Thesis, delineates unambiguously repressive strategies for controlling "opponents of the state." In defining degrees of oppositions to be countered, the framework begins with "antagonisms" such as illiteracy and then moves to more serious "vulnerabilities" and "pressures," such as strikes and violent demonstrations, before concluding with "dominant pressures" such as guerrilla warfare (Schirmer, 1991). As such, it is a language of the tactics of war.

The mythical language of camouflage, in turn, is a language of systematic distortion for "defending the indefensible," characterized by intentional "euphemism, question-begging and sheer cloudy vagueness."[6] Labels for the opposition shift from "subversive-Marxist" (*subversivo-marxista*) to "delinquent-subversive" (*delincuente-subversivo*) to "delinquent-terrorist" (*delincuente-terrorista*), depending upon internal and international circumstances. Asked whether there is a difference between "terrorism" and "delinquency" in this context, Gramajo's response reveals that the Guatemalan army, despite its notorious isolationism, has learned to fine-tune its vocabulary for international acceptability:

> It's only a matter of semantics that we [in the army] had to adapt to, given what was happening in the international [political] environment. We began with [the term] "delinquent-subversive" as someone who was against the order, subverting the order. . . . All the bad things against the State, anti-establishment, that [occurred] in Guatemala. But then, terrorists killed the poor Jews in Germany [at the Olympics], because Reagan railed against international terrorism, the terrorism of the Red Army—all of that was making it into an international thing. So, we quit using [the term] "subversive" and replaced it with "delinquent-terrorist." We thus show our international support by our vocabulary. (1990 interview by author)

Sophistries, or what former President Cerezo has referred to as "apparently a wordgame" (1991 interview by author), abound in this world where words signify their opposites: National Security is renamed "National Stability"; areas of conflict become "areas of harmony"; mandatory Civilian Defense Patrols are legislated as "Committees of Peace and Development"; and a village that was destroyed in order to save it from "subversion" is reborn as a "model village" in "liberated territory" within a "Pole of Development."[7] Linguistic looting encompasses even the appropriation of revolutionary slogans, with officers referring to the "class struggle" and replacing the leftist "The People, United, Will Never Be Defeated" with proclamations that "The People, United with the Army, Will Win." Finally, contradictory terms are merged into curious, hyphenated forms, as when the Civilian Defense Patrols are described as "forcibly-voluntary"; a president is "elected-appointed"; and the political transition is referred to as "a violent peace" or "a civil-militarized society" with "coercive consensus." Such sophistry is part of the reality and language of psychological warfare. At one point during a

1990 interview with the author, General Gramajo proclaimed in English: "We [the army] are experts at deception!"

Similarly, in 1986, the exiled Guatemalan Human Rights Commission (GHRC) denounced the military occupation of the town Santiago de Atitlan and the bombing of the nearby volcano. In response, the army public relations chief, Captain Fernando Cifuentes, first stated unequivocally that "the Army is obliged to strengthen its image, as is all of Guatemala, before the eyes of the world, and never could occupy an entire town as the GHRC claims." Yet he then proceeded to justify the army's actions, contending that "any [counterinsurgent] maneuver is plainly justified before the constitutional command which the Army must comply with."[8]

This contention exemplifies a form of political-psychological warfare that Gramajo calls a "reversal of Clausewitz," revealing the new international awareness of Central America's most isolated army. On the one hand, the military argues that it cannot violate human rights because it is "obliged to strengthen its image . . . before the eyes of the world." On the other hand, the military declares that if it were to take such action, it would be justified by virtue of its constitutional mandate.

A significant part of the psychological warfare campaign includes the opportunistic appropriation of human rights language with little if any commitment to improving standards. The linguistic looting has gone so far that army intelligence has written the human rights reports submitted to the Human Rights Commission in Geneva since 1986, resulting at times in votes favorable to the Guatemalan government position. According to Gramajo, the most significant by-product of this exercise,

> which is why we decorated the officers who wrote the [1989] report and argued it in Geneva, . . . was the educational message it conveyed within the army: that we can fight ideas with ideas. That we don't have to be so rude but [that we can be] sophisticated in defending Guatemala. I believe there is a big difference between the warrior and the soldier; anybody can be a warrior, learn to use a weapon, cut out the liver and kill everyone. That's a waste of energy. Now, a soldier comes to use a weapon consciously, intelligently, and only in the interest of the nation, not for personal interest or anything like that. That is what a soldier is all about. So the soldier can not only defend his country with a weapon but also, by being in constant preparation and in constant struggle, defend his country even though he doesn't have a weapon. . . . This is the concept that must be inserted into the Guatemalan military: A soldier is minimum force, as I mentioned in the Thesis. . . . Clearly, if there is someone who is against the interests of Guatemala and you appear like this (he glares) and do nothing else, and the police appear ready to act (he slaps his hands together quickly), the will to act against the interests of Guatemala quickly evaporates (he chuckles). They can't say you are using force then. . . . One always uses force but in a much more sophisticated way (this he says in a low voice). You needn't kill everyone to complete the job. (1990 interview by author, emphasis added; see also Mazariegos, 1990)

QUERIES: HUMAN RIGHTS, DEMOCRATIC RULE OF LAW, AND NATIONAL SECURITY?

How do we confront a project in which a world of disinformation and ever-increasing levels of opposition and political pressures create a violence called democracy? And what does the notion of "rule of law" mean when law itself is used to legitimate official repression?

Doctrines of national security have traditionally been viewed as tailor-made rationalizations for the overthrow of civilian governments or as justifications for using "exceptional law" as a form of law enforcement. Little, however, has been written about how such doctrine can become an integral part of traditional, democratic, legal structures and discourse. Also insufficiently discussed is the role that national security establishments—the military and the intelligence apparatuses—have played in the past and should play in the future within new democracies. Rather than see this issue in terms of democracy or national security, we need to examine precisely how national security becomes, or remains, structured within democratic governing apparatuses (Zagorski, 1992).

This focus on the relationship between national security and democracy has profound implications not only for the strategic approaches of the international human rights movement but also for the legal community. Across much of Latin America and elsewhere, a struggle is under way for the appropriation and control of the persuasive and coercive aspects of law in order to gain legitimacy, both internally and vis-à-vis the international community. This struggle is especially evident now, as domestic and international human rights organizations persist in using law as an instrument for advancing inherently moral claims.

The rule of law and the administration of justice are not timeless ideals but, rather, specific social forms of regulation at certain historical and political moments. They are instruments for the realization of particular political projects. In the past, however, at least in the Guatemalan case, there remained a gap between the traditional ideals of liberal, just legal structures and the executive use of law. Herein lies the difference between the previous order and the more recent form of counterinsurgent-constitutional order: That gap has been closed by the total immersion of "security" within constitutional structures. As a consequence, the human rights community must learn not only to contextualize the perceptions and practices of "rights" but also to understand how legal structures and constitutional orders themselves are appropriated and redefined as instruments for repressively humanitarian purposes.

The sophisticated doctrine and language deployed by the Guatemalan military in support of its project for National Stability pose a challenge to the human rights community. Knowledge of how that military thinks and acts in regard to law, human rights, and democracy suggests a particular set of queries as to how the human rights community should deal with the situation in Guatemala; but it also poses a number of questions about the nature and direction of human rights discourse and inquiry in general. In short, those concerned with human rights must, in the future, attend to issues of internal politics as well as international standards, to the problem of language in a world where the language of human rights is expropriated by those who repress those very rights, and to the problems of order, stability, and democratic freedom in a world perceived by many, including especially the militaries of Latin America, as being increasingly dangerous, unstable, and threatening.

Notes

As a 1991 John D. and Catherine T. MacArthur International Peace and Security Fellow, I would like to thank the foundation for its generous research support.

1. The author conducted interviews with more than thirty high-ranking military officers, including six defense ministers and heads of state, in addition to a series of thirteen interviews with former Defense Minister Hector Gramajo. The findings from these interviews are reported in greater detail in Schirmer (forthcoming).

2. Similarly, Colonel Garcia, chief of Civil Affairs in 1988, explained that "we [the army] are what give laws their force." And General Garcia Samayoa, vice-chief of the National Defense Staff in 1991 (and defense minister in 1992), referred to the law of forced recruitment of the army as "empowering us to proceed to carry away [recruits] forcibly, [although this procedure] can be violent and excesses do occur. We are not perfect" (1991 interview by author).

3. An illustration of the extreme right-wing view of law as an application of force is the letter pushed under the door of CERJ President Amilcar Mendez in August 1988. Its text reads in part: "Laws are made by men, and it is they who violate them and who use them whimsically. But the law of life is the strongest of all [natural] laws and that will be the law that our commandoes will apply to you. It is only a matter of time and opportunity, but we'll get you" (Amnesty International, 1989: 12; translation by the author).

4. CERJ, the Council of Ethnic Communities Runujel Junam, is an anti–civil patrol human rights group; GAM, the Mutual Support Group, consists of family members of the disappeared; and CONAVIGUA stands for the National Coordination of Guatemalan Widows of Political Violence. Further information on the latter two groups can be found in Schirmer (1988, 1992).

5. This assumption has been echoed by the civilian presidents, who believe that "illegal" dissenters (i.e., those outside the boundaries of law) fall within the bounds of justifiable killing. For example, in July 1991 President Cerezo stated nonchalantly that military intelligence had informed him that, although the leader of CERJ, Amilcar Mendez, was a *guerrillero militante,* his life was to be spared (1991 interview by author). President Serrano repeated that labeling in September 1991 in response to a question about the safety of human rights monitors in Guatemala.

6. George Orwell, quoted in Clark and Dean (1984: 99).

7. See also *Revista Cultural del Ejercito* (n.d.) and "Polos de Desarrollo y Servicios" (1984), both of which are official publications from the army's public relations office.

8. Reported in *La Hora* (October 6, 1986), p. 1.

References

Amnesty International. (1989). *Guatemala: Human Rights Violations Under the Civilian Government.* London: Amnesty International.

Cifuentes, Juan Fernando. (1982) "Operacion Ixil." *Revista Militar* 27 (September-December): 25–72.

Clark, Gordon L., and A. M. Dean. (1984). *State Apparatus: Structures and Language of Legitimacy.* Boston: Allen & Unwin.

Committee of Santa Fe. (1980). "A New Inter-American Policy for the Eighties." Washington, D.C.: Council for Inter-American Security.

Cruz Salazar, José Luis. (1988). "Perfiles militares." Mimeographed.

Dahl, Robert A. (1971). Polyarchy. New Haven: Yale University Press.

Damaška, Mirjan. (1986). *The Faces of Justice and State Authority.* New Haven: Yale University Press.

Ejercito de Guatemala. (1987). "Foro nacional de contrainsurgencia." Tape transcription. Guatemala City.

Hart, H.L.A. (1977). "Positivism and the Separation of Law and Morals." In R.M. Dworkin (ed.), *The Philosophy of Law.* Oxford: Oxford University Press.

Linares Morales, Arquiles. (1985). "La Constitucion Guatemalteca de 1985." *Cuadernos* 2, no. 7 (Ciencia y Tecnologia para Guatemala [CITGUA], Mexico, D.F.).

Mazariegos, Jorge A. (1990). *El estado, su estabilidad y el desarrollo de una estrategia nacional.* Guatemala City: Editorial del Ejercito.

Montealegre, Hernan. (1979). *La seguridad del estado y los Derechos Humanos.* Santiago: Academia de Humanismo Cristiano.

O'Donnell, Guillermo, Philippe C. Schmitter, and Laurence Whitehead (eds.). (1986). *Transitions from Authoritarian Rule: Comparative Perspectives.* Baltimore: Johns Hopkins University Press.

Schirmer, Jennifer. (1988). "'Those Who Die for Life Cannot Be Called Dead': Women and Human Rights Protest in Latin America." *Harvard Human Rights Yearbook* 1 (Spring): 41–76.

———. (1991). "The Guatemalan Military Project: Interview with Gen. Hector Gramajo." *Harvard International Review* 13, no. 3 (Spring): 10–13.

———. (1992). "The Seeking of Truth and the Gendering of Consciousness: The Co-Madres of El Salvador and the CONAVIGUA Widows of Guatemala." In S. Radcliffe and S. Westwood (eds.), *Viva! Women and Popular Protest in Latin America.* London: Routledge.

———. (Forthcoming). *A Violence Called Democracy: The Guatemalan Military Project 1982–1992.* Philadelphia: University of Pennsylvania Press.

Shklar, Judith. (1964). *Legalism: Law, Morals and Political Trials.* Cambridge, Mass.: Harvard University Press.

Tapper, C.F.H. (1973). "Powers and Secondary Rules of Change." In A.W.B. Simpson (ed.), *Oxford Essays in Jurisprudence.* Oxford: Clarendon Press.

Washington Office on Latin America. (1989). "The Administration of Injustice: Military Accountability in Guatemala" (December). Washington, D.C.: WOLA.

Zagorski, Paul. (1992). *Democracy Vs. National Security: Civil-Military Relations in Latin America.* Boulder: Lynne Rienner Publishers.

PART THREE

Citizenship in Democracy: Some Conceptual Issues

Citizenship Revisited: Solidarity, Responsibility, and Rights

ELIZABETH JELIN

It is fairly easy to recognize violations of citizens' rights in the context of dictatorship. But what about those perpetrated in democracies? The question arises because a considerable distance separates the legal provision of rights and their implementation in practice. A great many social struggles are geared toward closing this gap. There is also a great distance between the legal definition of rights and the understandings and practices of the assumed subjects of rights. It is precisely in this context that we see the importance of discussing the construction of a culture of citizenship "from below." How do those who are formally defined as citizens carry out the practices of citizenship? In which arenas or spaces do these practices occur, and in relation to which institutions? What social relationships are involved? What do the citizens expect, and what is being asked from them?

In this chapter I analyze the social processes through which citizenship is constructed—that is, the ways in which the formally defined "subjects of law" actually become such—in social practices, institutional systems, and cultural representations.[1] My central concern is with the process of construction of individual and collective subjectivity, in relation to "others" in general and to one "privileged other," the state, in particular. What takes place in the system of social and institutional relations during that process? This question and the preceding ones are the central analytical questions addressed in the following pages. The answers—both theoretical and empirical—are exploratory and provisional, based on the challenges raised by the transition to democracy in two spheres: the processes of learning about rights and responsibilities, and the development of a democratic institutional framework.

A related question concerns the means by which a person acquires reciprocal expectations in interactions with others: What rights do I have, and what are my responsibilities? In this case, the answer implies a dual process in which one must simultaneously become aware of the responsibilities of others toward oneself and learn about one's responsibilities toward others. At the same time, the process entails a shared definition of the scope of the responsibilites assumed by each subject.

This process takes place not in a vacuum but, rather, within concrete institutional frameworks, which in turn must be (re)constructed in transitions to democracy. Although the full range of institutional spaces is strongly affected by the type of political regime, there are important variations across institutional domains: The family is relatively less permeable to the repression of dictatorship than is the school, and the school is perhaps less permeable than are networks of youngsters on a street corner. The linkages between institutional spheres are complex: Mechanisms of contagion and of interpenetration operate alongside processes and spheres of institutional differentiation.

Dictatorial regimes and the state terrorism they sanctioned penetrated deeply into Latin American society, invading private spaces and daily practices beyond those commonly associated with the sphere of politics. They also generated hidden and clandestine spaces of resistance and solidarity. Although these spaces were not defined as public or political, they provided for both democratic socialization and instruction in patterns of behavior suitable for participation in the public sphere.

The transition to democracy has involved the reconstruction of state institutions and the transformation of the institutions of civil society. It implies dismantling antidemocratic forms of exercising power, which may be authoritarian, corporatist, and/or purely coercive in nature. It also entails a change in the rules governing the distribution of power, the recognition and legal sanction of rights, and the legitimation of social actors. People must embrace beliefs and practices that are suitable to, or consistent with, the notion of democracy; they also must learn how to act within the renewed institutional system. In turn, political leaders and dominant classes must learn to recognize and respect the rights and identities of diverse social actors, and to abandon not only their recourse to arbitrariness but also their impunity.[2] The challenge of democratization lies in the capacity to combine formal institutional changes with the expansion of democratic practices and the strengthening of a culture of citizenship. Herein lies the practical relevance of the issues under discussion.

HUMAN RIGHTS AND THE CONCEPT OF CITIZENSHIP

In democratic theory, the notion of citizenship is anchored in the legal definition of rights and obligations. There are two key issues around which the ideological, theoretical, and political debates revolve: the nature of the "subjects," and the content of their "rights." The former takes as a point of departure the tradition of liberal individualism, with further theorizations aiming to reconsider the relationship between individual subjects and collective rights—particularly in the case of ethnic identities, as discussed by Rodolfo Stavenhagen in Chapter 8 of this volume. The second issue involves the question of the existence of "universal" rights (a question that challenges positions of extreme cultural relativism and pluralism), as well as the relationship among human, civil, political, socioeconomic, collective and global rights.

Both issues have often been presented as irreducible theoretical-ideological antinomies: on the one hand, the "negative" rights of liberalism versus rights that require a "positive" intervention of the state; on the other, human rights anchored in a universal "human nature" versus cultural pluralism leading to international recognition of the "rights of nations," whatever they may consist of. These antinomies can be reinterpreted as follows: The individual right of freedom of expression is also the right of a community to hear different opinions and positions; and the guarantee of "negative" rights implies "positive" state decisions of budgetary assignments (i.e., for spending on public security). Insofar as such decisions invariably differ according to class and other social criteria, they erode the material basis for the argument presented by "minimalist" interpreters of the state as the guarantor of negative rights (see, for example, Stavenhagen in Chapter 8 of this volume; and Lechner, 1986).

Historically, human rights have been treated in the West as an issue raised by modernity, specifically by the bourgeoisie (and its philosophers) in the process of confronting the power and privileges of monarchies. Both the French Revolution's *Declaration of the Rights of Man* and the American Constitution reflect concepts grounded in natural law. The American version—based on the Founders' perception of English citizens' freedom and rights (as in Locke's conceptualization of the rights to life, freedom and property)—implied a recognition of man's "natural" freedom and potential, with the intention of reducing political (i.e., state) interference to a minimum. Natural rights, imminent in society, were expected to operate in an unconstrained manner. In contrast, the French version is a manifesto against a hierarchical society and against privilege, a univeralizing bourgeois pronouncement grounded in the general will of "the people," establishing the distinction between man (as depositary of natural rights) and the citizen with rights, integrated into a political system. In the latter view, political citizenship is a necessary condition for the recognition of human freedom (Ansaldi, 1986; Lefort, 1987).

Since its beginnings in the eighteenth century, the history of human rights has been long and complex, in terms of both political and ideological struggles (Ansaldi, 1986; Oliveira, 1989). Historical and comparative analyses go to considerable lengths to explain the changes in the contents of such rights. The mandatory reference here is to T. H. Marshall (1964), who shows the interconnection between the development of the English nation-state and the expansion of citizenship rights. Marshall presents a historical progression: First comes the extension of civil rights; next, political rights expand; and finally, social rights are increasingly recognized. In this view, the development of the welfare state can be conceived of as the public face of the process by which the socioeconomic rights of citizens are expanded (Marshall, 1964; Offe, 1985; Lefort, 1987).

Marshall's hypothesis about the historical expansion of rights is consistent with the terminology used in the United Nations, which refers to *generations* of rights.[3] This sequence, however, is not a universal, historical rule. At times, the development of social citizenship rights through the welfare state has replaced the ideal of the responsible citizen with the reality of the "client" (Habermas, 1975; Reis, 1993). The prevalence of populist regimes and of social and political authoritarianism in twentieth-century Latin America has fostered a culture in which awareness of citizens' rights is limited. Thus, the noteworthy expansion of labor and social rights in the region has not always been the outcome of full enforcement of civil and political rights (Collier and Collier, 1991); indeed in the 1980s the recovery of political rights in the transition to democracy coexisted with widespread violations of civil rights, as discussed by Teresa P.R. Caldeira in Chapter 11 of this volume. In general terms, until the 1980s, a decade characterized by structural adjustment policies and economic restructuring, socioeconomic rights were more prevalent than political ones (and these, in turn, were more so than civil rights), although there was significant variation among the countries in the region.

The notion of citizenship is a useful theoretical starting point for a consideration of rights, provided that one avoids a "positivization of natural right" (Habermas, 1991: 76). The danger lies in reifying the concept, and in identifying citizenship rights with a group of concrete activities—voting, enjoying freedom of speech, receiving public benefits of any kind, and so on. Even though these practices are key features of the struggles for the expansion of rights in specific historical situations, from an analytical perspective the concept of citizenship refers to a conflictive practice related to power—that is, to a struggle about who is entitled to say what in the process of defining common problems and deciding how they will be faced (van Gunsteren, 1978). Citizenship as well as rights are forever undergoing the process of construction and transformation.

This perspective implies a specific premise: that the basic right is *"the right to have rights"* (Arendt, 1973: 296 [emphasis added]; see also Lefort, 1987). Citizens' action must be conceived of in terms of its self-sustaining and expanding qualities: "The actions pertaining to citizens are only those that tend to maintain and, as far as possible, increase the future practice of citizenship" (van Gunsteren, 1978: 27; see also Lechner, 1986, and Lefort, 1987). As Claude Lefort has pointed out, that self-reference was already implicit in the formulations of the eighteenth century:

> The naturalist conception of law concealed the extraordinary fact that it was a declaration which was also a self-declaration, that is, a declaration in which men . . . were at the same time the subjects and the objects of the statement . . . and by so doing, they became the witnesses and judges of each other. (Lefort, 1987: 39)

An important element in the tradition of human rights in the West is the absence of transcendental references—hence the rise of the democratic debate. As

Lefort (1987: 40) explains, "Modern democracy invites us to replace the notion of a regime regulated by laws, of a legitimate power, by the notion of a regime based on the *legitimacy of a debate between what is legitimate and what is not*—a debate that by necessity has no guarantor and no deadline" (emphasis added).

Without sacred powers or superhuman reference points, there is no authority above that of society itself, no "transcendent judge" to settle conflicts. Accordingly, justice must be grounded in the existence of a space for public debate, and participation in the public sphere becomes both a right and a duty. In the words of Hannah Arendt:

> The fundamental deprivation of human rights is manifested first and above all in the deprivation of a place in the world [a political space] which makes opinions significant, and actions effective. . . . We became aware of the right to have rights . . . and a right to belong to some kind of organized community, only when millions of people emerged who had lost and could not regain those rights because of the new global situation. . . . Man, as it turns out, can lose all so-called Rights of Man without losing his essential quality as man, his human dignity. Only the loss of a polity expels him from humanity. (Arendt, 1949; cited by Young-Bruehl, 1982: 257)[4]

This approach to the notions of rights and citizenship has important consequences for the struggle against discrimination and oppression: The contents of demands, the political priorities, and the scenarios for struggle are broadened if and when the right to have rights and the right to a public debate of the contents of both norms and laws are upheld.[5]

Another broad issue is the tension between the universality of rights and the cultural, gender, and class pluralism that generates diversity. Modern history, encompassing the colonialism and racism of the past two centuries, was the ideological backdrop for the Universal Declaration of Human Rights. Proclaimed in the context of the postwar period, it was part of the efforts to prevent new horrors. This is explicit in its introduction: "Considering that the disregard and contempt of human rights gave way to acts of outrageous brutality for the consciousness of humanity . . ."

According to some theorists, the challenge of the times was to enter an era of cultural pluralism, to demonstrate scientifically the falseness of claims of white racial superiority, and to discover the complexity of "primitive" cultures. Recognition of pluralism was to become an antidote to the recurrence of massive crimes, genocide, and cultural annihilation, committed on the basis of ideologies and interests that implicitly or explicitly denied victims the status of "human beings with rights." The ideology of universal human rights would thereby serve to protect actual as well as potential victims.

Yet to raise the flag of universalism in defense of the rights of those who were different, in a struggle against those who wanted to impose uniformity and the idea of universal progress, was somewhat paradoxical. The implicit tensions soon were reflected in a lively academic and political debate. How could cultural relativism be reconciled with the defense of universal human rights? How could the alleged objectivity of science be squared with an ethically rooted defense of principles? The Universal Declaration began to be criticized on the grounds that its underlying notion of human rights was individualistic and Western, and that the will to extend it worldwide was an act of an imperialistic, discriminatory, and ethnocentric power. This anti-Western argument would in turn be deployed politically to justify rights violations, under the shield of cultural relativism and with an insistence on national sovereignty and self-determination, all of which could lead to a rejection of humanitarian interventions and international monitoring and controls.

The foregoing provides the context for contemporary reassessments of issues of cultural relativism, tolerance, and respect for differences. The positions that can be taken on these issues cover the whole spectrum, from radical cultural relativism (where "everything goes") to the search for universal biological roots of human behavior. In this process of reassessment, one entailing considerable political and moral urgency, the debate about ethnocentrism has been rekindled (Geertz, 1984; Rorty, 1986).

These general issues have been and remain the core of the debate and social struggles about the (formal) definition of the citizen—that is, about the boundary between those included and those excluded, be they "foreigners" or people who are marginalized or discriminated against for some particular reason (e.g., income level, education, race, gender, or culture). The debate and the struggles also revolve around the content of the rights to which citizens are entitled.

The expansion of the social base of citizenship (e.g., the granting of voting rights to women or illiterates), the inclusion of minorities or of dispossessed social groups as members of the citizenry, and the claim of "equality before the law" are ever-present issues in contemporary history. The most visible and best known examples of these social struggles include resistance to the "final solution" of Nazism, the U.S. civil rights movement during the 1960s, the ongoing fight against apartheid in South Africa, the demands of feminists for eradication of all forms of discrimination against women, and the demands of ethnic minorities for full citizenship and legal pluralism.

Finally, citizenship encompasses not only rights but also the responsibilities and duties of citizens, a subject less studied by theorists in this field. (Even Marshall [1964] merely mentions duties, and then neglects to discuss them.) Duty and obligation bear a coercive imperative; but responsibilities, as we shall see later, are broader and extend beyond duty. The later dimension includes a civic commitment, centered on active participation in public life (the responsibilities of citizenship), as well as symbolic and ethical aspects that confer a sense of identity and of belonging, a sense of community. Indeed, it is the sense of community that promotes the consciousness of being a subject with the right to have rights. The civic dimension of citizenship is anchored in the subjective feelings that unite or bind a community, in contrast to the seemingly more rational elements of civil and social rights (Kelly, 1979; Reis, 1993; see also Chapter 7 of this volume).[6]

Taking rights and responsibilities at face value, we find that the full development of citizenship may be in contradiction with the process by which such subjective feelings emerge, revealing the impossibility of reconciling the ideals of creation of autonomous subjects with those of a more just community (Rorty, 1991). This ambiguity is summarized by Fabio Reis:

> The ideal of the citizen includes, on the one hand, an egalitarian and consensual element that corresponds to the status derived from the involvement in a community, an element related to solidarity, to civic virtues and to the duties and responsibilities of the citizen. However, it also includes an element of autonomous self-assertion of each individual member of the community—and this element is potentially conflictive, instead of expressing solidarity or social convergence. (Reis, 1993: 294)

In the transitions to democracy that are taking place around the world today, concurrent with the secular process by which individual and collective subjects are created, both aspects of the citizenship process are present: the open expression of demands about respect for (and expansion of) citizens' rights—rights that have been restricted and violated during the dictatorships—and symbolic demands for a sense of belonging, anchored in collective identities.[7] In the context of the democratic order, the articulation between the need for governability and representation, on the one hand, and participation and citizens' control of government administration, on the other, are often portrayed as incompatible. But the construction of democracy requires both processes. Unless they endeavor from the outset to institutionalize the means of citizen participation and control, new and weak democracies cease to be democratic.

There continues to be an enormous gap between formally defined rights and everyday practices in Latin America. In everyday life, subordinated social sectors tend to consider their subordination as "normal," a naturalizing view of social hierarchy predominates, and the relationship with the state is expressed more often in terms of clientelism or paternalism than in terms of citizenship, rights and obligations. Yet the region has undergone a rich and complex history of popular struggles for the expansion of citizenship and rights. Peasant rebellions, workers' protests, old and new popular movements, political mobilizations (such as that of October 17, 1945, in Argentina, or the popular movement for the impeachment of Fernando Collor in Brazil, in 1992), even revolutions, cannot be discounted. This long experience of resistance and opposition to domination has gained salience against the historical (and continuing) backdrop of acceptance and naturalization of domination.

Yet the culture of domination-subordination has a significant and very deep historical continuity. The legacies of colonialism and of racial, ethnic, and cultural domination on the part of local oligarchies and bourgeoisies are evident in everyday relations among classes, as well as in clientelistic and populist forms of interaction between state and society. By the middle of the twentieth century, Latin American populist regimes had established a pattern of relationships between the state and subordinate classes in which the expansion of social services was associated with increasing state regulation and intervention in the living conditions of diverse social strata. It was to the state, transformed into a provider of services (education, health, housing, utilities and transportation services, pensions, etc.), that one went in search of solutions to daily problems of reproduction and survival. Sometimes this search for solutions took place in the context of clientelist relationships;[8] at other times, it reflected a clear awareness of social rights.[9]

In Latin American states that gained legitimacy and social consensus on the basis of their active role in the provision of services, issues of political democracy and civil rights were pushed into the background.[10] In cultural terms, even the tension between civil rights and social rights took on the appearance of antinomy: social justice versus formal justice. Given such a cultural matrix, it is hard to find historical evidence of citizens who constructed themselves as "subjects of law," with relatively high degrees of personal or group autonomy. This pattern of power relationships has overlapped with a decidedly patriarchal culture, thus taking a double toll on the social condition and rights of women (Valdés, 1990).

The situation began to change, however, by the 1970s. The struggle against military dictatorships and for democracy created space for the demand of political rights; massive violations of human rights created a new language, a new code. Until this time, the ideal of citizenship had barely extended beyond urban, educated middle-class men; but now the surge of popular mobilization and social movements, of feminism and women's movements, of indigenous organizations and urban mobilizations, prompted the emergence of new ways of expressing social, political, and cultural demands. Increasingly, civil society became mobilized, generating actions and demands rooted in the rights and responsibilities of citizenship.[11]

Social struggles are slowly changing the conditions of subordinate classes, at least when measured in terms of legal frameworks and formal definitions of citizenship rights. Their impact on everyday culture and practices is not so clear, however, especially in cases where democratic transitions have coincided with adjustment and economic restructuring, increasing societal polarization, exclusion, and poverty. How have democratic transitions affected cultural representations of domination-subordination? Is there any change in the relationship between the citizenry and the state? Is the state still seen as an institution of "naturalized" domination, in a paternalistic vein? Or is it increasingly considered to be an arbiter and legitimate guarantor of solutions to social conflicts (and not just an agent of repression)? Finally, is the state perceived to be accountable before the citizenry?

Notwithstanding the rich history of popular struggles, people often do not exercise citizenship rights in their everyday lives—even when such rights are formally and legally recognized. The population rarely demands them, does not act according to them, and does not take these rights as their own. In general, subaltern social classes take their subordination to be "normal," given their predominantly naturalistic vision of social hierarchies.[12] Yet the fact remains that political and institutional will can encourage the practice of collective citizenship responsibility, and can establish mechanisms for the expression of demands for rights, by fostering the legitimacy of public spaces for such expression.

DILEMMAS IN THE CONSTRUCTION OF CITIZENSHIP

The Individual and His or Her Interpersonal Environment

At the individual and interpersonal level, responsibility toward others is an inherent component of intergenerational relations.[13] Dependency is unavoidable for the initial survival of the child. It continues throughout life, since the individual establishes his or her subjectivity within the framework of a relationship of need vis-à-vis others. The development of social and affective adult spaces is marked by this relationship to others.[14] The process of individuation consists of differentiating oneself from others—of "liberating" oneself from maternal and paternal tutelage—while at the same time involving oneself in groups and social institutions, where new inequalities and power relations are the rule. A broader identity develops in this process, a sense of "we/us" that generates links of responsibility toward the others who belong to that wider collective body.

The question of individual moral behavior implies going beyond a "universal human nature." It also implies breaking with a positivistic and deterministic approach that seeks linear causality in such indisputable principles as "given such and such early childhood, there ensues such and such emotional or social adult behavior" or "from a given social circumstance, a fixed individual reaction follows." Rather than searching for uniform patterns or regularities in behavior, we must recognize that the human condition is permeated by hiatus and tensions (Heller, 1990). Within this context, circumstances and coincidences—as well as the different ways in which people confront them—help explain why some subjects express solidarity toward strangers, feel responsible for the fate of others, or are more inclined to care for and help those who suffer. The ethical question to be asked, then, is as follows: "Good people exist—How is this possible?" (Heller, 1990: 8).

One issue here concerns the way the "we/us" is defined, where its boundaries lie, and thus which people constitute the "others." A second issue refers to the moral principles that guide the actions of the subject toward that "we/us" as well as toward the "others," the excluded. Beyond the "we/us" and the "others," it is necessary to consider the reference to a third party, the authority (the state)—a dimension that becomes essential when dealing with the public sphere and with macrosocial relationships.

Patterns in the formation of responsibilities toward others vary across cultures, as do the content of responsibilities and the definition of the "moral tasks of responsibility." In Western culture, concern about the issue of responsibility emerged in the social sciences after World War II, when the need to unveil the enigma of the roots of violence and evil—as a way of preventing their recurrence and of finding a solid base for solidarity and democracy—became urgent. The brutality of Nazism and racism inspired the classical psychosocial project on the authoritarian personality (Adorno et. al., 1950), along with experiments attempting to gauge the limits of conformity and obedience to arbitrary (and immoral) orders (Asch, 1951; Milgram, 1974). But in recent years, a shift has occurred toward a more explicit concern with the "positive" side—namely, the roots of altruism, moral commitment, and solidarity (Kohlberg, 1981; Gilligan, 1985; Oliner and Oliner, 1988; Kelman and Hamilton, 1989; Bauman, 1991).

Studies of the development of moral consciousness have taken a cognitive (and liberal-individualist) perspective, which stresses the acceptance of rules as a basic feature of morality and has led to the development of tools for measuring "moral development."[15] However, cognitive and intellectual attachment to universal values is only one possible source of moral behavior, the ideal behavior of Western males. Even without venturing into intercultural or class considerations, we find that the inclusion of gender differences is sufficient to show the presence of alternative sources of moral behavior. Carol Gilligan contrasts the male morality of rights to a female morality of responsibility and care: "This conception of morality as concerned with the activity of care centers moral development around the understanding of responsibility and relationships, just as the conception of morality as fairness ties moral development to the understanding of rights and rules" (Gilligan, 1982: 19). Although different, the two logics are interconnected:

> To understand how the tension between responsibilities and rights sustains the dialectic of human development is to see the integrity of two disparate modes of experience that are in the end connected. While an ethic of justice proceeds from the premise of equality—that everyone should be treated the same—an ethic of care rests on the premise of nonviolence—that no one should be hurt. . . . Just as inequality adversely affects both parties in an unequal relationship, so too violence is destructive for everyone involved. (Gilligan, 1982: 174)

A recent study of non-Jews who helped and rescued Jews in Nazi Europe (Oliner and Oliner, 1988) was similarly concerned with identifying the roots of responsibility and care for others as a manifestation of morality. The study demonstrates that there is no single explanation for altruism and moral courage:

> The rescuers . . . were and are "ordinary" people. . . . Most have done nothing extraordinary before the war nor have they done much that is extraordinary since then. . . . They were not heroes cast in larger-than-life molds. What most distinguished them were their connections with others in relationships of commitment and care. . . . Their involvements with Jews grew out of the ways in which they ordinarily related to other people—their characteristic ways of feeling; their perceptions of who should be obeyed; the rules and examples of conduct they learned from parents, friends, and religious and political associates; and their routine ways of deciding what was wrong and right. . . . They remind us that such courage is not only the province of the independent and the intellectually superior thinkers but that it is

available to all through the virtues of connectedness, commitment, and the quality of relationships developed in ordinary human interactions. (Oliner and Oliner, 1988: 259–260)

In more general terms, the central question concerns the impact of ties of sociability and group bonds on the consciousness of the subject. The key elements of this morality are a sense of responsibility toward others and of solidarity with those who suffer. Cultural, class, and gender variations reveal themselves in distinct types of expected behavior and in the breadth of the definition of "we/us," varying from an intimate to a more public scope (Larrabee, 1993).

Authority figures and images are significant throughout the process of socialization. Learning involves rewards and punishment from an authority: the father (and mother as a secondary figure) in the patriarchal family, a school official, a policeman on the streets, God. The process of individuation entails, on the one hand, the internalization of ethical principles and, on the other, those of the authority, whether legitimate and legal or arbitrary. An autonomous moral subjectivity, prepared to challenge power when it is arbitrary or illegitimate, implies a strong self that has managed to internalize criteria of moral authority. And such subjective autonomy is sustained throughout life by intersubjective reinforcement, anchored in participation in social networks, groups, and institutions.

The Institutional Context and Citizenship Responsibility at the Level of Society

At the macrosocial level, the frame of reference for the process of construction of rights and responsibilities is the state, embodied in such apparatuses as its Judiciary and welfare institutions. In democratic theory, these institutions derive their power and legitimacy from their representativeness, from the power that citizens bestow on them. Nevertheless, no mechanism of formal democracy can guarantee that these institutions will be an effective means of citizen representation. In fact, the Latin American state has traditionally been, and remains to this day, mostly alien and distant from the citizenry, appropriated by some but not by all. The implication is that recognition of state institutions and their legitimacy by the "subjects of law" is an uncertain result of a long historical process of social struggles, without any guarantee of a "happy" and harmonious ending.

The tasks of the democratic transition are, in this respect, very arduous. State institutions have to change hands: Having been appropriated by authoritarian actors, they must now become responsive to society at large. At this juncture, the relationship that the citizenry establishes with state institutions is crucial. Yet in contrast to the daily operation of stable democracies, where relatively clear and ordered expectations are the rule, during periods of transition it is difficult to know in advance what to expect from different state agencies and what the responsibilities of the citizenry are to be. Recognizing the urgent need for democratization of the state, actors in civil society confront a difficult double task: They must demand, push, promote, and monitor the changes, while at the same time learning democratic practices and to constructing their own citizenship.

In stable democracies, the legal structure operates with relative predictability and effectiveness, thereby allowing debates about state legitimacy to be raised to a higher level.[16] But this is not the case in the new democratic regimes of Latin America (at least in large sectors of them). Legality, often experienced as unjust and illegitimate, is not usually enforced in the first place. Violations of human rights and state violence, corruption of public authorities, the questionable means by which powerful Executives seek to limit the autonomy of legislatures and the Judiciary, as well as the more traditional forms of electoral fraud and the buying off of governmental positions—all are well-known practices and need no further discussion here. These phenomena do not disappear with transition to an electoral system; on the contrary, they linger and sometimes even strengthen.

The construction of democratic institutions must therefore become a priority for elected authorities and politicians. But this is not enough. The citizenry and the organizations of civil society must also actively promote the transformation of state institutions. The creation of democratic institutional contexts can then be simultaneously the outcome of and the stimulus for the strengthening of a culture of democratic citizenship. How is such a daunting task accomplished? Where can the will and the power to carry it out be found?

Theoretically, the question of whether the notion of (public) responsibility toward others is or is not an intrinsic feature of citizenship can be debated. What is not debatable is the crucial need for practices of solidarity and responsibility toward others during periods of transition and change, as such practices become primary vectors for the transformation of the relationship between citizens and the state.

What kind of responsibility are we talking about? And what kind of solidarity? At the interpersonal level, solidarity refers to a practice anchored in the identification of others who suffer as "one of us" (Rorty, 1991).[17] At a wider level, one that includes the state and legitimate authority, solidarity requires the participation of groups and organizations that, in the process of challenging formal obligations and established norms, are willing to run considerable risks based on a very special sense of social responsibility. Let us consider this issue further.

The difference between responsibility and accountability is significant here.[18] For instance, Alfred Schutz (1974) clearly distinguishes between the responsibility *for* what someone does or does not do (responsibility) and the responsibility *vis-à-vis* someone (accountability). In short, accountability implies a reference to "objective" and institutionalized duties. It is analogous to "prospective" responsibility (Heller, 1990), which refers to the commitments associated with a position or office, or to a publicly known formal obligation (such that ignorance cannot be claimed as a justification for not obeying). Although meeting one's obligations does not bring rewards or recognition, infringing upon societal imperatives, tied to the fact of "being in charge," may bring about punishment. Clearly, a central demand of citizenship movements in transitions to democracy (and one that must be nurtured continuously in stable democracies as well) is for the accountability of public officials. But such accountability is no minor task, considering the tradition of arbitrariness of power and the persistent strength of authoritarian enclaves.

Another type of responsibility is even more relevant to this context. Here, the subject is responsible for what he or she does—a case of Heller's "retrospective" responsibility, which involves going beyond specific obligations and acting in a way that is guided by personal consciousness. It may even involve challenging and infringing upon current norms. There are circumstances in which the subject commits (or neglects) certain public actions, even when he or she has no obligation to do so and could retreat in inaction. To act or not to act, then, becomes an option dependent mainly on one's own conscience. There are no costs involved in not assuming that kind of responsibility; inaction can also be justified by ignorance or the claim of personal interest. This type of responsibility toward others is the source of solidarity in everyday life. It becomes politically meaningful when, in times of repression and change, some people and groups run the risk of defying established obligations and breaking rules, guided by values and ethical commitments other than those of the authority in power at the time. Through such acts, new values or social virtues might be introduced into the world. Thus, the responsibility involved is immense. Agnes Heller refers to these acts as situations of enormous responsibility or even of world historic responsibility (Heller, 1990: 78–80).[19]

Let me conclude by illustrating these points in the context of two significant issues that have emerged during processes of democratization in Latin America: the violation of human rights, and political corruption. It is never easy for a state (even in a democracy) to admit to violations of human rights committed by the state apparatus itself. The strength of security agencies and the Armed Forces, as well as strategic considerations and political negotiations, often lead governments to do the "least possible" to clarify such circumstances (see Chapter 2 of this volume). Individual victims, without a voice in dictatorships, remain politically weak. Their denunciations will be heard only when magnified by national and international solidarity organizations that support and coordinate acts of denunciation. Such organizations are able to give voice and legitimacy to the demands for redress, while at the same time challenging the legitimacy of state action (Jelin, 1993).

How can this confrontation be transformed into a new institutional framework at the state level, leading to societal recognition of the rights of victims? The human rights movement is a paradigmatic case of the decisive role played by a "third party" in the legitimation of its demands. This third party has no formal obligation or established role. Rather, it is a movement encompassing solidarity organizations founded on the social responsibility of their members—organizations that have resorted to universal ethical appeals. These organizations play a dual role: While legitimating demands vis-à-vis the state, they promote changes in state practices. In addition, through their systematic and unremitting monitoring of government actions in relation to the protection of human rights, they perform a dual citizen-education role, teaching simultaneously how rights should be claimed and how citizenship control should be exercised over the state apparatus.

Formally, the roles of legitimating citizens' demands, settling conflict, and imparting justice belong to the state, and specifically to the Judiciary. In democratic theory, the autonomy of the branches of government and full access to the Judiciary when rights are violated (even by the state) are central to full citizenship; but of course the reality of everyday life remains far from this ideal. It is here that we see the significance of the "educational" role performed by civil society, which teaches citizens how to relate to the legal system while simultaneously fostering the democratization of access to the Judiciary.

Corruption poses a different challenge. Its victims are seldom directly identifiable, and solidarity with them is rarely an important motivation for collective action. Two distinct responsibilities are at stake here: the responsibility of state officers, who may (or may not) behave according to the obligations linked to their positions, and the social responsibility involved in citizens' participation in overseeing the management of government. The formal provisions for institutional control of the administration commonly exist on paper only. The problem lies in the degree of autonomy exercised by such regulatory bodies in relation to the Executive branch; so the question becomes, Who is in charge, and what is the role of the citizenry in these monitoring agencies?

This area, too, is one in which social movements and organizations of civil society can play a significant role. Yet it has received very little study, perhaps because those who are concerned with social movements tend to emphasize societal dynamics (collective identities, social conflicts, opposition movements) rather than the role of such movements as intermediaries between citizens and the state. Social movements always include a large measure of solidarity and of responsibility toward others. In periods of transition to democracy, then, one of the new tasks of social movements is to center their efforts on both the democratization of the state apparatus and the construction of citizenship.

Notes

This chapter was prepared as part of a project entitled "Human Rights and the Consolidation of Democracy: The Trial of the Argentine Military," carried out at CEDES from 1989 to 1992 with the support of the John D. and Catherine T. MacArthur Foundation and the Ford Foundation. I thank Susana Kaufman, Silvia Rabich de Galperín, and Marcelo Leiras for their comments and suggestions.

1. It is necessary to distinguish clearly between this line of inquiry about the construction of citizenship and the legal issues raised regarding both the rights of immigrants and the emergence of new nation-states. This chapter deals with individuals who have formally

recognized rights and obligations toward a nation-state. The issues discussed here thus revolve around the content of their rights and duties.

2. Obviously, not everybody has to learn something entirely new: There are people who remember democratic practices of the past and are prepared to exercise them once again. Nevertheless, dictatorships have lasted long enough that the younger cohorts have had neither the chance to learn democratic political practices (e.g., how to vote) nor the experience of asserting their citizenship in everyday life. Furthermore, even in countries where political democracy has been functioning regularly, the democratic ethos and culture may not have been very strong. Decades or even centuries of arbitrary rulers and a cultural pattern of submission in hierarchical interpersonal relationships (patriarchy in the family, ethnic submission of minorities, etc.) have left legacy that is not easily modified.

3. The rights of the *first generation* are basically civil and political rights; those of the *second generation* are economic, social, and cultural rights, necessitating an active participation of the state in order to secure the material conditions required for the operation of the previous rights. These two categories refer mainly to individual rights. The rights of the *third generation* (to peace, development, and a clean environment) and of the *fourth* (people's rights) are of a different nature, inasmuch as they refer to global and collective phenomena. This sequencing of rights is a matter of historical discussion within the international agencies and should not be interpreted as a statement about priorities.

4. In her text on revolution, Arendt refers to the *public* nature of the notion of freedom during the French Revolution, and to "public happiness" (the right of the citizen to gain access to the public sphere, to participate in public power) during the American Revolution. Later in history, "this disappearance of the 'taste for political freedom' can be considered as the retreat of the individual into an 'intimate sphere of consciousness' where he finds the only appropriate region for human freedom'; from that region, as from a collapsed fortress, the *individual, having prevailed over the citizen,* will then defend himself against a society which, in turn, 'prevails over individuality'" (Arendt, 1965; emphasis added).

5. The realization tht there are no ultimate criteria for choosing among alternative values implies the need to find a space where we can recognize the contingency of our own beliefs and values and simultaneously admit the urgency of an ethical-political commitment to the central issues of our times. Avoiding suffering, expanding the bases of solidarity, widening the spaces for public and responsible action, as well as promoting tolerance, respecting autonomy and difference, and giving voice to the excluded and silent—all such actions may not have a final transcendental justification and can therefore, in a sense, be contingent. But they are not for this reason less necessary (see Downing and Kushner, 1988; Baumann, 1991; Rorty, 1991; Heller, 1990; Levinas, 1982; and, especially, Schirmer, 1988).

6. In the classical *polis,* civic responsibility could be referred to as an intense and direct involvement of the individual in the social and political affairs of the collectivity (Kelly, 1979). And, indeed, modern nationalistic movements have attempted to build civic commitment through identification with the nation-state. The result, however, has not always been successful, given the development of intolerant nationalism, rigidity, and racism in some cases (Kelly, 1979; Reis, 1993). The current challenge is to find a way to ground the sense of community and belonging in an ethical sense of equity, in a human concern for others, and in a concern for rights and reciprocal recognition.

7. The interaction between these demands of citizenship and the requirements of the construction of a new order is analyzed by Lechner (1993). He points out that the social

"demand for community," involving a search for a new collective identity, is a major component of the challenges facing the new democratic state.

8. *"Ahí [cuando llegó Perón] uno aprendió a pedir!"* (Then [when Perón arrived] one learned how to ask! [for things]), says an interviewee in a popular quarter of Buenos Aires (Rubinich, 1991).

9. In Argentina, what grew under the first Peronism (1946–1955) was the awareness of labor rights (Jelin et al., 1995). In Brazil is what Santos (1979) refers to as *regulated citizenship.*

10. On this point, the positions of populist regimes and of the left often coincided. Both tended to identify civil liberties and "negative" rights with "bourgeois freedom," "formal" democracy, and outdated liberalism (Oliveira, 1989).

11. As analyzed by Kathryn Sikkink in Chapter 4 of this volume, international networks—whether led by the United Nations, by nongovernmental organizations, or by transnational information agencies—play a meaningful role in this area.

12. Empirical evidence for this assertion can be found in studies of everyday life in different contexts. Especially relevant are the cases of Villa El Salvador in the outskirts of Lima and of Buenos Aires where, in spite of expectations, the practice of citizenship is limited (Jelin et al., 1995). The former had a record of self-government and community autonomy, which could hardly be consolidated when changes in the political and institutional context were running in the opposite direction (Zapata, 1989; Blondet, 1991; Jelin, 1993).

13. This section of the paper is the result of theoretical interdisciplinary discussions held over two years' time with Susana Kaufman and Silvia Rabich de Galperín.

14. From a psychoanalytic perspective, it can be claimed that a strong need for security governs our internal world—a security we seek as protection from our catastrophic primitive anxieties. In searching for that security in external reality, we become vulnerable and dependent, often beyond our will (Amati Sas, 1991).

15. Thus, in Kohlberg's stages of moral development, that of helping and pleasing others (the third stage) comes before and is developmentally inferior to the stage in which relationships are subordinated to rules; and full moral development is defined as the stage in which rules are subordinated to universal principles of justice (Kohlberg and Kramer, 1969; Kohlberg, 1981).

16. Habermas, for example, asks about the necessary conditions under which legality becomes a source of legitimacy: "Legitimacy can only generate legitimacy if the judicial order reacts reflexively to the need of justification that emerges with the positivization of law, so that judicial procedures of justification permeable to moral arguments become institutionalized" (Habermas, 1991: 163). In current transitions, it would be utopic—or even "extraterrestrial"—to imagine legal arrangements that react reflexively to the need of justification, or to ask for the institutionalization of legal procedures of justification permeable to moral arguments. Furthermore, it is only when minimal legality is operating in everyday experience that "violence of law" can be critically analyzed (Sarat and Kearns, 1992).

17. The hope of expanding human solidarity lies in "the ability to perceive with increasing clarity that traditional differences (based on tribe, religion, race, custom, and others of the same kind) are of no relevance when compared to the similarities referred to pain and humiliation; it is conceived as the capacity to consider people who are very different from us an included in the category 'us'" (Rorty, 1991: 210).

18. This distinction does not have a linguistic form in Spanish, which considers both to be "responsibilities."

19. Further complexities are introduced when the relationship between responsibility and guilt is brought to the fore. Who is responsible for redressing injuries when there is no way to establish guilt? Who is responsible for *preventing* harm? (Camps, 1990).

References

Adorno, Theodore, Else Frenkel-Brunswik, Daniel J. Levinson, and R. Nevitt Sanford. (1950). *The Authoritarian Personality.* New York: Harper and Row.

Amati Sas, Silvia. (1991). "Recuperar la vergüenza." In Janine Puget and Rene Kaes (eds.), *Violencia de estado y psicoanálisis.* Buenos Aires: Paidós-Asociación pro–Derechos Humanos.

Ansaldi, Waldo. (1986). "Una reflexión sobre los derechos humanos desde una perspectiva de las ciencías sociales." In Waldo Ansaldi (ed.), *La ética de la democracia.* Buenos Aires: CLACSO.

Arendt, Hannah. (1949). "The Rights of Man: What Are They?" *Modern Review* 3, no. 1 (Summer).

———. (1965). *On Revolution.* New York: Viking Press.

———. (1973). *The Origins of Totalitarianism.* New York: Harcourt, Brace and World.

Asch, Solomon. (1951). "Effects of Group Pressure upon the Modification and Distortion of Judgements." In U.S. Office of Naval Research, *Groups, Leadership and Men.* Pittsburgh: Carnegie Press.

Ballon, Eduardo E. (1986). *Estado, sociedad y sistema político: El caso de Villa El Salvador.* Paper presented at "Movimientos sociales, democracia y sistema político en América Latina y el área andino," a seminar in Cuenca, Ecuador (November).

Bauman, Zygmunt. (1991). *Modernity and the Holocaust.* Oxford: Polity Press and Blackwell Press.

Blondet, Cecilia. (1991). *Las mujeres y el poder: Una historia de Villa el Salvador.* Lima: IEP.

Brubaker, Rogers. (1984). *The Limits of Rationality: An Essay on the Social and Moral Thought of Max Weber.* London: Allen & Unwin.

Camps, Victoria. (1990). *Virtudes públicas.* Madrid: Espasa-Calpe.

Collier, David, and Ruth Berins Collier. (1991). *Shaping the Political Arena.* Princeton: Princeton University Press.

Downing, Theodore E., and Gilbert Kushner (eds.). (1988). *Human Rights and Anthropology.* Cambridge, Mass.: Cultural Survival.

Geertz, Clifford. (1984). "Distinguished Lecture: Anti Anti-relativism." *American Anthropologist* 86, no. 2 (June).

Gilligan, Carol. (1985). *In a Different Voice: Psychological Theory and Women's Development.* Cambridge, Mass.: Harvard University Press.

Gingold, Laura. (1991). *Crónicas de muertes anunciadas: El caso de Ingeniero Budge.* Buenos Aires: Documento CEDES No. 65.

Habermas, Jürgen. (1975). *Legitimation Crisis.* Boston: Beacon Press.

———. (1991). *Escritos sobre moralidad y eticidad.* Barcelona: Paidós.

Heller, Agnes. (1990). *General Ethics.* Oxford: Basil Blackwell.

Jelin, Elizabeth. (1993). "La política de la memoria: EL Movimiento de Derechos Humanos y la construcción de la democracia en la Argentina." In *Juicio, Castigos, y Memorias: Derechos humanos y justicia en la política argentina*. Buenos Aires: Nueva Visión.

Jelin, Elizabeth, and Pablo Vila. (1987a). *Podría ser yo: Los sectores populares en imagen y palabra* (photographs by Alicia D'Amico). Buenos Aires: CEDES/Ediciones de la Flor.

———. (1987b). "Política y cotidianeidad." *Punto de Vista* 10, no. 29 (April-June).

Kelly, George A. (1979). "Who Needs a Theory of Citizenship?" *Daedalus* 108, no. 4.

Kelman, Herbert, and V. Lee Hamilton. (1989). *Crimes of Obedience: Toward a Psychology of Authority and Responsibility*. New Haven: Yale University Press.

Kohlberg, Lawrence. (1981). *The Philosophy of Moral Development*. San Francisco: Harper and Row.

Kohlberg, Lawrence, and R. Kramer. (1969). "Continuities and Discontinuities in Child and Adult Moral Development." *Human Development* 12: 93–120.

Larrabee, Mary Jeanne (ed.). (1993). *An Ethic of Care: Feminist and Interdisciplinary Perspectives*. New York and London: Routledge.

Lechner, Norbert. (1986). "Los derechos humanos como categoría política." In Waldo Ansaldi (ed.), *La ética de la democracia*. Buenos Aires: CLACSO.

———. (1993). "Modernización y modernidad: La búsqueda de ciudadanía." In Centro de Estudios Sociológicos, *Modernización económica, democracia política y democracia social*. Mexico City: El Colegio de México.

Lefort, Claude. (1987). "Los derechos del hombre y el estado benefactor." *Vuelta* (July).

Levinas, Emmanuel. (1982). *Ethique et infini*. Paris: Librairie Artheme Fayard.

Marshall, T. H. (1964). *Citizenship and Social Democracy*. New York: Doubleday.

Milgram, Stanley. (1974). *Obedience to Authority*. New York: Harper and Row.

Offe, Claus. (1985). *Contradictions of the Welfare State*. Cambridge, Mass.: MIT Press.

Oliner, Samuel, and Pearl M. Oliner. (1988). *The Altruistic Personality*. New York: Free Press.

Oliveira, Luciano de. (1989). "Derechos humanos y marxismo: Breve ensayo para un nuevo paradigma." *El Otro Derecho* 4.

Reis, Fabio Wanderley. (1993). "Ciudadanía, estado y mercado: Democracia social y democracia política en el proceso de transformación capitalista." In Centro de Estudios Sociológicos, *Modernización económica, democracia política y democracia social*. Mexico City: El Colegio de México.

Rorty, Richard. (1986). "On Ethnocentrism: A Reply to Clifford Geertz." *Michigan Quarterly Review* 25: 525–534.

———. (1991). *Contingencia, ironía y solidaridad*. Barcelona: Paidós.

Rubinich, Lucas. (1991). *Apuntes sobre nociones de derecho en sectores populares urbanos*. Buenos Aires: Documento CEDES 71.

Santos, Wanderley Guilherme dos. (1979). *Cidadania e justicia*. Rio de Janeiro: Editora Campus.

Sarat, Austin, and Thomas R. Kearns (eds.). (1992). *Law's Violence*. Ann Arbor: University of Michigan Press.

Schirmer, Jennifer. (1988). "The Dilemma of Cultural Diversity and Equivalency in Universal Human Rights Standards." In Theodore E. Downing and Gilbert Kushmer (eds.), *Human Rights and Anthropology*. Cambridge, Mass.: Cultural Survival.

Schutz, Alfred. (1974). "Algunas ambigüedades de la noción de responsabilidad." In *Estudios sobre teoría social.* Buenos Aires: Amorrortu.

Valdés, Teresa. (1990). *Mujeres y derechos humanos "Menos tu vientre."* Santiago: FLACSO Work Document, Social Studies Series No. 8.

van Gunsteren, Herman. (1978). "Notes on a Theory of Citizenship." In Pierre Birnbaum, Jack Lively, and Geraint Parry (eds.), *Democracy, Consensus, and Social Contract.* London: Sage.

Young-Bruehl, Elisabeth. (1982). *Hannah Arendt: For Love of the World.* New Haven: Yale University Press.

Zapata, Gastón A. (1989). "Una estrategia de desarrollo alternativa basada en la participación social y la organización comunitaria: La experiencia de Villa El Salvador." In Bernardo Kliksberg (ed.), *¿Cómo enfrentar la pobreza? Estrategias y experiencias organizacionales inovadoras.* Buenos Aires: CLAD/UNDP/GEL.

◀ 7 ▶

The State, the Market, and
Democratic Citizenship

FÁBIO WANDERLEY REIS

Political scientist Adam Przeworski has advocated a minimalist conception of democracy as a means of avoiding analytical confusion and of facilitating effective action to address practical problems in the real world. Speaking at a symposium held in Mexico City in 1990,[1] Przeworski insisted that what matters ultimately is "that people shall not be killed!"—that proper guarantees shall exist for certain fundamental rights, which add up to the Rechtstaadt or "state of law."

Difficulties arising from Przeworski's position provide a useful starting point for the discussion that follows. Should we seek to ensure only those rights that are usually called "civil" rights? What about political rights, such as the right to vote or to run for office? One could hardly claim to have truly guaranteed civil rights in the absence of these rights—that is, under conditions of political dictatorship. But what about the social rights that complete the expansion of citizenship in T. H. Marshall's (1965) classic discussion? Of course, if social inequality is rampant, power will be distributed unequally, thus inevitably undermining prospects for the full enjoyment of civil and political rights by all.

Furthermore, Przeworski himself argues, in his studies of social democracy in the developed capitalist countries of Western Europe, that democracy is rooted in a social compromise, whereby the fundamental conflict between capitalists and workers is attenuated: Workers accept private property and the control of investments by capitalists, whereas capitalists accept political democracy and the ensuing enactment of social policies by the state in the interest of workers (Przeworski, 1985). Clearly, this way of conceptualizing democracy poses the question of the social conditions in which such a compromise can be achieved and is made to last, thus bringing us to the age-old query about the "social conditions for (political) democracy." But there is no reason to adopt the "sociologism" implicit in this phrase, which may just as easily be turned the other way around: What are the political conditions for social (and political) democracy? Such an inversion of the old formula (which highlights the sequence "initial social conditions → institutions → modified social conditions) is indispensable if we are to identify what must be done to attain the goal of democracy. It calls attention to the need both for deliberate institution building and for proactive measures undertaken through and by the state.

Przeworski's minimalist stance is thus clearly inconsistent—as is any position that claims to favor "merely" political (or liberal) democracy and refuses to see the call for action and construction contained therein. The opportunity for a maximalist (or at least an ambitious) view of democracy is undeniable, insofar as it is imperative for the achievement of liberal or "minimal" democracy itself. But one underlying insight in Przeworski's position is certainly correct. If our goal is democracy, we are concerned fundamentally with the achievement of conditions affirmed in a minimalist conception: The aim is ultimately to produce the conditions needed for free decisionmaking by multiple and autonomous agents. Yet there is a risk that, when actively intervening in pursuit of this goal, the state itself may become the chief obstacle to its realization. The tension and ambivalence at the core of this perspective highlight some of the complexities that emerge at the level of practice. They also point up the most important issue in fledgling democracies: not the size of the state per se or its capacity for action but, rather, the need for institutional guarantees to ensure the openness, social sensitivity, and democratic character of the inevitably complex and activist state. The aim, then, is not to contain and restrict the state but to strengthen it appropriately.

THE MARKET, CONCENTRATION OF POWER, AND THE STATE

The emergence and expansion of capitalism produce the context within which the tension between the social and political aspects of democracy takes form. Many observers have examined the relationship between capitalism and political democracy, often emphasizing their supposed incompatibility at the level of underlying principles (Offe, 1985). But the matter can also be seen in a different light—within a context crucial to the issues that concern us in this volume. I refer to the socially democratizing character of capitalism itself. The crucial foundation of capitalism is the (at least potentially) egalitarian principle of the market, which tends to erode those inequalities pertaining to the traditional world of status, ascription, and domination. Indeed, the contradictory features commonly associated with capitalism can be attributed to the operation of this egalitarian market principle simultaneous with institutional acceptance of the new inequalities that are inherently generated by the concrete operation of any real market. Thus, capitalism is bound to produce both a new spirit of equality and peculiar forms of inequality. The latter are translated into class society—a particular type of social stratification that differs from caste-based or status-based society precisely because of the operation of the market principle.

Socialism was the historically most important attempt to respond to the contradictions of capitalism. The recent breakdown of socialism in the USSR and Eastern Europe can clearly be understood as evidence that attempting to dispense with the market was an enormous mistake. This lesson forces itself upon us not only on the grounds of efficiency but, more important, on the basis of accumulating evidence—which the experience of socialist countries has corroborated in a lasting and unequivocal manner—of the fundamental affinity between the principle of the market and the ideal of democracy.[2] For, notwithstanding the many negative connotations associated with the idea of the market, in contemporary ideological debates this idea fundamentally involves notions of contract and of free and autonomous deliberation by individual agents engaged in transactions. In this sense it connotes the egalitarian principle emphasized earlier. An additional implication is that, strictly speaking, an oligopolistic or monopolistic market is not a real market. Thus, in contrast to the usual opposition between market and state (whereby the expansion of one is thought of as necessarily taking place at the expense of the other), the affirmative operation of the state can be seen as indispensable to neutralization of the tendency of real markets to be penetrated by oligopolies and monopolies—that is, to neutralization or mitigation of power mechanisms within the market.

THE MARKET, INTERESTS, AND DEMOCRACY

This approximation of democracy and the market, which some readers will probably resist, requires further elaboration. Otherwise, it may seem akin to a conventionally Liberal (or neo-Liberal) point of view, whose adherents would be eager to avoid restrictions on entrepreneurial "free enterprise" and may exhibit limited sensitivity to social concerns. Such a conventional liberalism has little to do with the outlook I am trying to sketch here, however. Resistance to the argument I am making also might reflect the common tendency to link democracy to an altruistic and civic sort of solidarity, whereas the notion of market inevitably emphasizes the self-interested component of transactions or interactions among agents.

A crucial reason for presenting the idea of the market as a point of reference for the discussion of democracy concerns the equilibrium it implies between the realistic element of self-interest and the solidaristic elements that critics would be likely to stress. Such an equilibrium, in which the distinctive logic of each of the contrasting principles weakens somewhat in practice, is clearly present in Max Weber's conception of the market. As is well known, Weber places this category in an intermediate position between, on the one hand, the concepts of "society" and "societal action" (which refer to the rationally motivated mutual adjustment of interests) and, on the other hand, the concepts of "community" and "community action" (which refer to the feeling of participants of belonging to a whole) (Weber, 1984: 33–35). Thus, although the market is unequivocally the arena for the generalized pursuit of interests, this quest takes place under conditions that presuppose the underlying operation of a principle of solidarity and the adherence to norms that regulate and mitigate it. Such conditions ensure that interest-based exchanges and interactions may recur and endure without degenerating into a Hobbesian situation of generalized fraud and, eventually, belligerence. Given the aforementioned equilibrium, the category of the market, understood in such a way as to prevent its "contamination" by elements of power (oligopolies and monopolies), can become the point of reference for a sort of "realistic utopia."

Moreover, by stressing the notion of market as distinguished by the autonomy and equality of agents, I can ascribe to it a scope and a relevance that go far beyond the sphere conventionally thought of as "economic," making it appropriate to speak of a "political market" as a regulating idea capable of encompassing important aspects of the democratic ideal. This suggestion can best be appreciated through a reevaluation of the basic notion of interest itself. Current usage tends to link "interest" above all to the "economic" sphere defined in a rather narrow way, in connection with values or objectives of a "material" nature. I propose, instead, to approach the notion of interest as generically equivalent to what Jürgen Habermas has called "self-affirmation" (Habermas, 1975a, vol. 2: 104). In this sense, the idea of interest is intertwined with the ideas of strategic interaction and of power—and there clearly is no reason to restrict the category of the market, seen as the locus of the play of interests, to the economic arena. Actually, the reference to "interests," "strategy," and "power," as well as to the affinities among them, turns out to provide a fundamental criterion for an analytic definition of politics as such. According to this definition, politics would consist of strategic interactions and the search for self-affirmation or for power among individuals and collectivities in any concrete institutional or social context, independent of the specific content of goals that may be the object of conflict or cooperation in one sphere of interaction or another—that is, of religious, material or "economic" goals relating to class, race, ethnic group, gender, generation, and so on. In other words, politics, understood as the interplay among interests, has no content of its own and is socially ubiquitous. It penetrates social relationships of all kinds and pertains to the "social basis" of conflicts as well as to the potential or actual foci of solidarity and group identification that become engaged in conflicts. At the same time, politics necessarily entails the organizational expression of conflicts and solidarities at the level conventionally referred to as "political" or "politico-institutional."[3]

ASCRIPTIVE IDENTITIES, AUTONOMY, AND PLURALISM

At this juncture a third set of observations is in order. Resorting to the "realistic utopia" conceived in reference to the market allows us to avoid important mistakes commonly found in debates about questions of rights. The basic point is that there is an analytic correspondence between the pursuit of interests and the condition of individualism, a correspondence that has important consequences. Indeed, if the condition one aims to achieve entails the autonomy of individual agents, it necessarily includes the idea that the opportunities faced by any particular agent (his or her "life chances," to resort to a celebrated phrase by Max Weber) should not be determined by his or her inclusion in a certain group or social category—that is, by factors of ascription. The insight here is that relationships of power or domination in social life are usually linked to the operation of such ascriptive factors and to the corresponding restrictions on access to various occupations or activities, or to free social interchange. Under such restrictions, the opportunities for general social interchange and social promotion that are opened up (or closed) to the members of society do not, of course, depend on their individual characteristics or efforts. Indeed, a crucial aspect of the penetration and expansion of the market principle is its opposition to principles of ascription, for it characteristically favors free involvement in transactions on the part of individuals (in accordance with the "liberty of factors" that is usually stressed in conventional economic discussions).

These ideas are of great relevance to the problem of collective identities and the relationship of this problem to individual identities and autonomy. In this regard, discussions of citizenship and human rights tend to emphasize the role played by ascriptive factors of collective identity. From the same standpoint, ascriptive collective identities, understood in terms of the rather naive or uncritical immersion of individuals in groups or social categories taken as "given," are seen as natural entities that, in a democratic society, should be granted the right to express themselves freely in the sociopolitical arena. The underlying logic of this perspective is based on a conception of a society in which partial collectivities built around ascriptive factors (racial or ethnic groups, for instance) confront other groups of the same nature (natives and conquerors, or blacks and whites in a racist society) and are made the object of discrimination, exploitation, and so on. In contrast to such a negative condition is a scenario in which the previously subordinate groups, through mobilization and struggle, come to affirm their collective identities (i.e., as groups distinguished by ascriptive attributes) and to establish egalitarian relationships with their former oppressors, recognizing the latter as members of another similarly ascriptive category. The resulting condition might well be described—in the conventional way of looking at these problems—in terms of "pluralism."

Let us concede that the open confrontation between social categories based on ascriptive criteria is both justified and, probably, inevitable in cases where relationships of inequality and domination actually prevail. Domination is apt to ensure the salience and visibility of the ascriptive traits that distinguish competing groups; therefore, the definition of the personal identities of individuals will be conditioned decisively by reference to the ascriptive, unequal, and at least latently hostile categories to which the individuals belong. Nonetheless, such a confrontation, whether in the open and dramatic form pertaining to the moment of mobilization and struggle or in the quiet and stable form that would supposedly ensue, should not be seen as a desirable goal or as an adequate way of realizing the ideals of liberty and democracy. Indeed, the full achievement of these ideals should not imply a sort of confrontation of collective "powers" constructed around ascriptive criteria such as race or ethnicity; if this *were* the goal, outright segregation would probably be the best means to accomplish it, as often occurs in the sphere of international relations. Instead, the result to be expected is the elimination of the social relevance of any criterion of this kind—that is, its elimination as a factor capable of influencing or in any way restricting social intercourse. In other words, the links between individual identity and collective identities of whatever nature, with their unavoidable appeal to some form of ascription, stand in the way of the fully open and democratic society. From a normative point of view, therefore, they can be admitted only insofar as reference to them may turn out to be a necessary step in the process of seeking the final suppression of their social relevance (especially in connection to power relationships) and the fullest possible affirmation of choices that, in the last analysis, can only be the choices of individuals. It would also be necessary to emphasize the degree to which the more or less rigidly ascriptive character of different identities affects the prospects they may face with regard to such a liberating process. We are able to imagine the "classless society" being achieved by means of class struggle, because the ascriptive "ingredient" is less intense in the case of collective identities defined through the social division of labor, which, in principle, can change through personal effort or achievement. "Race struggle," in contrast (absent total segregation or the absurd hypothesis of the physical elimination of some of the races involved), will inevitably conclude with the coexistence of the previously struggling races. This coexistence may turn out to be egalitarian; but it will hardly be harmonious and brotherly. Analogous observations apply, of course, to relations between ethnic groups.

In short, the kind of pluralism to be sought is that in which the links of individuals to given social groups reflect decisions made voluntarily in connection with freely chosen goals. Stated differently, the collectivities or social groups making up this sort of pluralistic structure can only be voluntary associations; even though these associations may turn out to be durable, individual participation in them is by necessity provisional and varied in nature. Conversely, the pluralist ideal is undermined when the existence of groups is linked to the operation of asymmetric and coercive mechanisms for stigmatizing individuals and restricting their opportunities to decide freely such basic matters as what to do and with whom to interact (from the level of merely economic interchange up to the level of love or intimate affairs)—and hence how to build oneself up or what to make of oneself. By implication, the ideal of autonomy requires, above all, extension of the sphere of free will and reflexive deliberation to the very level of personal identity. Of course, all that which is socially given, as a consequence of the immersion of individuals in various collectivities, is the essential "raw material" for this process of reflexive self-construction. But any effort at artificially or deliberately producing collective identities should be greeted with suspicion, all the more so if it is based on rigidly ascriptive criteria—unless, I must repeat, it is a tool in the very struggle against the ascriptive foundations of relations of domination. In this case it should contain an important element of self-criticism and aim clearly at the elimination of the social relevance of attributes or traits of an ascriptive nature.

The suggestions made in this section help us to better understand several aspects of the themes discussed by Rodolfo Stavenhagen (in Chapter 8) and Carlos Hasenbalg (in Chapter 9). The case of race relations in Brazil, for instance, offers a contrast between two different points of view. One favors an attitude of combative affirmation of black identity and intransigent denunciation of the Brazilian official ideology of racial democracy. The other is inclined to make that ideology effective and consequential, and to use it as a real instrument in the construction of a society where racial characteristics of individuals indeed become irrelevant. Despite what is arguably a mystifying component in the ideology of racial democracy, we cannot deny that it describes a goal that is clearly preferable to egalitarian racial hostility.[4]

CIVIC AND CIVIL DIMENSIONS OF CITIZENSHIP

A basic ambivalence characterizes the notion of citizenship (a notion that is clearly crucial to the theme of rights), as discussed in the literature of both the social sciences and political philosophy. An article published some years ago by George Armstrong Kelly (1979) illustrates the point.

Kelly contrasts the civic and civil dimensions of citizenship. In his view, the civic dimension is linked to the duties and responsibilities of citizens—specifically, to the propensity of the latter toward solidaristic forms of behavior and the observance of civic virtues. This civic dimension involves a process of identification with the collectivity, or with a conception of personal identity deeply marked by the individual's insertion into the community. The most advanced case of civic citizenship is that of the classical Greek *polis,* but the modern nation-state also seeks to mobilize such feelings and attitudes on the part of its members. By contrast, the civil dimension of citizenship corresponds to the modern search for the affirmation of rights by individual members of the national collectivity. Following T. H. Marshall's (1965) analysis of the sequential realization of various kinds of rights, the civil dimension of citizenship corresponds either to the moment of the emergence of civil rights proper or to the moment in which political and social rights appear on the scene.

The essential point here is that the meaning of citizenship varies widely depending on whether we emphasize one or the other of these two dimensions, for the values expressed by notions of civil and civic citizenship are in clear contrast with one another. Clearly crucial to real citizenship is the "civil" (or "liberal") component whereby the members of the collectivity affirm themselves autonomously, in the private sphere (i.e., in the market), in a way that not only dispenses with the state but may even involve acting effectively against it. Actually, this component is present even in the classical world, as shown by the Aristotelian notion, further elaborated in recent times by Hannah Arendt, that the Athenian citizen qualified as such by being, above all, a private "monarch" or "tyrant"—that is, by controlling the family and the slaves and having the freedom, as a result, to devote himself to public affairs (Arendt, 1968: ch. 3).

Be that as it may, in the current literature on citizenship the necessity of accommodating the needs of those whose general social condition does not allow them to affirm themselves autonomously leads to a shift in which the notion of citizenship is reformulated so as to include an unavoidable paternalistic ingredient—one inherent in the idea of "social protection" and in the social aspect, as such, of citizenship. The meaning of *citizenship* thus introduced is opposed to the autonomist and liberal sense of the word, and the idea of social protection or social assistance is then defined (or redefined) in terms of a right stemming from egalitarian insertion into the community—that is, as something linked to a shared status, as stressed by Marshall (1965), rather than to market interactions. This shift signifies a return to the solidarity of traditional civic virtues; the real citizen is no longer the bearer of rights that are exercised in the private sphere and affirmed, if necessary, against the state (and against other citizens). Rather, the individual becomes the one who acknowledges his or her responsibilities before the collectivity (particularly its destitute members) and who is willing to deliver to the state the resources and the authority needed for it to act on behalf of the collectivity. Obviously, we are dealing here, above all, with the operation of the welfare state in response to the "social rights" of Marshall's expanded concept of citizenship.

However, the tension between the two dimensions, and the values affirmed in each of them, is so severe that they often appear contradictory. If the private, market, or civil sphere is the sphere of autonomy, it is also that of egoism and particularism; and if the civic sphere is where solidarity occurs, it is simultaneously the sphere of dependency. The relevant literature, especially that portion devoted to social policy, provides disappointingly little guidance for resolving the contradictory implications deriving from the contrasting assumptions about citizenship.

Two examples will support this contention. The first is provided by George Armstrong Kelly (1979), who elaborates on the distinction between civil and civic citizenship. Analyzing the citizen's claim for social rights in the welfare state, Kelly contrasts "negative citizenship" (which would be involved in this claim) to the "positive" or genuine citizenship associated with the civic virtues of the classical world.[5] This analysis parallels the denunciation by Habermas (1975a) of the posture of the "client" as contrasted with that of the supposedly "authentic" citizen (Santos, 1979: 74ff). Habermas's evaluation is clearly antagonistic toward the elements of egalitarianism, consensus, and solidarity that mark much of the literature devoted to the social dimension of citizenship, including, most notably, the classic essay by Marshall (1965). And it is perplexing to note that some people are willing to associate the institutionalized welfare state, distinguished by universalist traits developed under the aegis of expanding citizenship rights, with notions of "clientelism," which traditionally refer to expressions of more or less spurious particularism. Equally noteworthy is the faulty idealism contained in the vision of a virtuous "authentic" citizen who does not make rights-based (or, more "realistically," interests-based) demands upon the state.

The second example is taken from the work of the Brazilian political scientist Wanderley Guilherme dos Santos, whose influential use of the category of *cidadania regulada* (regulated citizenship) for characterizing certain supposedly basic aspects of social policy in Brazil illustrates the ambiguities found in much of the Latin American literature on the subject (Santos, 1979: 75–76.) The purpose of the phrase is clearly to emphasize a certain ingredient of authoritarian manipulation and control on the part of the state, which Santos achieves by stressing the densely intertwined linkages between Brazilian welfare policies and corporatist mechanisms. In this case, we are dealing with a concept of citizenship whose roots are to be found in "a system of occupational stratification . . . defined by legal norms," whereby the state regulation of professions, the professional identification papers, and the state-regulated trade unions constitute "the three parameters within which citizenship comes to be defined" (Santos, 1979: 74). Santos calls attention to the importance of the principles through which the Brazilian state created welfare programs for retirement and allowances during the 1930s. By linking individual benefits to contributions and by providing differential treatment according to earnings, the state has "consecrated in practice the inequality of welfare benefits given to occupationally defined stratified categories of citizens" (Santos, 1979: 77). But this occupationally stratifying mechanism is nothing other than what the welfare literature usually calls social insurance, an arrangement in which benefits are proportional to contributions. Of course, social insurance inevitably rewards the individual for having the capacity to mobilize resources by himself or herself—that is, to succeed in the "market." The denunciation contained in the concept of regulated citizenship thus suffers from a clear contradiction: On the one hand, those who employ this concept as a denunciation have claimed that citizenship should not be regulated, so as to escape state tutelage or authoritarianism; on the other hand they have criticized mechanisms created by the state for merely sanctifying differences that come from the market—which means that more regulation is called for.

This issue leads to difficult arguments, not unlike those arising from the confrontation between the perspectives of contractarianism and utilitarianism. An important point about the concept of citizenship merits emphasis here: What appears to be a tension between the consensual and civic elements concerning insertion into a community, on the one hand, and the autonomous self-affirmation of every individual member of society, on the other, is a tension that pervades politics, as such, and is therefore inevitable. For whatever the circumstances, political life necessarily involves permanent stress and accommodation between the instrumental affirmation of interests (ultimately, of individual interests) and the definition of foci of solidarity and of collective identities on different levels. (The coexistence of these identities results in the definition of collective interests.) The great challenge of modern political life, then, is to reconcile the conflicting demands involved therein by means of the rich but ambivalent standard provided by the expanded ideal of citizenship, so as to make of the latter both a basis for the egalitarian coexistence of individual and social agents and an arena for the autonomous pursuit of objectives or interests of whatever nature.[6]

CIVIL SOCIETY AND CITIZENSHIP

Let us take a very brief detour to consider the discussion of "civil society" in *Civil Society and Political Theory,* by Jean Cohen and Andrew Arato (1992). In my view, some relevant aspects of citizenship can indeed be captured by reference to the concept of civil society. But Cohen and Arato, among other scholars, claim a rather special status for "civil society" as the focus for a new theoretical perspective, in which it would be added to the categories of "market" and "state" as the privileged space of operation of distinctive principles. All in all, I think that this view turns out to be more harmful than beneficial. At stake is a question of scientific parsimony—that is, whether the "space" of relevant problems can be adequately "mapped out" by means of the market-state dichotomy, and whether the reach of the concept of market can be expanded so as to recover the space that would correspond to "civil society." Actually, the attempt to "scissor" out and define the place of civil society turns out to dilute the crucial interplay between the aspects of solidarity and interests, consensus and conflict, "community" and "society," that I stressed as pervading the different levels or spheres of society, thus permitting an analytic definition of the very idea of politics.

The difficulties associated with Cohen and Arato's position emerge, for instance, when "civil society" is linked to the contrast discussed earlier between the "civil" and the "civic." The intention of much of what Cohen and Arato propose is to emphasize the role played by aspects related to the problem of identity, which are clearly akin to the solidarity and civic dimension. But it would clearly be improper to exclude the operation of interests from the realm of civil society: Think of "civil society" in the Hegelian sense; of the concept's obvious affinity to Kelly's (1979) notion of the "civil," prone to degenerate into clientelism and particularism; and, above all, of the fact that Cohen and Arato are explicitly concerned with social movements that strategically seek an objectiveness of their own while resisting other actors. On the other hand, to divest the concept of the elements of solidarity and civic virtue, which presuppose community and thus also identity, is to miss something essential, making market transactions equivalent to virtually belligerent interactions.

CAPITALISM AND DEMOCRACY

Capitalism and its expansion have provided the most general context for our discussion. From this perspective, the challenge outlined earlier in reference to citizenship can be described in terms of a basic constitutional problem that imposes itself on modern nation-states as a consequence of capitalism's affirmation of the principles of the market and of the "civil." How, we must ask, is a "civic" accommodation of that affirmation to be achieved? At the crux of the problem is the fact that we cannot expect the solution to be merely the result of some sort of moral, ideological, or sociopsychological "conversion" to a certain "civic culture" considered appropriate to democracy. Rather, the prevalence of civic virtues will have to issue from a propitious process of development and maturation of the very logic of the "civil" and of interests. In short, the problems of democracy, especially with respect to ensuring that various rights are upheld, will hardly have a stable solution if the problems of capitalism are not resolved and if capitalism itself is not made to flourish and mature.

The specifically social feature of this constitutional issue gives rise to a crucial reflection. It turns out that the socially democratizing character of capitalism, which is found in the very affirmation of the principle of the market, also leaves its imprint on the operation of the aforementioned logic of the "civil" and of interests. The reason is that social character operates in such a way as to define foci of potentially antagonistic collective interests (or of opposed nuclei of solidarity). Specifically, it generates and reproduces social classes as a form of inequality specific to capitalism. From this outcome derives the latent aggravation of social conflict, which will tend to crystallize around encompassing forms of solidarity as the general logic of capitalist development evolves. The latter will happen, however, only up to the point where the maturation of capitalism itself produces the necessary conditions for the effective emergence of the social component of citizenship and, hence, for a twisting of that logic. The latter step in this pattern of evolution will probably be accompanied by what can be described as the institutionalization of the very contradictions of capitalism. Such institutionalization, in turn, may take place through the operation of mechanisms akin to the "neocorporatist" patterns of many contemporary European countries.[7]

In this sense, the decisive test of the successful solution of the constitutional problem, and thus of the consolidation and stabilization of "merely" political democracy, is demonstrated by the extent to which issues relating to the social confrontation can be processed and solved institutionally—that is, through the routine operation of the appropriate legal-institutional apparatus and the mechanisms it establishes. A negative example of sorts is provided by the recent Brazilian experience of the impeachment of President Fernando Collor. As Teresa P.R. Caldeira suggests in Chapter 11 of the present volume, this event augured well for the prospects of democratic consolidation in Brazil. The experience of seeing political institutions at work in a normal and effective way under crisis circumstances is likely to promote broad support for democratic institutions. Nonetheless, the crisis of Collor's impeachment is far from representing the crucial test mentioned earlier, for it was born and exhausted itself in the corrupt practices of intimate power circles: Even the denunciation of corruption came from the same circles, specifically from the president's brother. The dimension of social confrontation was clearly not present in such circumstances. By contrast, the crisis of the Getulio Vargas government in 1954, which featured analogous denunciations of corruption involving individuals close to the president, ended less favorably. In this case, the corruption issue emerged at a time when Vargas's socially "progressive" populism was being opposed by the electorally weak conservatism of the União Democrática Nacional (UDN). In the aftermath of Vargas's suicide were serious political disturbances.

By emphasizing the problematic connections between the dynamics of capitalism and democracy, I aim to highlight a number of important lessons concerning the general theme of human rights. These are summarized in the following pages, in which the central points revolve around the tension and eventual accommodation between a doctrinaire approach to human rights and an outlook that might be described as a realistic sociology of interests and power.

1. The process of instituting and enshrining human rights must not be analytically blinded by a solidaristic and civic idealism. And the concern with efficiency must not be avoided in the pursuit of such lofty objectives. In this connection, the fundamental premise should be the proposition that, for better or for worse, what is at stake in social and political life very often involves the affirmation of interests. Moreover, when properly considered, this affirmation of interests appears, through its connection with the value of autonomy, to be intrinsic to the very ideal to be realized through the promotion of human rights. The reference to the model of a "market" to be created and guaranteed, then, is justified not only because it points toward autonomous agents who, as such, are the bearers of rights but also because it provides a "realistic utopia" that is attentive to the element of interests and power.

Without ignoring the potential contribution of pedagogic or edifying efforts of various sorts, this outlook implies recommendations at the level of practical action—recommendations emphasizing the idea that even the objective of creating a propitious collective psychology or "culture" will be better served if this culture is recognized as the by-product of realistic efforts at institution building. Rather than counting upon or actively seeking the "conversion" of agents, these efforts will be oriented by concern about the need to foster an institutional environment through which the pursuit of interests and the egoistic (or particularistic, even if collective or solidary) calculations on the part of either private or public agents lead to favorable aggregate results.

2. The state will necessarily be a crucial immediate target of such efforts at realistic institution building, given the need to make the institutional apparatus socially effective. Of course, not all initiatives should be in the hands of the state, but even those initiatives arising spontaneously from various segments of society will, one way or another or at some moment, have to go through the state or assert a presence in some state arena. In my discussion of Przeworski's democratic minimalism at the outset of this chapter, I mentioned the need for democratically containing a necessarily large and active state that would probably tend, as a conse-

quence, to emerge as an autonomous focus of dictatorial power. However, the perspective allowed by the problematic connections between capitalism and democracy suggests that we face a new and opposite difficulty that deserves at least as heavy an emphasis—to wit, the obstacles that the state may have to overcome so as to be able to act autonomously.

The central issue here is the classic Marxist concern with the autonomy or dependence of the state in relation to certain social forces, and hence the possible limits that might be placed either on any attempt to shape the state or on the state's capacity for initiative and efficacy—particularly if it is thought of as an instrument of change. These limits point to the reasons for the ambivalence (clearly present in much of the literature) that characterizes observations of state autonomy in connection with the goal of democracy. In an egalitarian society, whose members are liable to be conceptualized as the homogeneous "public" of certain contractualist fictions, democracy supposes that the state does not become autonomous. In an unequal society, however, the state's autonomy is a condition for the advancement of democracy, to the extent that democracy necessitates neutralization of the tendency for the state to be privately appropriated by the powerful.

A paradoxical feature emerges here. Even if we ignore the doctrinal connections between democracy and the market, the plausibility of seeking to establish and guarantee democracy is limited in the absence of capitalism. The problem of democracy must therefore be solved under conditions of capitalism, conditions that in turn give special relevance to Przeworski's (1985) view of democracy as a social compromise, first and foremost between labor and capital. So, in setting aside the notion of anticapitalist revolution, we see that a paradoxical aspect of the general question stems from the fact that affirmative action by the state in support of democratization and the enshrinement of ever-expanding rights will by necessity take place under circumstances characterized by the "structural dependence" of the state on private capital. As has been stressed by many Marxists and non-Marxists alike, capitalism—regardless of specific institutional arrangements—inevitably promotes asymmetries in the sensitivity of the state apparatus toward different social forces (Offe and Ronge, 1985; Przeworski, 1985; Lindblom, 1977). Capitalism institutes a bias in favor of entrepreneurial interests specifically because investment decisions are in the hands of capitalists—who can thus control the rhythm of economic activity, with pervasive consequences for all.[8] However, what is achieved through the democratic compromise (besides the suppression of the revolutionary threat to capitalism) is precisely the attenuation of that bias and of the general effects of the structural dependence of the state. For under conditions of political authoritarianism the "elective affinities" between the state and entrepreneurial interests are intensified, with the latter powerfully shaping public policymaking through the informal and clandestine articulation between entrepreneurs and state bureaucracy that takes place in the "bureaucratic rings" described by Fernando Henrique Cardoso (1975: ch. 6). A reasonable bet that the state will be able to act as a democratizing tool requires only the acknowledgment that, despite its theoretically dependent character under conditions of capitalist inequality, the state is also a complex and rather plastic entity; and its many interstices afford plenty of room for efforts to build democratic institutions. Moreover, such efforts can intensify this trait of plasticity, with a corresponding strengthening of the democratic variety of state autonomy.

3. In order to grasp the general logic of the process discussed here, we must acknowledge the existence of thresholds in the process of penetration and diffusion of market relationships and of the corresponding "civil" posture. If such thresholds have not yet been crossed, the "autonomist" assumption implied by Marshall's (1965) proposed sequence for the emergence of various rights turns out to be inadequate. In his view, once civil and political rights have been ensured, the popular strata engage in autonomous struggles and eventually conquer social rights. But under circumstances of great social inequality, the inequality itself may have to be reduced in order to produce the sociopsychological conditions needed for the "civil" component of autonomy to occur in any minimally effective way.

As an example, consider the second-class citizenship that remains the lot of many poor people in Brazil today, partly as a consequence of the country's long experience with slavery. Hence we come to understand why the general attitude of the Brazilian popular strata is still predominantly conformist and submissive in nature. Indeed, the popular strata help to preserve a situation in which even the most basic civil rights of the Brazilian poor are permanently in jeopardy, especially in their daily dealings with the police.[9] Under such circumstances, the presence and intensity of the paternalistic element—an element inherent in the social protection provided by a properly institutionalized and effective welfare state that guarantees the social aspects of citizenship—must be evident beforehand, so that the appropriate operation of the "civil" may take place.[10]

The analytic significance of this observation concerns the duration and complexity of the period of time in which (1) a supposed initial moment of market-based penetration of the sense of personal autonomy (and of the corresponding propensity toward interest-oriented behavior) is separated from the breaking up of traditional and conformist norms and the customs this implies; and (2) a "final" moment of effective establishment of new norms is adjusted to the continuous operation of a "market" that no longer runs the permanent risk of deteriorating into a generalized "praetorian" disposition toward fraud and, perhaps, belligerence.

By way of illustration, consider Guillermo O'Donnell's (1986) elaboration on some suggestions of Roberto da Matta (1978) concerning the alleged differences in typical attitudes among Brazilians, Argentineans, and Americans confronted with situations that call into question the egalitarian character of social relations. O'Donnell and da Matta remind us that the Brazilian question "Do you know who you are talking to?" carries a powerful message of domination that is likely to be met with fearful silence, whereas to the same question an Argentinian would answer "Who cares?" and an American would take offense, saying, "Who do you think you are?" My point is simply that these proposed differences reveal so-ciopsychological (or "cultural") crystallizations that would result from the inter-play between the social and civil-political dimensions, and that might be seen as corresponding to three different "phases" or "moments" of the process in which the above-mentioned "lapse" tends to occur: the naive acquiescence and con-formism in the face of real or alleged authority (Brazil), cynical affirmation of personal autonomy (Argentina), and a "civil" sense of autonomy tempered by a certain "civic" moderation that precludes, without further arrogance, an unduly authoritarian posture on the part of the other (United States). What appear to be "cultural" peculiarities would thus constitute a consequence of the general logic at play in the overall process. Indeed, it is the operation of this logic that we must try to grasp in a more detailed and careful way.

Finally, let us ponder the promising questions raised by the special case of Eastern Europe and the former Soviet Union. Here, the fall of socialism and the consequent reopening of the "constitutional problem" occurred under circum-stances in which the market principle did not operate in a significant way, despite the comparatively significant level of social development. Some authors, such as Adam Przeworski (1991), have characterized as "Latin Americanization" the combination of poor capitalism and political instability that is likely to result from current developments in these countries. But I think this characterization suggests another set of circumstances. Indeed, many observers of the problem of institutional and political stability tend to think of the stable condition as the "nor-mal" one. They also sometimes fall prey to the related illusion that such a condi-tion should be easy to achieve and consolidate, if only certain peculiar traits shared by the countries of Latin America and other similarly "wrong" nations are duly corrected.[11] By contrast, the "Latin Americanization" formula contains the suggestion that we (in the developing world) are the rule! In other words, the most widely operative and applicable "model," is the Latin American one, given the unsolved constitutional problem and the multifaceted praetorian instability that beset the region. And those countries that prove to be exceptions to the rule, but cannot sustain themselves as such, will tend to fall again within the grip of this rule.

Notes

1. This symposium, entitled "Democracia Política y Democracia Social," was spon-sored by the Centro de Estudios Sociológicos at the Colegio de México and took place on October 17–19, 1990.

2. Given this affinity, the socialist experience can be shown to have suffered from its own contradictions—namely, those between the undeniably democratic inspiration of so-cialism and socialism's aversion to the market.

3. A suggestive ramification of this definition of interests in terms of the search for "self-affirmation" (and thus of the linking of interest to power in the widest and most en-compassing sense of the word) is that the contradictory feature previously pointed out in

capitalism—as a consequence of a "betrayal" of the market principle—appears to be inherent in the *depurated* (unadulterated) idea of market itself, thus accentuating the tension contained in the Weberian view of the market as a synthesis of "society" and "community." For even though the market is the place where the egalitarian principle affirms itself, making it possible to say that markets are less evident where monopolies or oligopolies are more widespread, it is also the place of self-affirmation and thus of power. Of course, the latter trait accounts for the fact that the real operation of any market is bound to deny the egalitarian principle. Thus, the idea of the egalitarian market is inevitably no more than an ideal, notwithstanding the importance it may have from both an analytical and a practical point of view.

4. Moreover, it would be improper to liken Brazilian conditions to those prevailing in the United States and then to simply imitate American solutions. The relationships between the "identity" approach to politics and the presumably opposed one of "rational choice" are discussed more fully in Reis (1988, 1991).

5. Actually, Kelly designates the claim for welfare rights as "civil II" and the modern and liberal enjoyment of civil and political rights as "civil I."

6. See Reis (1974) for a fuller elaboration of the basic ideas involved in this compressed presentation. Among recent attempts to retrieve and reexamine the concept of "civil society" in connection with the issues discussed in this chapter, that of Cohen and Arato (1992) is especially provocative.

7. Commenting on an initial version of this chapter, Hilda Sábato criticized what she took to be two assumptions behind this argument: first, the tendency toward a "universal" affirmation of a logic of the market, or toward an "inclusive" capitalism: and second, the tendency toward the polarization of interests under capitalism.

8. Given the specific concern with Latin America that frames the discussions in this volume, it is worth stressing that the thesis of the overall dependence of the state apparatus clearly applies to the special sector made up by the military. As Manuel Antonio Garretón maintains in Chapter 3, the fear of the continuity or reaffirmation of an important military presence in Latin American political life (particularly that of Chile) would involve conceiving of the military as a sort of "autonomous arbitor," a view that is unacceptable given the new complexities of the present political and socioeconomic structure of the countries in the region. However, Garretón's position is open to the rebuttal that the decisive role played by the military is far from requiring the status of autonomous arbitrage; rather, the acting out of this role has long been marked by dependence and special sensitivity with regard to entrepreneurial interests and views, which strongly condition the general direction that military political action will continue to assume—provided that the crucial social dimension of the unsolved constitutional problem is activated.

9. This problem is discussed further by Teresa P.R. Caldeira in Chapter 11 of this volume.

10. Commenting on an earlier version of this chapter, Hilda Sábato stressed the tendency for civil rights to shrink under the authoritarian conditions associated with a paternalistic state that conceives of society in organic terms. There is much to be said for this piece of conventional wisdom, yet it overlooks the nuances and complications emphasized in the chapter.

11. In this connection, it seems instructive to emphasize the haste with which social scientists have begun to talk about "consolidated democracies," so soon after the painful experience of military rule and, sometimes, in reference to countries that have not been

able to get rid of even the formal political presence of the military. As a case in point, consider the discussions about Uruguay and Chile that took place at a November 1991 conference in São Paulo, under the coordination of Guillermo O'Donnell. In attempting to elaborate the conditions producing democratic "consolidation," a number of senior scholars appeared to overlook the fact that the countries in question did suffer military coups and dictatorships in the recent past.

References

Arendt, Hannah. (1968). *Between Past and Future*. New York: Viking Press.

Cardoso, Fernando Henrique. (1975). *Autoritarismo e democratização*. Rio de Janeiro: Paz e Terra.

Cohen, Jean, and Andrew Arato. (1992). *Civil Society and Political Theory*. Cambridge, Mass.: MIT Press.

da Matta, Roberto. (1978). *Carnavais, malandros e heróis*. Rio de Janeiro: Zahar.

Habermas, Jürgen. (1975a). *Théorie et pratique*, vols. Paris: Payot.

————. (1975b). *Legitimation Crisis*. Boston: Beacon Press.

Huntington, Samuel. (1968). *Political Order in Changing Societies*. New Haven: Yale University Press.

Kelly, George Armstrong. (1979). "Who Needs a Theory of Citizenship?" *Daedalus* 108, no. 4 (Fall): 37–54.

Lindblom, Charles. (1977). *Politics and Markets*. New York: Basic Books.

Marshall, T. H. (1965). "Citizenship and Social Class." In (ed.), *Class, Citizenship, and Social Development*. New York: Doubleday.

O'Donnell, Guillermo. (1986). "E eu com isso?" In (ed.), *Contrapontos: Autoritarismo e Democratização*. São Paulo: Vértice.

Offe, Claus. (1985). "Competitive Party Democracy and the Keynesian Welfare State," in Claus Offe, (ed.), *Contradictions of the Welfare State*. Cambridge, Mass.: MIT Press.

Offe, Claus, and Volker Ronge. (1985). "Theses on the Theory of the State." In Claus Offe (ed.), *Contradictions of the Welfare State*. Cambridge, Mass.: MIT Press.

Przeworski, Adam. (1985). *Capitalism and Social Democracy*. New York: Cambridge University Press.

————. (1991). "The 'East' Becomes the 'South'? The 'Autumn of the People' and the Future of Eastern Europe," *Political Science and Politics* 24, no. 1 (March).

Reis, Fábio W. (1974). "Solidaridad, Intereses y Desarrollo Político." *Desarrollo económico—Revista de ciencias sociales* 14, no. 54 (July-September): 227–268.

————. (1988). "Identidade, política e a teoria da escolha racional." *Revista Brasileira de Ciências Sociais* 3, no. 6 (February): 26–39.

————. (1991). "Para pensar transiçôes: Democracia, mercado, estado," *Novos Estudos* (CEBRAP), no. 3O (July): 76–98.

Santos, Guilherme dos, Wanderley. (1979). *Cidadania e justiça*. Rio de Janeiro: Editora Campus.

Weber, Max. (1984). *Economía y sociedad*. Mexico City: Fondo de Cultura Económica.

PART FOUR

Structures of Discrimination: Individual and Collective Rights

◀ 8 ▶

Indigenous Rights:
Some Conceptual Problems

RODOLFO STAVENHAGEN

The recent emergence of indigenous peoples' ethnic rights as a special case of human rights poses two conceptual questions that need to be addressed from different angles. How does the notion of "ethnic rights" relate to the generally accepted concept of human rights? And if indigenous peoples claim recognition of special rights specifically on the basis of their "indigenous" character, what is the value of the concept of *indigenidad,* or "indigenity?" Insofar as the recognition of ethnic rights has a collective basis, the relationship between individual and collective rights merits analysis, as does the ambiguity surrounding the use of the term *ethnic minority* and its application to indigenous peoples. Furthermore, the scope of the concept of a "people" in general, and of "indigenous people" in particular, should be delineated, especially as it relates to the broadly extended notion of "rights of peoples." Finally, the concepts of self-determination and autonomy should be specified in the context of indigenous peoples living confronting the boundaries of the modern territorial state. This chapter addresses each of these issues, but first it is necessary to consider the evolving demands of indigenous peoples on the American continent, along with the response that these demands have elicited from Latin American states.

THE NATIONAL-HISTORICAL CONTEXT

Although the term *indigenous* has many definitions, it is used in this chapter to refer to descendants of the original inhabitants of the Americas, those who preceded the European invasion and whose cultural characteristics distinguish them from the rest of society.[1] Generally occupying an inferior social position vis-à-vis the rest of the population, they suffer economic and social marginalization. Consisting of more than 400 groups, each with an identity of its own, the indigenous or Indian population of the Americas totals some 30 million people. Indigenous groups vary greatly, ranging from inhabitants of the Amazon jungle to highland peasant farmers.

In many Latin American countries Indians are but a small minority of the population. (This is the case in Argentina, Brazil, Chile, and Costa Rica.) Elsewhere, by contrast, Indians constitute a significant portion of the population (as in Ecuador, Mexico, and Peru) or even a majority (as in Bolivia and Guatemala). Indigenous people are dispersed among populations everywhere, sometimes to the point where their specific cultural traits have practically disappeared. But one of the fundamental elements of indigenous identity in the Americas is its territoriality: To belong to an indigenous group means to have the consciousness of possessing a territory and of maintaining special ties to the land.

For reasons that are well known, indigenous peoples occupy a disadvantaged position in the social hierarchy. Poverty, malnutrition, poor health conditions, and a lack of adequate medical care and sanitation are endemic. These problems are rooted in the unequal position of Indians in the economic structure—especially in agriculture. Indeed, since the colonial era Indians have been stripped of their lands and subjected to brutal forms of exploitation. Although the most egregious abuses have declined gradually as a result of continuing struggles for justice, their effects remain evident in the hardships that characterize the daily lives of indigenous people today.

The origins of discrimination and human rights violations against the Indians can be traced to the productive structure as far back as the colonial era, and to the social, political, and legal institutions developed by Latin American states following independence. Dominant ideologies rejected the specificity and even the existence of indigenous peoples. The concept of "nation" that swept the region during the nineteenth century excluded indigenous and ethnic groups from the national community, giving rise to racist, nationalist, and positivist ideologies that lacked a place for indigenous peoples—even though they often constituted a numerical majority. As a result, by the beginning of the twentieth century indigenous peoples had become minorities, discriminated against and subordinated, exploited and rejected, by dominant groups as well as by the mestizo and creole populations.

The dominant society has never been without voices to defend the Indians, and both active and passive resistance from indigenous people themselves is a recurrent theme in Latin American history. In recent decades, governments in the region have grown more aware of the terrible social and economic situation faced by the great majority of the indigenous population, and numerous measures have been implemented in an effort to improve living conditions for Indians. Yet contemporary conceptions of the Indian differ only in nuance from those of the modern period. To this day, a common belief is that the state must be culturally homogeneous and that development policies for Indian communities must reflect a strategy of integration and assimilation. Indeed, the official vision of the future of Latin American societies remains one of nations without Indians. Of course, museums will remain as silent testimony to the greatness of the Indian past, and crafts and folklore will be preserved or recreated for the pleasure of tourists. But specific Indian groups, along with their cultures, languages, idioms and artistic expressions—in short, their very identities—will presumably disappear, inevitable victims of progress, modernization, economic development, and national integration.

Processes of acculturation are thus evident; indigenous cultures persist. Buttressed in recent years by a growing sense of collective identity and by strategies of political resistance, such cultures constitute a significant element in the sociopolitical landscape of contemporary Latin America. This fact, however, has been acknowledged only recently in official descriptions of the region, a delay that can be seen as one of the structural causes of human rights violations against the Indian peoples of the continent. Often the weakest sectors in society, indigenous people are frequent victims of the most flagrant violations of human rights.

Beyond the question of human rights, however, lies that of collective rights. Although constitutions and legislation have adopted the principles of equality before the law and of nondiscrimination and proclaim, at least formally, absolute respect for individual human rights, Latin American countries rarely recognize the collective rights of ethnic groups, indigenous or otherwise. Indeed, most constitutions in the region do not recognize even the existence of indigenous populations.

Recently, several states adopted new constitutional texts in which for the first time reference was made to indigenous rights and indigenous peoples were recognized as such (Stavenhagen, 1988). In Brazil, for example, the eighth chapter of the 1988 Constitution refers to indigenous peoples; in Nicaragua, following the conflict between the Miskito Indians and the Sandinistas during the 1980s, the autonomy of the Atlantic Coast communities was established; and in Mexico, Article 4 of the 1991 Constitution was modified to include a section on the rights of indigenous peoples. In addition to reiterating individual rights, the new charters recognize some collective rights, including those relating to language, culture, common law (Stavenhagen and Iturralde, 1990), and, in some cases land.

In contrast to the long-standing neglect of the indigenous question in Latin American constitutions, virtually every Latin American state has enacted one or another law or decree, or even packages of legislation, referring specifically to the indigenous population. Of a diverse nature, this legislation generally obligates the state to favor the economic and social betterment of indigenous populations.

Agrarian law warrants special mention, since the problem of land is fundamental for indigenous peoples throughout the continent. Several countries maintain special arrangements for Indian lands dating back to the colonial era. Beginning in the nineteenth century, indigenous communal lands have had access to an ever-diminishing supply of natural resources, due to pressures from latifundias as well as to colonization by mestizo farmers, commercial plantations, and multinational enterprises. Many indigenous peoples have lost their lands and their ecological basis for sustenance in this manner. It is for this reason that the agrarian struggles of indigenous peoples are so deeply etched in the modern history of Latin America.

Responding to this situation, some governments have adopted agrarian legislation favorable to indigenous peoples, especially with regard to the protection of collective or communal property. This legislation is particularly evident in the experience of Mexico, Bolivia, and Peru, but it has emerged to a lesser extent in Ecuador, Venezuela, and Colombia and, during democratic periods, in Guatemala and Chile. Other countries, in contrast, have destroyed indigenous property rights and promoted private landownership. Although the Universal Human Rights Declaration recognizes the right to collective or individual property, legislation in many Latin American countries denies the right to collective ownership of land. Individual property rights—with their associated processes of accumulation and concentration, on the one hand, and of atomization and fragmentation, on the other—have been a powerfully destructive force in the history of indigenous peoples in the Americas.

The educational and cultural policies of Latin American governments have been highly "integrationist," as have the legislative frameworks through which these policies are implemented. By failing to take into account the specific cultural characteristics, goals, and aspirations of indigenous groups, educational policies, characterized by obligatory castilianization (linguistic assimilation), have imposed Western models that observers have deemed ethnocidal because of their support for unilateral acculturation and, hence, the disintegration of indigenous groups. Questioning of these educational policies, by the indigenous people and others, has led some governments to bestow official status on indigenous languages, paving the way for bilingual and bicultural education long demanded by Indian organizations.

There is much debate over the question of whether an educational policy respectful of indigenous cultures and supportive of their development can be compatible with the dominant conception of national unity and development. Do the social and cultural rights of peoples enshrined in international law translate into the rights of Latin American indigenous groups to receive education in their own language, along with protection and respect for their culture by society as a whole? The debate rages on in many Latin American countries; yet in a world characterized by ever greater integration and cultural homogenization, the cultural rights of peoples have taken on increasing importance as basic human rights.

The rights of indigenous peoples to land, property, and a culture of their own constitute one set of issues for legislation in contemporary Latin America, but the case of criminal law highlights a separate and perhaps even more complex problem. This problem concerns the applicability of juridical norms belonging to a specific (Western) sociopolitical tradition. At stake is not only the scope of state jurisdiction but also the applicability of customary law as it emerges from indigenous communities and the degree to which the legal order can accommodate these particularities. Penal codes in some Latin American countries grant special recognition to the "customs" of indigenous peoples; in other countries, juridical practice is relatively flexible with regard to practices and customs internal to indigenous communities. Nevertheless, indigenous organizations protesting human rights violations decry the countless instances in which the law, particularly criminal law, has been applied inflexibly in situations where sociological or cultural context should have constituted a mitigating factor. Beyond these issues, however, lies the fundamental question of whether indigenous peoples can or should have the right to govern themselves in accord with their own norms of conviviality, and whether and to what extent these norms conflict with those imposed by the national state.

Closely linked to this question is one of even greater importance, concerning the political representation of indigenous people. In most Latin American countries, Indians enjoy "on paper" the rights of all citizens to participate in the political process. But the modes of discrimination against indigenous peoples are so numerous and profound that these individuals remain, in practice, politically marginalized throughout most of the region. Only rarely are there legal mechanisms to enable indigenous groups to participate as collectivities in the political order. In most countries, the liberal doctrine of individual representation leads to an explicit rejection of even the possibility of according collective rights or representation on the basis of ethnic or other ascriptive categories.

Liberal democratic theory was designed for societies in which all individuals are effectively equal, and in which socioeconomic differences can be confronted through social and economic policies. Ethnic differences, by contrast, are destined either to disappear through integrationist or assimilationist policies, or to stimulate the creation of political mechanisms designed to strengthen ethnic and cultural pluralism. These mechanisms remain largely absent in Latin America, despite advances in several countries over the past decade.

For the most part, indigenous organizations have shown little interest in legislative questions, aside from instances in which laws affect them directly, as in the case of the *Estatuto do Indio* (Statute of the Indian) in Brazil or the *Ley de Comunidades* (Law of Communities) in Paraguay. These organizations are gradually becoming more aware of legal issues, however, and have begun to put forth proposals that go beyond the traditional demands for greater attention to the economic and social needs of indigenous communities. Yet their calls for political representation, territorial autonomy, and self-determination have seldom received sympathy from state authorities, who contend that the civil, cultural, and political rights of ethnic groups can be satisfied within the framework of existing political systems.

Calls for self-determination and autonomy, in particular, are becoming more frequent in declarations of indigenous peoples' organizations in national and international forums across much of Latin America. Yet whereas leaders of the movement cite rights enshrined in international agreements and in UN declarations, Latin American governments frequently perceive a risk to territorial integrity posed by "separatist" and secessionist demands. This debate is likely to continue, and to become more pressing, in much of Latin America during the coming years. Thus the issue of indigenous rights will require greater attention on the part of human rights specialists, lawyers, and social scientists. At the same time, this issue cannot be separated from the debate over democracy, justice, and citizenship in Latin American countries.

HUMAN RIGHTS AND ETHNIC RIGHTS

The classic human rights paradigm—as embodied in the Universal Declaration and the International Conventions at the international level, and in the American Declaration and the San Jose Convention in the American sphere—refers basically to individual rights, the rights of the human being. The principle underlying the modern conception of human rights is that of their universality, which in turn refers to the principles of equality among all people and of nondiscrimination in the areas of gender, race, language, national origin, and religion. Recall that these principles, which today are accepted almost universally (at least at the rhetorical level), were revolutionary when first enunciated. As recently as the 1950s, the colonized peoples of Africa, Asia, and the Caribbean did not enjoy the same rights as citizens of the colonizing empires; until the 1960s, in the United States, the civil rights of blacks (now known as African Americans) were not entirely won; and only now is apartheid (a negation of human rights) being dismantled in South Africa. Meanwhile, the notion of "human rights" is still not accepted in some current Islamic theories. Even if the Holocaust and the genocide of gypsies by the Nazis deserves a separate historical chapter, the postwar world has not been exempt from massacres, repression, or territorial expulsion of specific groups of people for ethnic, racial, religious, or national reasons. The crimes committed in Rwanda during 1994, and the brutality of the ongoing Serbian aggression against the Muslims of Bosnia Herzegovina, attest to the distance that remains to be traveled before the most basic human right, the right to life, becomes respected everywhere.

It is generally accepted that the enjoyment of so-called political and civil rights will be greater where the state intervenes in them only minimally, limiting its role to guaranteeing the full exercise of these rights and maintaining an atmosphere in which they can be freely exercised. In other words, what is required is a passive, restrained, reduced, and cautious state. According to this view, an interventionist state can always represent a danger to human rights. Such is the interpretation of those who seek greater rights from the state for themselves, especially if they already enjoy them widely and if they occupy a dominant position in society.

The so-called economic, social, and cultural rights present a different problem. Participants in the historical debate on human rights acknowledge that the exercise of civil and political rights is illusory in the absence of conditions conducive to the enjoyment of economic, social, and cultural rights, the "second generation" of human rights. Second generation rights complement rather than displace first generation (civil and political) rights. Nevertheless, there are those who deny that economic and social rights are "human rights," suggesting instead that they are merely social policy objectives.

In contrast with the first generation of rights, the second generation requires an "active" state that is responsible, redistributive, and regulatory, and that provides the resources and services necessary to the exercise of economic, social, and cultural rights. When the state abdicates its responsibility in this area, the conditions for the full exercise of such rights are reduced. Thus, the structural adjustment policies being implemented by Third World governments at the behest of international financial agencies, which seek to reduce the role of the state in the economy, are considered by some observers to violate human rights. To the extent that such policies affect especially the most vulnerable and poorest sectors of society, thus increasing poverty and marginality, they can be deemed discriminatory and therefore in violation of the principles of equality inscribed in the International Human Rights Charter (Gros Espiell, 1986.)

As noted earlier, the indigenous peoples of the Americas have traditionally been victims of the greatest human rights abuses. Rather than going back to the "struggles for justice" involved in the conquest of America or to the legacy of Bartolomé de las Casas, I will limit my analysis to the twentieth century. Two broad objectives can be attributed to the *indigenista* government policies of this period: promotion of the economic and social development of indigenous peoples, and acceleration of their integration into national society (i.e., into the dominant society, whose cultural parameters are defined by the ruling classes of the country).

The desired "integration" largely has meant the destruction of indigenous cultures and identities through assimilationist policies, with ethnocidal consequences. Even if ethnocide does not appear in any juridical instrument as a human rights violation, it is generally considered as such, since it represents a form of "cultural genocide" contradictory to the right of culture proclaimed in Article 15 of the International Convention on Economic, Social, and Cultural Rights.

The notion of "ethnic rights" emerges, then, as a necessary frame of reference from which to proclaim the human rights of ethnic groups whose situation is particularly vulnerable—due precisely to the disadvantages and violations that they suffer as collectivities with ethnic characteristics distinct from those of the dominant society. Reflecting the collective effort of the international community to enrich and consolidate the basic edifice of human rights protection, the United Nations Human Rights Commission has been developing instruments relating to the rights of indigenous peoples and of minorities.

Given the universality of human rights, it is frequently heard in the contemporary debate on this subject that treatment of specific rights or of specific groups should be considered not a "broadening of human rights" but simply an instance of application of these rights to specific cases. Therefore, it is argued, these rights cannot be considered human rights in the strict sense. Yet because human beings are not abstract entities living outside their time, context, and space, the concept of "human rights" acquires significance only in a specific contextual framework—one that yields the following conclusions:

1. There does indeed exist a core of basic universal human rights (for all people in all circumstances).
2. In addition to this "core" there exists a "periphery" of human rights specific to distinctive categories of the population (e.g., children, women, workers, migrants, disabled people, refugees, ethnic minorities, and indigenous groups).
3. Basic universal human rights cannot be fully enjoyed, exercised, or protected in every instance if the "peripheral" rights specific to the groups in question cannot simultaneously be enjoyed, exercised, and protected. In other words, there are circumstances in which it is illusory to speak about the basic "core" of universal human rights (except at a totally abstract, theoretical, or philosophical level) if the "periphery" is not taken into account.[2]

Note that the second point in this list refers specifically to groups that have traditionally been marginalized, oppressed, or discriminated against. The proposal to acknowledge human rights specific to such groups has been the result of long historical struggles. In the process, the conceptualization of these specific rights has been recognized as a response to historical and structural realities of many kinds. The "rights of men" or the "rights of adults" do not appear in the list precisely because these dominant population categories have always been identified with "human rights" in general and thus have not required a specific conceptualization in their favor. In fact, the conceptual and theoretical construction of human rights historically reflects the asymmetries and inequalities of human society. From this perspective, ethnic rights, including indigenous rights, are inscribed in a framework where the basic core of human rights has been expanded and consolidated.

THE CONCEPT OF *INDIGENIDAD*

If the word *indígena* refers to "native," all human beings can be considered indigenous to some place or another. Nevertheless, in sociological, political, and, increasingly, legal terminology, *indígena* is used to refer to sectors of the population that occupy a certain position in the greater society as a result of specific historical processes. In Latin America, as elsewhere, the label *indígena* has been transformed from a word with discriminatory connotations (used mostly pejoratively by the representatives of dominant societies) into a term of recognition of cultural and sociological distinctions. On many occasions it has even served as a symbolic call for resistance, defense of human rights, and societal transformation.

The colonial origin of the concept of *indígena* is beyond question. Indigenous peoples are simply the descendants of the peoples who occupied a given territory when it was invaded, conquered, or colonized by a foreign power or population.[3] In cases where this process took place relatively recently and can be historically documented, the use of the concept is quite straightforward. Thus, for example, the invasion and colonization of America in the sixteenth century marks the beginning of the division of the population between indigenous people (also referred to as natives, aborigines, or Indians) and "Europeans" (or Spanish Americans, creoles, whites, Spaniards, English, etc.). The same differentiation applies in other parts of the world, as in the cases of the aborigines (in Australia) or the Maoris (in New Zealand) versus English colonizers, and the "Native Hawaiians" in Hawaii or the Eskimos (Inuit) in Alaska versus American colonizers.

In other contexts, however, the use of the term *indígena* becomes more complicated. During the period of the colonial empires in Africa and Asia, the colonized population as a whole was frequently denominated as "natives" by the colonizers. And to this category was generally added the economic, political, and legal disadvantages particular to the colonial situation, which operated in favor of the colonizer. With the decolonization and political independence that followed World War II, the "natives" were transformed into "nationals," a metamorphosis that was as much political as semantic. Of course, this process characterizes only the territories in which the colonizer ceased to ccupy a dominant position after independence (Africa, Asia), in contrast to those in which the colonizers themselves declared their own political independence (America, Australia, New Zealand, South Africa).

Must we therefore conclude that *indígena* is strictly a colonial category that ceases to have validity in the postcolonial condition? An affirmative answer would apply to some cases, but not to those in which the structure of domination within the independent country can be conceptualized as "internal colonialism," as in Latin America, North America, and Australia.

In several South Asian and African countries, a dominant and majoritarian sector of society that is identified with the national state coexists with ethnic minority groups that have a long historical presence in certain regions and are relatively isolated and marginalized. These ethnic minorities, who possess a culture that is distinct from the national hegemonic model, are victims of exploitation and domination by the economic and political representatives of the national society. They are often known as tribal populations (a category imposed by the colonial or national state), and their situation is similar to that of indigenous groups in other parts of the world. Known as *adivasis* in India, as mountain tribes in Thailand and the Philippines, and as aborigines in Malaysia and Sri Lanka, these groups have come to identify themselves as indigenous peoples. In recent years they have joined forces with the indigenous peoples of the Americas to secure their human rights—for example, by increasing their participation in the annual sessions on indigenous populations held by the United Nations Subcommission for the Prevention of Discrimination and Protection of Minorities, and by participating in nongovernmental organizations at the international level.

Nevertheless, governments generally avoid the word *indigenous* in reference to these peoples, since they reject the conceptual construct that accompanies the use of this word. India, for example, disputes the claim that the *adivasis* of the tribal regions (a concept introduced by British colonialism) are more indigenous than the Hindu population present for a thousand years in these areas. The Bengali population in Bangladesh takes a similar stance vis-à-vis the communities of the region of Chittagong Hill Tracts. And in Sri Lanka, Singhalese and Tamils dispute the original occupation of the island (an event that occurred more than two thousand years ago), even though the state officially recognizes the existence of the aboriginal Veddas.[4]

As currently used, the term *indigenous* carries with it the idea of the original occupant of a given territory. Indigeneity is thus an ambiguous category, since in many cases the dates of original occupation cannot be documented and no one can know with certainty who the first inhabitants of a given territory were. For that matter, those people who currently claim to be indigenous could have displaced previous occupants in the even more distant past. Yet the use of *indigeneity* for specific political purposes is not precluded. In the nineteenth century, for example, the United States witnessed the rise of "nativism," a political movement among whites of English origin opposed to immigrants from Ireland and Central and Southern Europe. Of course, the authentic natives (indigenous peoples) of North America were equally rejected by this political group. Today, Malaysians assert their status as "sons of the land" (*bumiputra*) to defend their rights and privileges in opposition to the population of Chinese origin in Malaysia, even though the small aboriginal population continues to be marginalized. And during the 1980s, a military coup overthrew a democratically elected government in Fiji on the pretext that rights violations were being inflicted on the native population of the island. In reality, this group felt threatened by the demographic growth (and increasing political presence) of the population of Indian origin introduced as sugarcane workers by British colonizers (Howard, 1991; Premdas, 1992).

The concept of indigeneity also suggests a historical continuity between the original indigenous population and that which presently identifies itself as directly descendant from the original population. This continuity can be either genetic (via biological reproduction) or cultural (relating to maintenance of cultural forms such as the language and the religion that are derived directly from the original group). In most current cases of indigeneity, both genetic and cultural continuity have experienced changes. The biological mixtures among peoples have been extensive (as a result of *mestizaje,* or miscegenation), and indigenous cultures everywhere have been profoundly modified by various processes of acculturation. Who are the authentic descendents of the Inca? Who are the bearers of the authentic culture of "deep Mexico" (Flores Galindo, 1988; Bonfil, 1987)? How can populations dispersed in multiple villages and possessing their own parochial traditions be brought to see themselves in this "imaginary community" (Anderson, 1983) now conceived as an "indigenous or indian people or nation"?[5]

Indigeneity, independent of origins and of both biological and cultural continuity, is frequently the result of government policies imposed from above and outside. It is also the product, more often than not, of a discourse that is constructed by emergent intellectual elites of the indigenous peoples and by their sympathizers among other sectors of the population (Mires, 1991).

In any case, the discourse of indigeneity has led to the denunciation of historical injustices and crimes committed against indigenous peoples (genocides, plunderings, servitude, discriminations) as well as to the advocacy of specific rights that derives from these injustices. As reflected in such phrases as "First in time, first in rights," and in the quest for "recuperation of historic rights," the discourse of indigeneity forms the basis of and legitimates the demand for human rights specific to indigenous peoples.

INDIVIDUAL AND COLLECTIVE RIGHTS

The classic doctrine holds that since human rights are individual, of the person, collectivities cannot be the subjects of human rights. They may have other rights, but "human rights" in the strict sense do not apply to social groups, whatever their characteristics. On the surface this assertion seems logical; nonetheless, it should be questioned. In the first place, we must recognize that it is *only* in a collective form that certain individual human rights can be exercised fully. Examples include political rights (e.g., the right to free association) and economic rights (e.g., the right to belong to a labor union). Moreover, since human beings are by nature eminently social, and since the principal activities around which the human rights debate has been constructed are carried out in groups or collectivities with their own legal status, the exercise of many human rights can be undertaken *only* in the framework of these collectivities, which for this reason should be recognized and respected by the state and by society as a whole. In short, certain types of human groups must be thought of as subjects of human rights, in addition to other kinds of rights. Exactly what type of groups, under what circumstances, and for what class of rights are questions at the center of the current debate.

The Liberal and individualist views of human rights exclude the notion of "collective rights." As Jelin discusses in Chapter 6 of this volume, individual and universal human rights constitute a historical victory for individual freedom against the absolutist state. In its most recent form, Liberal doctrine holds that the culmination of individual rights is found in the operation of political democracy, the free market, and private enterprise.

Yet the history of the last hundred years has demonstrated, at times dramatically, that the enjoyment of individual rights is illusory or at least problematic in highly stratified societies characterized by socioeconomic and regional inequalities and ethnic divisions (i.e., along cultural, linguistic, religious, and/or racial lines). These are precisely the societies in which recognition of group and collective rights has been deemed an indispensable mechanism for the protection of individual rights. In such societies, individual rights cannot be fully realized if collective rights are not recognized; yet, conversely, acknowledgment of individual rights leads necessarily to recognition of collective rights. Similar interpretation may have guided the framers of the two international human rights agreements, given that the first article of both begins with the same assertion: "All peoples have the right to self-determination." The implication is that all other rights proclaimed in these international instruments are subject to and derived from the primordial collective right to self-determination. Of course, this proposition should be understood in the context of the anticolonial struggles that occurred in the years following World War II. Recall that the two agreements were passed by the UN General Assembly in 1966, when the international community was beginning to recognize that individual rights could be difficult to exercise if people were collectively subjugated by colonial regimes.

The situation of the various ethnic minorities and indigenous peoples within the framework of national or multinational states represents another instance in which the full exercise of individual rights can be achieved only through collective rights. The "equality of rights" of individuals is nothing more than an illusion if this equality is negated by the varying circumstances of the collectivities to which these individuals belong. In turn, the equality of rights among ethnic collectivities creates the necessary, if perhaps insufficient, condition for the exercise of individual liberties and rights.

From the prior discussion a provisional and normative conclusion can be derived: *Group or collective rights should be considered human rights to the extent that their recognition and exercise promotes the individual rights of their members.* For example, the right of the members of an ethnic minority to use their own vernacular language is based on the right of a linguistic community to maintain its language in the context of the national state (as a vehicle for communication, literary creation, education, etc.).

But there also are instances in which the rights of a community to the preservation of customs and traditions can mean the reduction or violation of the individual rights of some of its members. I am thinking specifically of the case of sexual mutilation of girls in some African societies (Dorkenoo and Elworthy, 1992). From this a corollary of the previous conclusion can be derived: *Those collective rights that violate or reduce members' individual rights should not be considered human rights.* This declaration, however, presents a dilemma that is not easily resolved in the present situation: How can we identify the circumstances under which the individual or the collectivity has priority? Even in the most liberal societies, the so-called collective good can be invoked to limit individual rights—and not just in cases of war or national emergency.[6]

The international community has recognized the existence of other collective rights that can be considered rights of humanity as a whole, without which the exercise of individual rights does not go beyond a well-meaning intention. A clear example of this "third generation" of human rights, also called "solidarity rights," is the right to the environment, also proclaimed by the UN General Assembly. As demonstrated during the "Earth Summit" meeting of June 1992 in Rio de Janeiro, humanity risks collective and planetary suicide if it does not care for and conserve the environment. Thus, the right to the environment is simultaneously a collective and an individual right. As an individual right it can be protected only in collective form, so it must also be considered a collective human right. After all, the entire conceptual framework of human rights rests on a moral imperative: the intrinsic value of life, liberty, and the dignity of the human being. To achieve this imperative, individual and collective rights must complement one another.

ETHNIC MINORITIES AND INDIGENOUS PEOPLES

The issue of minorities has preoccupied the international community for some time, even though the United Nations has addressed this question at considerably less length than the League of Nations had previously. With the recent changes in Eastern Europe, the question of national minorities and the national state has emerged anew, in the face of disproportionate violence. In 1992, after many years of discussions, the UN Human Rights Commission ratified a declaration of rights of people belonging to national, ethnic, religious, and linguistic minorities. This declaration is derived from Article 27 of the International Convention on Civil and Political Rights, the only section that addresses the rights of members of ethnic minorities. Although the scope of this article is limited (Stavenhagen, 1990a: 60–65), it constitutes a valid basis for the development of a section on protection of minorities' rights. Consistent with the conceptual dispute discussed in the previous section, neither Article 27 nor the declaration proposal recognizes collective rights, referring instead to "the people who belong. . . ."

More important to the issue of human rights for indigenous peoples is the implication in these documents that there exist "minorities" in need of "protection" from the state or the international community. The notion of a minority can be understood in the numerical sense as a population whose number is "less than the majority." Given that we live in an era of "majority rule" (itself a foundation of democracy), the identification of a given ethnic group as a "minority" places it in an inherently disadvantageous situation, especially if the majority controls the state apparatus. The notion of minority may also be understood in the sociological sense of a marginalized, discriminated against, excluded, or disadvantaged group independent of its demographic weight. Here, the minority *would* require the protection or tutelage of the state—either temporarily, while it achieves complete equality with the majority, or permanently, if the characteristics that distinguish it from the majority persist. (In this connection, note that several states have legislated measures for the protection of minorities, yet many of these are considered insufficient by nongovernmental organizations representing such groups.

Accordingly, the NGOs have pressed their demands before international organizations, such as the United Nations, the Conference on Security and Cooperation in Europe, and others.)

The notion of minority bears directly on the territorial and administrative unit of the state and state policies. Some national minorities, embedded in the territory of another nation, are in fact the result of historical processes and the arbitrariness of borders, as dramatically demonstrated by current events in the former Yugoslavia. Other minorities (defined along racial, linguistic, or religious lines) are dispersed throughout a national territory. The protection of their human rights cannot be reduced to territorial arrangements but instead requires the use of electoral, institutional, and cultural mechanisms.

To what extent should the rights of indigenous peoples be considered in the framework of the rights of minorities? Are national and international measures for the protection of minorities adequate to guarantee the human rights of indigenous peoples? The controversy represented by these questions is significant. Indigenous peoples' organizations maintain that their situation is not comparable to that of other minorities. In the first place, they insist that as "original peoples or nations" they deserve historic rights that should not necessarily have to be shared with other minorities, such as ethnic immigrant groups. Second, they point out that as victims of past invasions, conquests, and plunderings, they demand restitution for lost rights (and for sovereignties denied) as opposed to the protection of rights conceded to them (a semantic distinction, but one that is politically significant). Third, they recognize that their ancestors were sovereign nations, subjugated against their will and incorporated into foreign political units (i.e., states and empires).[7] These considerations shaped debates leading up to the UN declaration of 1993 as "The Year of Indigenous Peoples," a year in which indigenous peoples' organizations demanded to be recognized as "peoples" rather than as "minorities" (Stavenhagen, 1990b).

THE RIGHTS OF PEOPLES AND OF INDIGENOUS PEOPLES

As noted, Article 1 of both international human rights agreements of 1966 reads forcefully: "All peoples have the right to self-determination." This international human rights order is based on two other sets of rights: individual rights and the rights of peoples. Yet, for the reasons discussed earlier, the rights of peoples have received less attention than individual human rights. It is common to confuse the notion of "people" with that of the "nation" (the organization is, after all, called the "United Nations") and, in turn, with the state (the United Nations is an arena for states). States jealously claim for themselves every kind of right—to sovereignty, equality, nonintervention, territorial integrity, and so on.

The concept of "people" as distinct from established states emerges in the context of struggles for decolonization and national liberation. Since international practice has conceded the right to self-determination to the peoples of colonized territories but not to minorities, indigenous peoples have come to demand that they be considered "peoples" in order to enjoy the right to self-determination. (Certainly many can marshal powerful arguments to demonstrate that they have been colonized peoples at one time or another during their history.) Clearly, however, this proposition could be rejected by states that perceive a potential danger to their own sovereignty and territorial integrity. Indeed, the world population is made up of thousands of peoples and only a handful of sovereign states.

What, then, is the legal and sociological value of the concept of "people"? What criteria are being used to determine which peoples will have the right to self-determination and which will not? Finally, who, and under what circumstances, decides these questions? Laws are made by states, but the fundamental principles that sustain laws are elaborated by peoples through their struggles and aspirations.

The speed with which some apparently immutable states have recently disintegrated, and the equally rapid emergence of peoples with demands of their own reveals that we are entering an era of rapid change in which the last word has not yet been written. The concepts of "peoples without a state" and of "unrepresented peoples" are now being introduced into debates about the rights of peoples, the right of self-determination, the protection of minorities, and the rights of indigenous peoples.

If the concept of "people" as a subject of international law is to be more than a simple euphemism for the population incorporated into a "state" that already exists, then it is necessary to develop sociological, cultural, and political criteria capable of defining, characterizing, and distinguishing peoples from one another. It is also necessary to construct mechanisms that will allow negotiated or consensual agreements regarding the rights of these peoples, so as to avoid the destructive violence that characterizes so many contemporary ethnic conflicts.[8]

The concept of "people" has two basic meanings. One concerns the totality of citizens that make up a country, as in references to the "sovereignty of the people," "government from the will of the people," and so on. Used in this context, the right of self-determination is exercised through political democracy or, in exceptional cases, through struggles for national liberation or the revolutionary transformation of the state. The second meaning refers to the set of traits that characterizes a conglomeration of human beings in territorial, historical, cultural, and ethnic terms, and provides a sense of identity that can be expressed through nationalist or ethnic ideologies. This identity is neither permanent nor fixed: It can emerge, become modified, and disappear according to the circumstances. In this second sense, the concept of "people" is similar to that of "nation," the main difference being that "nation" generally refers to the ideology and politics of "nationalism" linked to the constitution of a state whereas "people" implies no reference to control over state power.

There are valid reasons to consider the indigenous peoples of the Americas and elsewhere as *peoples* subject to legal and human rights as defined by the United

Nations. Some would even maintain that use of the term *nations* is justified. The North American Indians refer to themselves as *nations,* in part because this is what they were called by the U.S. government in earlier periods. However, in recent assemblies their Latin American counterparts have insisted on using the term *peoples.*

The American indigenous peoples were present at the birth of modern international law. Francisco de Victoria, Bartolomé de las Casas, and others laid the basis for international law precisely through their arguments about the position of the American "natives" in relation to the expansion of the Spanish empire. With the establishment of the modern interstate system, indigenous peoples ceased being independent actors on the world scene. Now it is proposed that they should once again become subjects of international law as a consequence of the legal instruments that are currently being elaborated.

TOWARD INDIGENOUS SELF-DETERMINATION

The self-determination of indigenous peoples is inscribed in the fundamental human right for self-determination of all peoples, but there persists a lack of clarity and consensus on this issue (Obieta Chalbaud, 1985). In its restricted sense, self-determination is often equated with the political secession of a people within an established state, who in this way "exercise their right to self-determination." In recent years such secession has taken place in the republics that previously formed the Soviet Union, as well as in the former Yugoslavia (although in the latter case the previous federation simply disintegrated without any official declaration of secession). But self-determination does not always mean political independence; sometimes, for instance, it entails negotiation with equality of circumstances between a people and the state to which it is connected. The outcome can be a new form of political coexistence within the framework of a different political unit. Quebec provides a contemporary example. Among the American indigenous peoples the case that comes closest to this possibility is the Comarca Kuna San Blas of Panama.

Self-determination can also be "internal," in that it can refer to the political and economic organization of a people without necessarily reflecting its relations with outsiders. The U.S. government uses the term *self-determination* to refer to the internal economic management of indigenous reservations. But this use of the term is mistaken, since the indigenous tribes of that country have been reduced to total dependence on the federal government and do not have any real power to exercise free determination in the sense of a human right.

In the international sphere, the conventional wisdom is that self-determination is exercised once and only once. A case in point is Namibia, which a few years ago acceded to political independence through an act of self-determination under the supervision of the United Nations. But in the sense of the term used here, self-determination can be seen as a process, as a complex web of relations between a people and the state in which they reside. In this way, the right to self-determination of an indigenous people can begin with the renegotiation of relations between that people and the national state, and end with a new democratic pact in which the interrelations are defined by common agreement. More current discussion centers on the topic of political, territorial, and economic autonomy than on that of secession or political independence (Díaz Polanco, 1991; Hannum, 1990). In this regard it is worth studying the recent experiences of Nicaragua and Brazil (where, after many years of struggle, the Yanomami people have received confirmation of their rights to their traditional territory).

Autonomy, self-government, and self-determination are relative concepts currently considered essential to the full development of the human rights of indigenous peoples. The hope is that, in coming years, new ways will be devised in which they can be used and exercised to the benefit of the American indigenous peoples.

Notes

1. This section draws heavily from Stavenhagen (1988: 341–353).

2. There is a dialectical relationship between the "core" and the "periphery" of human rights that needs to be made explicit in each case. Commenting on an earlier version of this paper, Fernando Rojas seemed to adopt an openly relativist position: that "our" (Western) conception of the law has nothing to do with indigenous law (or with that of other cultures). Taken to its extreme, this stance would negate the validity of any attempts to establish a set of human rights of universal scope—a position with which I do not agree. In addition, recognition of the fact that human beings live in unequal circumstances, as Rojas notes, does not diminish the value of establishing the moral principle of equality within the human rights framework.

3. The special rapporteur for the United Nations proposed the following definitions: "Indigenous communities, peoples and nations are those which, having a historical continuity with precolonial and pre-invasion societies that developed in their territories, are considered distinct from other sectors of the societies that now prevail in those territories or parts of them. They now constitute non-dominant sectors of the society and have the determination to preserve, develop and transmit their ancestral territories and their ethnic identity to future generations as a basis for their continued existence as a people, in accordance with their own cultural patterns, social institutions and legal systems" (Martínez Cobo, 1987: 30).

4. On the Sri Lankan case, see Dharmadasa and de A. Samarasinghe (1990); on the use of the term *tribes* in India, see Devalle (1992); and on the tribal peoples of Southeast Asia, see Lim Teck Ghee and Gomes (1990).

5. With respect to the quincentennary, the meeting of the *Alianza Continental Indígena* in Quito in July, 1990 declared: ". . . indian peoples, nationalities and nations are presenting an oppositional and committed response to reject this 'celebration' based on our identity, which should lead us to a definitive liberation" Comisión por la Defensa de los Derechos Humanos (1990).

6. Commenting on an earlier version of this chapter, Enrique Mayer correctly pointed out the difficulties in judging from outside whether or not a collectivity (seen as "the other") violates the individual human rights of its members (based on the criteria of those

judging from the outside). The reference here is to the old question of cultural and moral relativism, posed since 1948 about the "universality" of universal human rights. I agree with Mayer's response to the dilemma: So that collective rights can be recognized as human rights and be legally compatible with individual rights, they should be exercised voluntarily, without coercion, by all members of the collectivity. One implication is that, in order to be valid, this position can apply only to people "at the age of reason." Another proceeds from the generally accepted norm that individuals cannot, even voluntarily, give up their human rights (e.g., a person cannot even voluntarily become enslaved).

7. Many indigenous peoples at some point signed or were obligated to sign treaties with the invaders—treaties through which they lost their sovereignty. This was the case with the North American Indians, the Hawaiians, the Mapuches, and many others. Many of these treaties were later violated and/or abrogated unilaterally by the respective governments. For example, in the nineteenth century, the U.S. Congress declared null the treaties that the government had signed with the Indians, thus transforming them from members of sovereign nations (already battered by the wars of extermination of which they were victims) into mutilated minorities under tutelage, their rights restricted. The same thing occurred in many other countries. The United Nations has undertaken a study of the current state of such treaties in light of international law.

8. In this regard, it is useful to note the contrast between the killing in the former Yugoslavia, where the Serbian government denies other peoples' right of self-determination, and the peaceful separation of Czechs and Slovaks at the beginning of 1993.

References

Anderson, Benedict. (1983). *Imagined Communities: Reflections on the Origin and Spread of Nationalism.* London: Verso.

Bonfil, Guillermo. (1987). *México profundo, una civilizacion negada.* Mexico City: CIESAS/SEP.

Comisión por la Defensa de los Derechos Humanos. (1990). *Declaración de Quito.* Quito.

Devalle, Susan B.C. (1992). *Discourse on Ethnicity, Culture and Protest in Jharkhand.* New Delhi: Sage Publications.

Dharmadasa, K.N.O., and S.W.R. de A. Samarasinghe. (1990). *The Vanishing Aborigines: Sri Lanka's Veddas in Transition.* New Delhi: Vikas Publishing House (International Centre for Ethnic Studies).

Díaz Polanco, Héctor. (1991). *Autonomía regional: La autodeterminación de los pueblos indios.* Mexico City: Siglo XXI.

Dorkenoo, Erfua, and Scilla Elworthy. (1992). *Female Genital Mutilation: Proposals for Change.* London: Minority Rights Group.

Flores Galindo, Alberto. (1988). *Buscando un inca.* Lima: Instituto de Apoyo Agrario.

Gros Espiell, Héctor. (1986). *Los derechos economicos, sociales y culturales en el sistema interamericano.* San José: Libro Libre.

Hannum, Hurst. (1990). *Autonomy, Sovereignty and Self-Determination: The Accommodation of Conflicting Rights.* Philadelphia: University of Pennsylvania Press.

Howard, Michael. (1991). *Fiji: Race and Politics in an Island State.* Vancouver: University of British Columbia Press.

Lim Teck Ghee and Alberto G. Gomes (eds.). (1990). *Tribal Peoples and Development in Southeast Asia* (Special edition of *Manusia & Masyarakat.*) Kuala Lumpur: University of Malaya.

Martínez Cobo, José R. (1987). *Estudio del problema de la discriminación contra las poblaciones indígenas.* Vol. 5, *Conclusiones, propuestas y recomendaciones.* New York: United Nations.

Mires, Fernando. (1991). *El discurso de la indianidad: La cuestion indígena en América Latina.* San José: Editorial DEI.

Obieta Chalbaud, José A. (1985). *El derecho humano de la autodeterminación de los pueblos.* Madrid: Editorial Tecnos.

Premdas, Ralph. (1992). *Ethnic Conflict and Development: The Fascistisation of the State in Fiji.* Geneva: UNRISD.

Stavenhagen, Rodolfo. (1988). *Derecho indígena y derechos humanos en América Latina.* Mexico City: El Colegio de México y Instituto Interamericano de Derechos Humanos.

———. (1990a). *The Ethnic Question: Conflicts, Development and Human Rights.* Tokyo: United Nations University Press.

———. (1990b). "Los derechos indígenas: Nuevo enfoque del sistema internacional." In *Curso Interdisciplinario en Derechos Humanos: Antología Basica.* San José: Insituto Interamericano de Derechos Humanos.

Stavenhagen, Rodolfo, and Diego Iturralde (eds.). (1990). *Entre la ley y la costumbre: El derecho consuetudinario indígena en América Latina.* Mexico City: Instituto Interamericano de Derechos Humanos and Instituto Indigenista Interamericano.

◄ 9 ►

Racial Inequalities in Brazil and Throughout Latin America: Timid Responses to Disguised Racism

CARLOS HASENBALG

Throughout modern Latin American history, racism has perpetuated situations of economic, political, and social inequality, most notably in countries where non-whites constitute a significant portion of the population. Racism introduces categories through which people are differentiated from one another and judged to be deserving (or not) of rights, resources, and status. If the extension of citizenship rights to all sectors of the population constitutes a central goal of those who strive to put democratic ideals into practice, the stubborn persistence of racial discrimination across much of the region presents an especially daunting challenge.

In this chapter I analyze the significance of race for the extension of citizenship rights in contemporary Latin America, particularly in Brazil. First I review evolving perceptions of race relations in order to illuminate the degree to which issues of race were until recently obscured by widely held myths about the existence of "racial democracy." Then I offer an updated analysis of the position occupied by Afro-Brazilians in the social structure of Brazil, as an illustration of racial inequalities between whites and blacks in Latin America. Studies of race relations after the abolition of slavery are more developed in Brazil than in the remaining countries of Latin America. Nevertheless, the few available references to other countries point in the same direction, allowing me to identify the characteristics of a peculiarly Latin American type of race relations. Finally, I suggest a number of strategies that nascent democratic systems might pursue in an effort to improve conditions faced by victims of racial discrimination and, ultimately, to overcome such discrimination.

WHITENING AND RACIAL HARMONY: A KEY TO SIMILARITY

A great deal was written during the first half of this century about the peculiar and original nature of race relations in Brazil, particularly about their nonconflictive

161

character (Freyre, 1933; Pierson, 1942; Tannenbaum, 1946). So much was written and said in this respect that in the early 1950s UNESCO was prompted to sponsor several research projects on the subject. These investigations originally intended to transmit to the rest of the world the Brazilian recipe for harmonious race relations. But the results did not confirm original expectations. On the contrary, the self-image and racial idealizations of the country suffered considerable damage. The research was conducted in the north, northeast, and southeast of the country, and all of them verified a strong association between skin color—or race—and socioeconomic status. In the anthropological projects of the north and northeast, influenced by the views of Gilberto Freyre (1933) and D. Pierson (1942), the concept of race was given less priority than the generalized conditions of underdevelopment and poverty in explaining the concentration of blacks and "mestizos" at the base of the social hierarchy. In the studies carried out in the southeast, particularly in São Paulo, the existence of prejudices and discrimination was amply documented. For the first time in the history of either Afro-American studies or racial relations in Brazil, academic inquiry attacked the myth of racial democracy. The work originally sponsored by UNESCO was continued throughout the 1950s and 1960s with the investigations of the São Paulo school of racial relations, developed by Florestan Fernandes, Fernando Henrique Cardoso, and Octávio Ianni, among others. These social scientists were forced out of their positions at the University of São Paulo by the military dictatorship in 1969.

The first goal of this chapter is to suggest that Brazil, being an original case, presents a series of features common to the Spanish-speaking countries of Latin America—at least with respect to the historical experience of the descendants of African slaves and the relations between whites and blacks. In this sense, one could refer to a Latin American type of race relations, in contrast to the racial patterns that exist in the United States and in the Caribbean colonized by non-Iberian powers.[1]

The similarity between Brazil and other Latin American societies is demonstrable in at least two areas. First, political and intellectual elites developed an image of their own countries that presumed racial harmony, tolerance, and the absence of prejudice and discrimination (an image that coexists in all cases with the social subordination or the virtual disappearance of the descendants of Africans). Second, a pervasive "whitening" occurred throughout the region, taking the form both of a national project implemented through population and immigration policies, and of an obsession with portraying the respective societies as essentially or predominantly white and culturally European or Hispanic.

Analyzing the thought of José Martí, José Vasconcelos, and Gilberto Freyre, Michael Hanchard (1992) has compared narratives of exceptionality referring to the United States and to Latin America. In the first case, what is exceptional is the absence of a feudal past and of the class tensions distinctive of the European historical experience. In the second case, that of Latin America, the exceptional character is presented in terms of racial harmony and of cultural congruence. Focusing their attention on the system of racial segregation in the United States, these and other Latin American thinkers would not consider the possibility that racial conflict, like class conflict, could manifest itself in a variety of forms. As Michael Hanchard (1992: 4) explains, "Since the United States were seen as the model of racial hate in relation to which all other organized societies should be assessed, Latin American intellectuals never bothered researching the strong racist currents in their own countries."

Like the rest of the countries of the Americas that had experienced slavery, Brazil, following abolition, had to struggle with the "problem" raised by ex-slaves and the descendants of Africans. The solution devised by the nation provides the key to understanding race relations in Republican Brazil. Rather than involving a system of racial segregation similar to that of the United States, it entailed the whitening and symbolic integration of nonwhite Brazilians through the idea of racial democracy.

For many intellectuals and politicians during this time, at the end of the empire and the start of the republic, the harmonious solution to the race problem of the country involved the gradual disappearance of blacks by way of their absorption into the white population. Underlying this solution were racist suppositions regarding the biological superiority and predominance of white genes, suppositions leading to the expectation of an eventual elimination of nonwhites. This process was expected to be reinforced by the European immigration. Towards the 1950s, even though the intellectual legitimacy of the ideal of whitening had begun to erode (because of the defeat of Nazism in World War II and the emergence, in the Third World, of independent nations of nonwhite population), this ideal became deeply rooted in the very group whose disappearance was anticipated, favoring the trend toward self-denial of blacks.

Simultaneously, other sectors of the Brazilian elite were nurturing and shaping what was to become the myth of racial democracy. The main effect of this powerful ideological construction has been to prevent interracial differences from entering the political arena, thus creating severe limitations to blacks' demands for racial equality. Two practical results have ensued from the monolithic acceptance by whites of the Brazilian racial mythology. First, once the racial ideology and its corollaries—the absence of racial prejudices and discrimination—were accepted, evidence of prejudice toward blacks could be credited to differences of class and not of race. Inequalities between whites and blacks are thus perceived as related not to race but, rather, to class factors. Second, this official racial ideology produced a feeling of relief among whites, who could then regard themselves as exempt from any responsibility toward the social problems of the blacks and mulattos.

The notion of racial democracy, as conceived by the intellectuals, has been accepted by the state, which in turn provides the official definition of the situation. The state also shapes the racial common sense of the population, including that of the racially subordinated groups themselves. Talking or acting against this official definition may entail high political costs. One such cost is the widespread view in Brazil that anyone who refers to racism in that country is importing a set of assumptions from abroad to describe a situation that does not exist in Brazilian society.[2]

No other Latin American country constructed such an elaborate and persistent dogma as that of the Brazilian racial democracy. In the other countries of the region, only a weak version of the Brazilian racial myth took hold. For external observers, including those of Latin America, it must be difficult to understand how Brazilians even today can interpret their country along the lines fixed by Gilberto Freyre more than fifty years ago, much less how they can still think about racial democracy in a society where democracy, in contrast to *racial* democracy, has existed in such a limited way.

One ingredient of the racial myth, both in its strong Brazilian version and in the weaker versions associated with the rest of Latin America, is the idyllic reconstruction of slave society. Everywhere throughout the region are traditional historians proclaiming the benevolence of the slave system in their own societies. This image of benign slavery—pioneered in Latin America by Freyre and by historians Frank Tannenbaum and Stanley Elkins in the United States—was then projected forward, to the period following abolition. The Latin American racial myth, including such typical elements as the supposed absence of prejudices and discrimination, has been reinforced by the lack of overt racial conflict in the region, the nonexistence of legal discrimination, the presence of some nonwhite people among the elites, and racial intermarriage—as well as by the oft-mentioned comparison with the Jim Crow system of the American South. Two other ingredients of this racial myth are the emphasis on race mixture (understood as an indicator of racial tolerance) and the apology of the *mestizaje*. The strong parallel between Freyre's notion of a Brazilian *metarraça* (meta-race) and the *raza cósmica* (cosmic race) proposed by the Mexican José Vasconcelos still awaits in-depth study.

Nevertheless, as Hanchard suggests, the theoreticians of "miscegenation" seem to have confused racial mixture at the biological level with racial interaction in the sociological sense. Assuming that the biological event took place without conflict (a statement that can be empirically tested and rejected), they suggest that the sociological outcome could ensue without conflict. (Hanchard, 1992: 24). After all, until the abolition of slavery, much of the race mixture was the result of sexual violence toward black women.

Undoubtedly, the Latin American racial myth has fulfilled an important role of social control, pointing toward national unity and hiding the existence of racial and social divisions. It has also allowed the elites of Latin America to establish a field of moral superiority over their economically powerful Anglo-Saxon neighbors of the north. In addition, this racial mythology works as a conscious model of representation for Latin Americans, including Afro-Latins. But behind this conscious model there is a latent or unconscious one, in which nonwhite people of all colors occupy a perfectly determined place along the socioeconomic hierarchy.

The ideal of whitening, congruent with the tendency of many Latin Americans to think about themselves and their countries as white, was clearly shaped toward the end of the nineteenth century. It has been construed as a product of the tension between, on the one hand, racist theories that originated in Europe and in the United States but were absorbed by Latin America and, on the other, the racial reality of the Latin American countries, characterized by the strong presence of black, indigenous, and racially mixed populations (Skidmore, 1974; Wright, 1990). However, the oldest grounds of the ideal of whitening are found in the colonial systems, both Portuguese and Spanish. In these systems, characterized by the absence of racial dichotomies and of rules of hypo-descent, a certain number of nonwhites could ascend step-by-step in a highly hierarchic and color-conscious society. The first step in this long path consisted of abandoning the condition of slavery through *manumission* or escape; the last step, possible for only a few fair-skinned mestizos, involved gaining acceptance in the dominant white group. Outside Brazil, and from 1795 on, it was possible to become legally white through special certificates called *cédulas de gracias al sacar,* which were sold by the Spanish crown. And within Brazil, to this day, examples of renowned nineteenth-century nonwhites, such as Machado de Assis and André Reboucas, are remembered in anecdotes reinforcing the racial mythology.

In the past, as now, the counterpart of racial systems that allow for a slow ascent through a color gradient was a white racist aesthetics that undervalues the black end of the spectrum, thus conditioning the attitudes and behavior of nonwhites. As one observer notes, "Naturally, the hierarchical ordering of people in terms of their proximity to whiteness helped in the disdain that darker-colored people show of their African origin" (Rout, 1976: 132). Expressions such as *cabelo bom* (nice hair), *cabelo ruim* (bad hair), and *melhorar a raça* (to improve the race) are common to the Portuguese and Spanish spoken in the Americas. It is no surprise that this strong pressure toward whitening has created a situation in which "blacks and mulattos do whatever they can to look more white and put their energy into covering up or hiding their black origins" (Rout, 1976: 245).

The effort to resemble whites to the degree possible, and the social perception of race according to a continuum of shades of color, had led to a fragmentation of racial identities. In turn, this fragmentation is related to the difficulties involved in the construction of collective identities based on racial criteria and to the low degree of politicization of race conflict in the region. The Partido Independiente de Color (Independent Party of Color), established early in this century in Cuba (but repressed and violently eliminated in 1912), and the Frente Negra Brasileira (Brazilian Black Front) of the 1930s (eliminated in 1937 by the dictatorship of the Estado Novo) appear in the historical landscape as exceptions to the general trend of the region. Contemporary black movements, as well, are facing enormous difficulties in their efforts to mobilize mass support.

Another aspect of the Latin American ideal of whitening has been the attempt to cover up all traces of black presence following abolition. The purpose is not only to make blacks invisible in the mass media but also to prevent them from occupying key public positions. In Brazil, for example, the burning of documents on slavery was ordered by Ruy Barbosa. Historians still discuss the extent of damage to their sources caused by this decision, as well as the motives that prompted it: Was it intended to erase the black stain of slavery in past history, or to limit the demands for compensation raised by the last slave masters? The history of Brazilian demographic census taking, which started in 1872, illustrates this point. The 1900, 1920, and 1970 counts simply omitted the question about skin color of the population; then the question was included the 1980 census, in response to the pressures of social scientists and of the black movement.

A similar attitude may be identified in other Latin American countries. Argentina has not recorded the race or skin color of its population since the third national census, conducted in 1914. Bolivia has no figures on race since 1900; and Peru, since 1961. Ecuador eliminated the information on race from the 1950 and 1962 censuses. Venezuela has no data on race since the first national census, carried out in 1876. Nicaragua has not recorded this information since 1920, Honduras since 1945, and the Dominican Republic since 1950. Furthermore, there reason to suspect that in some countries the data are manipulated to reflect a racial composition that is whiter than actually the case. Where the black presence is undesirable, then, its record in the official statistics is simply eliminated—as is the possibility of detecting discrimination and racial inequality.

Specialists in the history of Latin America also seem to be imbued with the whitening ethos. The names of such historians as Rolando Mellafe, Gonzalo Aguirre Beltrán, Jaime Jaramillo Uribe, and Manuel Moreno Fraginals are sufficient to suggest the quality of the historiography on slavery in Latin America. Yet few names of this caliber can be mentioned in relation to the history of the black people in Latin America after abolition. In the words of one American historian:

> The history of Afro-Hispanic-Americans since emancipation is still to be written. Leslie Rout's efforts to produce a synthesis of available secondary sources on black people and on race relations in Spanish-American countries during the XIXth and XXth centuries show clearly the almost total absence of such studies. (Andrews, 1980: 201)

The situation is not very different in Brazil. Notwithstanding the growing number and sophistication of studies on slavery, blacks are included in Brazilian historiography only as slaves. Their social history after 1888 has been greatly neglected.[3]

In addition to the social and psychological aspects of the ideal of whitening, we must briefly discuss its role in the national project of Latin American countries. This project, with its goals of race mixture and the promotion of European immigration, was anticipated in Brazil as early as the period of abolition. In Brazil as well as in other countries of Latin America, whitening was not only an *ex post facto* rationalization of the advanced stage of racial crossbreeding of the population; it also reflected the racial pessimism being felt by the end of the nineteenth century:

> The colonial legacy of social degradation and racial prejudice turned in the XIXth century into an acute form of racial pessimism, in the belief that only immigration of

white Europeans through colonization could provide the industrious labor force needed to transform Latin America. (Stein and Stein, 1970: 119)

The "apathy, indolence and lack of foresight" of the predominantly colored population weighed heavily in the diagnosis of economic backwardness of Latin American elites. These presumed traits of the native lower classes were then isolated from the historical conditions that blocked their access to property and to socialization in the discipline of the free labor market, and were ascribed to their racial attributes. Accordingly, European immigration was considered a short-term solution way of solving the crisis of slave labor or of populating and economically occupying the territory; it was also deemed a long-term contribution to the whitening of the population. The work of Juan B. Alberdi and Domingo F. Sarmiento foreshadowed the thesis of European immigration in Latin America, anticipating by decades the ideas of João Batista Lacerda, Oliveira Vianna, and many other Brazilian intellectuals.

Between 1888 and 1930, approximately 3.76 million Europeans immigrated to Brazil. During the final crisis of slavery, the importation of Chinese workers was considered a solution to the scarcity of labor for the coffee plantations, but the various attempts made by the São Paulo landowners to promote Chinese immigration were rejected. To use the terms coined by Carlos Vainer (1990) the "racial logic" defeated the "economic logic." Table 9.1 shows the impact of European immigration on the racial composition of the Brazilian population.[4]

Notwithstanding the changes in the procedures involved in registering the color of people's skin in the various censuses, the figures in this table indicate two general trends. During the fifty-year period from 1890 to 1940, the impact of the European immigration was greatest. This was also a time of whitening of the population: The proportion of whites increased from approximately two-fifths to almost two-thirds of the entire population. Subsequently, in the years between 1940 and 1980, the main trend was toward *pardizaçao,* or crossbreeding of the population, during which the proportions of both whites and blacks diminished. Clearly, the whitening ideal is not being accomplished. Now that European immigration

TABLE 9.1   Composition of the Population According to Skin Color in Brazil, 1890–1980 (percentages)

	Year of Census				
Skin Color	1890	1940	1950	1960	1980
White	44.0	63.5	61.0	61.0	54.8
Mulatto	41.4	21.2	26.5	29.5	38.5
Black	14.6	14.6	11.0	8.7	5.9
Yellow		0.7	0.8	0.8	0.8
Totals	100.0	100.0	100.0	100.0	100.0

Note: "Yellow" includes categories for which data are not available.
SOURCE: Brazilian demographic censuses of 1950 and 1980.

has ceased, the crossbred group is the fastest-growing one. Nevertheless, as envisioned by adherents of that ideal, the black group is gradually facing extinction.

The European immigration to Brazil was not merely stimulated; in São Paulo, it was even financially supported. Complementing this promotion of white immigration was the restricted entry of nonwhites. Immediately following proclamation of the republic, a decree of June 28, 1890, provided free entry into the country to all individuals suited for work—"except for Asian or African natives, who would be admitted only with a special permit of the National Congress and according to the specific conditions thus stipulated."

Subsequently, the 1934 Constitution restricted immigration flows to a "limit of two percent of the total number of immigrants of the respective nationalities established in Brazil during the last fifty years." This measure specifically sought to control Japanese immigration, which had begun in 1908. Later, as soon as World War II had ended, a new decree, issued on September 18, 1945, stated in its first two articles that "all foreigners can enter Brazil satisfying the conditions established by this law. . . . [And] in admitting immigrants, the need to preserve and develop, in the ethnic composition of the population, the most fitting characteristics of its European descent, as well as the defense of the national worker, will be taken into consideration."[5]

It is well known that not all countries in Latin America were as successful as Brazil, Uruguay, and Argentina in promoting European immigration. Peru and Cuba, having less favorable conditions to attract Europeans, imported Chinese laborers in the second half of the nineteenth century. And blacks from the English-speaking Antilles entered Panama to work in the construction of the canal and came to other countries of Central America as a labor force for United Fruit. Nevertheless, these countries showed no less zeal than did Brazil in restricting nonwhite immigration.

In 1886, Uruguay prohibited the immigration of people of African origin. The 1903 Paraguayan immigration law outlawed the granting of visas to people of African or Asian origin; it was eliminated in 1924, but this unofficial immigration policy remained in force at least until the 1940s. In 1929, during the government of Juan Vicente Gómez, Venezuela restricted the immigration of people of African origin; the new immigration law of 1936 reiterated this restriction, which was eliminated as late as 1966. In Honduras, the 1934 and 1935 immigration laws prohibited the entry of blacks, gypsies, and unskilled laborers from the Far East. In Costa Rica, the 1911 and 1942 laws (repealed by decree in 1949) blocked the entry of blacks, North Africans, and Orientals. In Panama, the 1941 law forbade the granting of visas to blacks who were not native Spanish speakers. And in the Dominican Republic, apart from the massacre of Haitians promoted by Trujillo in 1937, a law placed a $500 levy on all immigrants who were not white or Amerindian.[6]

Having examined the similarities between Brazil and the other countries of Latin America with regard to race relations between whites and blacks, we now look at how the Latin pattern of relations operates in terms of racial stratification and inequalities. The situation in Brazil, where information on the race and color of the inhabitants is available, will be our frame of reference.

THE CONDITION OF AFRO-BRAZILIANS
A CENTURY AFTER ABOLITION

The following pages present an updated picture of racial inequalities in Brazil, based on household survey data gathered by the Pesquisa Nacional por Amostra de Domicilios (PNAD) of 1987, the year immediately preceding the centennial celebration of the abolition of slavery in Brazil. As we shall see, the two key factors for understanding these inequalities are differences in geographic distribution and in racial discrimination.

Only the distribution of the white, black, and mulatto groups will be considered in this analysis. (Orientals and people who have not declared their skin color are excluded, as they represent fewer than 1 percent of the population.). Table 9.2 provides the relevant figures.

For historical reasons linked to the economic cycles of the slave system and to international migrations in the decades following the abolition of slavery, the color groups have exhibited a very uneven geographic distribution. At present, three-quarters of the white population is concentrated in the southeast and in the south (the most developed regions of the country), whereas almost three-fifths of the nonwhite population live in the northeast, the north, and the centerwest (the most underdeveloped areas). The locational disadvantage of the nonwhites, which is more pronounced in the mulatto group, has meant lower educational and economic opportunities.

TABLE 9.2   Racial Inequalities in Brazil, 1987 (percentages)

	Whites	*Blacks*	*Mulattos*	*Nonwhites*
Population in southern and southeastern regions	75.3	62.8	37.1	40.5
Urban	78.1	73.4	62.9	66.6
Illiteracy in ages 10+	18.0	35.0	36.5	36.3
Completed primary education (8 years total)	29.5	11.5	14.0	13.6
Completed university education (4–5 years total)	9.2	1.2	2.3	2.1
Recipients of social security	57.3	43.1	37.4	38.2
Nonmanual workers	26.9	6.7	12.6	11.6
Holders of work card in urban labor	52.0	47.5	42.5	43.3

Note: The category of nonwhites includes blacks and mulattos but excludes Orientals. Other relevant data include average years in school (whites: 4.1, blacks: 2.2, mulattos: 2.6, nonwhites: 2.5) and average monthly income (whites: Cz$10,615, blacks: Cz$4,326, mulattos: Cz$4,984, nonwhites: Cz$4,888).

SOURCE: Pesquisa Nacional por Amostra de Domicilios, *Cor da População,* vol. 1 (1987).

Regarding educational achievements, Table 9.2 shows that in 1987 the proportion of illiterates among nonwhites (36.3 percent) was twice as high as that of whites (18.0 percent). In addition, the proportion of whites who completed the eight years of compulsory primary education (29.5 percent) more than doubled that of nonwhites (13.6 percent). Based on these data, the probability for whites to complete higher education was 4.4 times greater than for nonwhites.

In the decades following abolition, blacks and mulattos enjoyed very limited access to the better agricultural jobs in the coffee plantations and in the emerging manufacturing industry—particularly in the southeast, where the vast majority of the foreign immigration was settling. The entry of large numbers of nonwhites into the modern urban economy took place only after 1930. Today, blacks and mulattos are overrepresented in the urban manual occupations. They also participate disproportionately in the worst jobs of the informal sector, as can be inferred from the lower percentage of nonwhites with "work cards" (which guarantee the protection of labor legislation) among the total number of people employed in nonagricultural activities. According to this criterion, the proportions of whites and nonwhites employed in the formal sector are 52.0 percent and 43.3 percent, respectively. At present, the discriminatory barriers for access seem to have been transferred to higher levels of the occupational structure. This conclusion is suggested by the unequal participation of both groups in white-collar jobs—a proximate measure of membership in the new middle class, which in 1987 comprised 29.5 percent of whites and only 11.6 percent of nonwhites. The difference in the proportions of blacks (6.7 percent) and mulattos (12.6 percent) employed in white-collar jobs suggests that phenotypical traits are important considerations for access to these positions. Moreover, as could have been predicted, racial inequalities in educational and work opportunities have strongly affected the distribution of income in Brazil. In 1987, the average monthly income of nonwhites (Cz$4,888) was equivalent to a little less than half that of whites (Cz$10,615).

The lower socioeconomic standing of blacks and mulattos in contemporary Brazil has been explained in terms of the different points of departure of these groups and of whites at the time that slavery was abolished. This argument contrasts with the view that the explanatory power of slavery as a cause for the social subordination of blacks and mulattos decreases over time. In other words, contemporary racial inequalities are only residually linked to the legacy of slavery because the racist principles of social selection continue to operate. Recent studies of the social mobility of whites and nonwhites indicate clearly that these two groups have different degrees of access to social opportunities (Silva, 1981; Oliveira et al., 1983; Hasenbalg and Silva, 1988). Indeed, discriminatory practices and the symbolic violence inherent in the racist culture of Brazil have much more severely limited the educational opportunities for nonwhites than for whites of the same social origin (Hasenbalg and Silva, 1990). Furthermore, educational achievement has translated into proportionally lower occupational and income benefits for nonwhites than for whites. From these observations we can conclude that greater equality between racial groups in Brazil will likely be achieved through circumstances other than individual social mobility.

A recent study by Peggy Lovell (1992) presents highly significant results for the appraisal of racial discrimination and inequalities in Brazil in the years preceding 1980. Lovell uses 1960 and 1980 census information to estimate income differences according to race. Her estimates indicate that during this twenty-year period, nonwhite men and women obtained real gains in income due to improvements in education, occupation, and the regional distribution of this group. Yet inequalities relative to whites have persisted. By means of regression techniques Lovell divided the income differential between whites and nonwhites for 1960 and 1980 into three components: discrimination, composition, and interaction between the two. The discrimination component indicates what part of the difference in income is due to the fact of being nonwhite and of earning lower salaries than white workers who are equally qualified, whereas the composition component indicates what part of the income of nonwhites is lower due to their deficit in human capital.

Lovell's analysis shows that, in 1960, 12 percent of the difference in income between white and nonwhite women was due to discrimination and that 40 percent of the difference was due to disparities in composition. By 1980, however, the proportion of the income gap due to discrimination had risen to 16 percent, whereas the proportion attributed to disparities in composition had diminished to 35 percent. Moreover, in the case of men, in 1960, 17 percent of the difference in income between whites and nonwhites was due to discrimination and 48 percent resulted from differences in composition. In 1980, by contrast, the proportion of the gap due to discrimination was 32 percent and that due to disparities in composition was 34 percent (Lovell, 1992).

Contrary to theories that postulate a gradual disappearance of the racial factor as a consequence of economic development, these results show that, during the period of rapid economic growth between 1960 and 1980, racial discrimination in the labor market increased in Brazil. Despite the absence of published studies analyzing the evolution of the socioeconomic situation after 1980, existing data strongly suggest that the "lost decade" for economic and social development has not significantly altered either the absolute or relative situation of nonwhites in Brazil. If racism as a mechanism of social selection puts nonwhites at a disadvantage in the competitive process of social mobility and confines them to the base of the social hierarchy, the question we must ask is, What can be done to diminish or eliminate racial inequalities? As we turn to the next section for some suggested answers, it is useful to recall that the question is hardly a new one. As Leslie B. Rout, Jr. (1976), has written:

> Possibly the most striking factor in the history of the black man in Spanish America has been the absence of significant change in his overall position. Admittedly he is no longer in bondage, but, in his deprived state, the Hispanic black or mulatto is generally excluded from competing for society's premier awards and positions. The

Spaniards brought the African to the New World to perform manual labor; four hundred years later, this is still his primary function. (p. 318)

POSSIBLE SOLUTIONS

The main barrier to development of strategies and policies designed to combat racial discrimination against nonwhite Latin Americans is the absence of information on these groups. Indeed, data are lacking in several domains. Most significant is the deficiency of up-to-date official statistics regarding the demographic and socioeconomic situations of racial and ethnic groups in most Latin American countries. All countries that are signatories of the International Convention on the Elimination of All Forms of Racial Discrimination should begin to collect data and produce statistics on racial and ethnic groups, as such information has not been gathered in national censuses or yearly home surveys. As of March 1991, only Paraguay and Honduras among Latin American countries had failed to ratify this international convention. Information on the different racial groups of the region is indeed essential to the monitoring of unequal socioeconomic results generated by discriminatory practices.

The lack of official information is exacerbated by the inadequacy and scarcity of academic research on the contemporary situation of black populations in Latin America. Only very few studies have updated the national cases, and virtually none deal with the people in greatest distress. Noteworthy among the latter are the black communities living in peripheral and impoverished areas of such countries as Ecuador, Venezuela, and Colombia; the rural black communities that emerged from the traditional *quilombos* and *palenques,* where the guaranteed right to land is a basic demand; and the English-speaking black communities of Antillean origin living in Venezuela, Panama, and other countries of Central America.

Finally, there is only very limited circulation among Latin American countries of the few studies that do exist. One potential solution would be the establishment of a central clearinghouse from which regional documentation could be disseminated, thereby promoting the sharing of information about black populations across countries.

At least in theory, there are three additional solutions to the more general problem of racism affecting nonwhite Latin Americans. The first option is legal in nature, entailing the application of existing legislation against racism. Such legislation attempts to guarantee equal opportunities through elimination of the artificial barriers imposed on competition by racial discrimination. Through the Center for Human Rights, the United Nations Committee for the Elimination of Racial Discrimination recently collected and published all the national laws against racial discrimination in the countries of Latin America. This legislation varies widely from country to country. In some instances, the formal principle of equality is embedded in constitutions; in others, the laws are more specific and rigorous (as in Brazil, where such laws stem from the 1988 Constitution). Given that the elites in

Latin America lack a commitment to addressing the problem of racism, the effective enforcement of existing legal principles will depend more on the mobilization of interested sectors of civil society than on the spontaneous action of the state apparatus involved in guaranteeing the law.

A second solution is outlined in the "affirmative action" policies of the United States and the "positive action" policies of some European countries. These policies aim at equality of rights of groups; by granting preferential treatment to people belonging to certain groups (based on race, gender, or ethnicity), they attempt to compensate for past discrimination. But there is little cause for optimism in Latin America about the prospects for carrying out such policies in the short term. In Brazil, as in other countries of the region, difficulties would begin at the moment of negotiating the political agreements necessary to approve the relevant legislation; and they would continue when it became necessary to determine who is black and thus qualified to reap the benefits of the quota system. Much time will likely pass before Latin American societies modify their racial self-image, recognize that racism exists, and admit that racism and democracy are incompatible. Nevertheless, small improvements in this direction are perceptible.

The third solution has been suggested by William Julius Wilson (1987) in relation to the problem of the underclass in the United States. Specifically, Wilson calls for the implementation of nonracially specific policies—that is, social-democratic and redistributive policies designed to equalize the life opportunities of all people, independent of racial considerations. Given that racial inequalities are deeply embedded in the social and economic disparities common throughout Latin America (and especially in Brazil), such policies would be of direct benefit to the nonwhite populations subjected to the greatest deprivations. Yet even the eventual improvement of life conditions for these populations would not necessarily alter the racism etched into the culture itself. In the democratic projects of our times, the reduction of inequalities must indeed be tied to the recognition of differences.

Notes

1. An alternative analysis of the Spanish variant of racial relations, based on the concepts of segmented society, intersegment mobility, and "somatic" image, can be found in Hoetink (1967).

2. Regarding the historical conditions that favored the formation of the myth of racial democracy, see Costa (1985).

3. A significant body of literature on blacks and race relations in Brazil during the republic does exist, produced almost entirely by anthropologists and sociologists. One of the few historians who studied race relations in the postabolition period is Andrews (1991), who concentrated on São Paulo.

4. Given the lack of information on skin color or race in the most recent demographic census of most countries in Latin America, it is impossible to estimate the magnitude of the population of African descent in the region. The estimates presented here, however,

pertain to the Spanish speaking countries, as suggested by Rout (1976: 210): (a) A tiny black population (less than 1 percent of the total) disappeared or was completely absorbed into the white populations of Mexico, Argentina, Bolivia, and Chile. (b) A small minority of blacks (2–5 percent of the total) exists in Guatemala, El Salvador, Costa Rica, Peru, Paraguay, and Uruguay. (c) A meaningful black minority (6–30 percent of the total) exists in Honduras, Nicaragua, Venezuela, Colombia, and Ecuador. And (d) the largest population groups in Cuba, Santo Domingo, and Panama are probably black.

5. One of the few studies providing a detailed examination of the racist character of the immigration policies and legislation in Brazil is that of Vainer (1990). The most complete analysis of the whitening ideal in Brazil is that of Skidmore (1974). And the case of Venezuela is analyzed by Wright (1990).

6. These references to the restrictions imposed on the immigration of nonwhites are taken from Rout (1976: chs. 7–11).

References

Andrews, George Reid. (1980). *The Afro-Argentines of Buenos Aires 1800–1900.* Madison: University of Wisconsin Press.

———. (1991). *Blacks and Whites in São Paulo, Brasil, 1888–1988.* Madison: University of Wisconsin Press.

Costa, Emilia Viotti da. (1985). *The Brazilian Empire: Myths and Histories.* Chicago: University of Chicago Press.

Freyre, Gilberto. (1933). *Casa Grande e Senzala.* Rio de Janeiro: Maia & Schmidt.

Hanchard, Michael. (1992). "Taking Exception: Narratives of Racial Equality in Brasil, Mexico and Cuba." Paper presented at the international seminar on *Racismo e relaçoes raciais nos países da diáspora Africana,* Centro de Estudos Afro-Asiáticos, Rio de Janeiro.

Hasenbalg, Carlos A., and Nelson do Valle Silva. (1988). *Estrutura social, mobilidade e raça,* São Paulo/Rio de Janeiro: Vértice/IUPERJ.

———. (1990). "Raça e oportunidades educacionais no Brasil." *Estudos Afro-Asiáticos,* no. 18.

Hoetink, H. (1967). *Caribbean Race Relations: A Study of Two Variants.* London: Oxford University Press.

Lovell, Peggy A. (1992). "Raça, classe, gênero e discriminaçao salarial no Brasil." *Estudos Afro-Asiáticos,* no. 22.

Oliveira, Lúcia E.G. de, et al. (1983). *O lugar do negro na força de trabalho.* Rio de Janeiro: Instituto Brasileiro de Geografia e Estatística.

Pierson, D. (1942). *Negroes in Brazil.* Chicago: University of Chicago Press.

Rout, Leslie B. (1976). *The African Experience in Spanish America.* London: Cambridge University Press.

Silva, Nelson do Valle. (1981). "Cor e o processo de realização sócio-econômica." *DADOS* 24, no. 2.

Skidmore, Thomas E. (1974). *Black into White: Race and Nationality in Brasilian Thought.* London: Oxford University Press.

Stein, Stanley J., and Barbara H. Stein. (1970). *The Colonial Heritage of Latin America.* New York: Oxford University Press.

Tannenbaum, F. (1946). *Slave and Citizen.* New York: Alfred A. Knopf.

Vainer, Carlos B. (1990). "Estado e raça no Brasil, notas exploratórias." *Estudos Afro-Asiáticos,* no. 18.

Wilson, William J. (1987). *The Truly Disadvantaged, the Inner City, the Underclass, and Public Policy.* Chicago: University of Chicago Press.

Wright, Winthrop R. (1990). *Café con Leche: Race, Class and National Image in Venezuela.* Austin: University of Texas Press.

◀ 10 ▶

Women, Gender, and Human Rights

ELIZABETH JELIN

Two stories run parallel through the history of the last twenty years. The first concerns women's struggle for their liberation and for their rights: the story of feminism. The other is the story of development and expansion—through nongovernmental networks, governments, and societies—of the demand for human rights, including the key role played by women in the struggle to defend human rights. But can the two be put together? And if so, where do they meet? Doubts about which preposition or conjunction to use in relating gender and rights highlight the implications of this question: Are we speaking about the position of women in relation *to* human rights, *or* about the human rights *of* women? (It could also be human rights *and* women, human rights *for* women, etc.)

In the final analysis, there is no single solution, no uniquely correct way of relating women to human rights. Using this observation as a point of departure, the chapter presents two objectives. The first is to explore, through a theoretical-conceptual exercise, how women are situated vis-à-vis human rights and how human rights can be conceptualized from a gender perspective. The second is to consider the human rights issue in the more concrete context of contemporary Latin America. Following a review of the history of the relationship between feminism and the human rights movement in the region, the specific demands of women and the possibility of interpreting them in terms of the human rights paradigm will be explored. These objectives will point us toward more precise meanings for the prepositions and conjunctions that can be used to connect questions of gender and rights, thus enabling us to better recognize the tensions and contradictions inherent in these issues, and inducing some thoughts about the options the future may hold in store.

THE LOGIC OF DIFFERENCE: RIGHTS AND RELATIONS

Although "law has failed to resolve the meaning of equality for people defined as different by society." (Minow, 1990: 9), there are various ways of approaching the issue of difference from a legal point of view. One way is to conceive of difference as inherent in some persons, such that it becomes significant when identified with inferiority: Persons who are different cannot enjoy rights and are seen as "dependents" and "noncitizens." A second way is to secure "equality before the law"; but here, equality is defined in terms of a single set of (masculine?) traits, possibly resulting in the disregard, even denial, of many traits that indicate differences. But since differences do exist, this approach eventually leads to a search for the "real" differences—namely, those that deserve a "truly differentiated" treatment. A third way is to approach difference as a function of social relations, whereby it becomes situated not in categories of individual persons but, rather, in social institutions and the legal norms that rule them (Minow, 1990).

Social demands on the part of the "different" (inferior) actor—in the present case, women—express themselves first in a call for equality. In recent decades, this has meant demanding access to places and positions previously out of bounds for women (from exclusive clubs to traditionally male jobs), and condemning both discrimination (e.g., barriers blocking access to high-level positions in work or in politics) and inequality (unequal pay for equal work).

Much remains to be done if women are to attain equality before the law.[1] However, a literal interpretation of equality can be misleading or insufficient in many situations. For instance, in cases involving workers' pregnancies, is equality—in the sense of denying the differences between men and women—called for? Or should the law recognize the need for "special" treatment of specific groups of people? Alternatively, what does equality of educational rights mean for a disabled child? Or for one whose "mother tongue" is not the language used in public school?

Emphasis on the norm of equality reinforces a conception grounded in universal natural law: It reasserts that all human beings are naturally equal. This conception is politically effective insofar as it allows opposition to certain forms of discrimination, asserts individualities, and limits the exercise of power. However, there is another side to social reality, too. Not all individuals are equal, and the hiding or denying of differences tends to perpetuate the notion that there are two essentially different kinds of people: those who are "normal" and those who are "different" (the latter almost always implies "inferior"). The notion of equality, if maintained and stated in universal terms, entails risks: It may lead to an excessive formalization of rights, isolating them from the social structures in which they exist and acquire meaning. The passage from the universal to the social, historical, and contingent then becomes difficult.

One of the major contributions of feminism has been its profound critique and unmasking of the assumptions implicit in the dominant paradigm that takes (Western) men as the universal reference point and makes women (and others) different or invisible. In the process, feminism has moved on contradictory grounds. On the one hand, it has claimed equality of rights and equal treatment vis-à-vis men; on the other, it has demanded the right to a differentiated treatment and to the social recognition of women's uniqueness. Thus implied is an unavoidable tension between the principle of equality and the right to difference. Recognizing this tension stimulates debate and creativity, and helps avoid dogmatism.

In fact, the critique of the universalization of the "masculine" point of view runs the risk of incurring dangerous simplifications. Often, the assertion of difference implicitly or explicitly entails the right to affirm a universalistic "feminine" point of view, attributing equal or even superior standing to the masculine perspective. The danger here consists in responding to male supremacy with a claim to a feminine/feminist supremacy, reproducing a specific form of (masculine?) thought that cannot conceptualize difference without making it hierarchical (Minow, 1990).

Rather than talking about the *woman*, I am talking about *women*—and thus about the enormous variety of experiences and viewpoints, and differences according to race, class, and nationality, among women. Indeed, my critique of the claim to universal equality implies an incorporation of the perspectives and social positions of various women and men, considering also the intersections of differences and of the power relations inherent in those differences (Romany, 1991; Minow, 1990).

Feminist legal theorists are currently debating whether to pose the issue in terms of either women's rights or gender relations. Demands stated in terms of rights make reference to a paradigm of equality, yet this paradigm is increasingly difficult to maintain in light of all the progress that has been made in the recognition of difference. Demands posed in terms of rights cannot be abandoned, however. Such an abdication could entail strategic and political costs, since demands presented in terms of human rights have a very high moral and emotional legitimacy (Bunch, 1991).[2] From both a theoretical and strategic point of view, a way out could combine the critique of the assumptions of the discourse on rights with a permanent conceptualization of rights in systems of social relations, especially gender relations. Let us look at a case that is especially relevant to this type of analysis.

PRIVATE SPHERE AND PUBLIC LIFE: DOMESTIC VIOLENCE

The human rights paradigm rests on an implicit differentiation between public and private life: The civil and political rights of individuals are located in public life, but these rights are not recognized in the private sphere of family relationships. Unlike the structures of political domination and inequality among men, domination of men over women is socially and economically established in the sphere of private life, without basis in law or in explicit state actions, and often in intimate contexts defined as everyday life.[3] In fact, the dichotomization of life into public and private spheres leads to a mutilation of women's citizenship. Mistreatment of women is often described as the result of an emotional outburst by an enraged man, or as a symbolic manifestation of power resulting from men's need to display masculinity. Furthermore, insofar as it curtails the freedom of women and creates a climate of terror and submission that accentuates gender inequality and women's economic dependency, domestic violence reinforces the structural limitations on women's options. Yet the privacy of family life appears to justify the limitation of state intervention in this sphere.

The result is an inescapable tension between respect for privacy and intimacy, on the one hand, and for public responsibilities, on the other—a tension that requires a redefinition of the distinctions among public, private, and intimate. These distinctions have operated on a symbolic and ideological level, but not in practical terms, for the modern state has always had the power to police the family (Donzelet, 1979; Jelin, 1993). Consider the social recognition of, and moral indignation caused by, domestic violence in recent years; in this context it becomes clear that when human rights are violated in the private realm of family life, respect for privacy within the family cannot justify legal impunity for violence against women.

If the issue of women's rights can no longer be presented as a matter of equal rights but, rather, is framed in terms of demands related to an antisubordination principle, the role of the state must change. Whenever a contradiction appears between respect for privacy and defense of the victims of violence, the affirmative obligation of the state to protect the basic human rights of its citizens necessarily becomes the final criterion for defining state responsibility.

Yet state intervention does not resolve the tension or the contradiction. In the private sphere such interventions may be justified as a defense of the victims and the subordinate people in the patriarchal system. Under authoritarianism, however, it may imply arbitrary intervention, control, and even terrorism, on the part of the state. Thus it may be desirable to protect from state interference all the domains associated with arbitrary intervention, but not those that strengthen (gender) subordination. In short, the solution is to be reached not through the unyielding confrontation of the discourse of equality and the discourse of difference but through an approach that poses the issue of equality of rights in contexts of social relations in which differences, including those of power and marginalization, can be stated explicitly (Valdés, 1990).

LATIN AMERICAN WOMEN: STRUGGLES AND ACHIEVEMENTS

What are the most important demands put forth by Latin American women today? How should the priorities among these demands be established? And finally, is it possible to take advantage of the legitimate spaces opened up by the debate about human rights while at the same time promoting basic changes in the way of conceptualizing the very notion of rights? To begin to answer these questions, we continue in the next section with an analysis of the recent history of women's struggles, followed by a review of specific fields of human rights action.

History I: Women's Rights and Feminism

When feminist movements reappeared at the end of the 1960s in the developed countries, they confronted a dual challenge. On the one hand, they sought to understand and explain the various forms of women's subordination; on the other, they aimed to propose strategies for overcoming that condition. Women had to subvert the theoretical and conceptual order; they had to undermine power relationships at both the macro and the micro levels of society. This struggle necessarily took place on several fronts simultaneously.

What was (or is) the nature of gender subordination? How is it best understood, not only in theory but also in the context of efforts to design practical responses? There is no single conceptual approach or unified strategy. The debate within feminism has been intense, reflecting the permanent heterogeneity and theoretical and tactical conflicts of the movement. New perspectives and new themes are constantly being discovered, while old ones are recovered and redefined. Without pretending to offer an exhaustive history, I have attempted to pinpoint some key moments and turning points.

A first landmark was the discovery of the social invisibility of women: in the hidden realm of domestic work, against an active background of historical moments of struggle, "behind" great men. During the 1960s several influential books sought to make visible the invisible. Recognition and naming bestow social existence, which in turn is a prerequisite for self-esteem and for revindication. Women had to reveal and acknowledge the social value of everyday life, of anti-heroism, of the social web that supports and reproduces social existence. But these processes necessarily coincided with a theoretical debate. What do women produce when they dedicate themselves to their families and their homes? Who appropriates their work? In the 1970s, the recognition of the housewife as a "worker" and the demand for a definition of her labor rights became major topics of debate and controversy.

In the next stage of the struggle, women abandoned the private sphere. They left the house to participate in the public world—which, until then, was a masculine world. By the 1970s, historical trends were already occurring: All over the globe, educational levels for women were increasing as were rates of female participation in the labor market. In Latin America, this rise in women's participation took place with an unanticipated intensity.

Yet the labor market is still characterized by segregation and discrimination. Women have limited access to "good" jobs, their wages for equal work are unequal, and social definitions of "typically feminine" tasks still beset them. These tasks require women to occupy traditional domestic roles (e.g., as secretaries, teachers, and nurses), and female employment is concentrated in them. This second dimension of visibility—anchored mostly in access to the world of work and, to a lesser degree, to other forms of participation in public spaces—promotes a specific form of struggle: the fight against discrimination, and for equality vis-à-vis men.

Insofar as women's struggle for more favorable conditions failed to challenge the traditional sexual division of labor, it was increasingly seen as inadequate. Thus, the new goal of the 1970s was to transform those conditions—specifically, by asserting that the sexual division of labor is oppressive in itself and that it implies subordination and a lack of autonomy on the part of women who remain the "property" of the *patresfamilias*. Theoretical discussions of the history of patriarchy—a concept that focuses on power relations—were important landmarks in the 1970s. Indeed, liberation implied the transformation of patriarchy as a social system (Valdés, 1990).

Women have always been "in charge of" reproductive tasks within the family. Given the need to rely on collective consumption and on public services for performing such tasks, women of the urban popular classes have participated actively in neighborhood organizations and in local public activities demanding collective services from the state. And when the state became inefficient or was inaccessible, self-managed community provision of these services has been promoted. Yet this collective dimension of the domestic role has also been socially invisible and without recognized social value. A feminist analysis of the reproductive roles of women not only implies recognition of the (domestic) tasks of women as socially necessary but also considers participation in neighborhood activities to be a training ground for action in public spaces.

The movement of women out of their homes and into the workplace, along with their participation in organizations and in collective action with other women, seemed to anticipate a future of liberation, especially for women who had been marginalized. If oppression was grounded in the domestic-patriarchal domain, breaking the divide between the private and the public worlds, and learning to express needs and demands in work and in collective action, could become the means of shattering it.

As experience has shown, these practices are liberating at times, but they can also reinforce subordination. For instance, women's community work in collective dining halls, in cooperative child-care efforts, and in neighborhood activities is not remunerated. Nor is it considered to be evidence of autonomy or power in decisionmaking and management. Indeed, it often ends up reproducing subordination and clientelism. And entering the world of paid work generally means a double day's work (or triple, if there is also community work to do), leading not so much to liberation as to exhaustion, fatigue, and overwork. Badly paid and precarious jobs, lack of access to social benefits, little or no recognition of labor rights—all add up to segregation and discrimination.

The struggle against both explicit and implicit forms of discrimination against women and their segregation in the labor market and elsewhere (the 1979 United Nations Convention mentions *all* forms of discrimination against women) represents an important fight for equality of opportunities and living conditions. It is a struggle in behalf of which much remains to be done. Since the 1980s, women's efforts to achieve equality vis-à-vis men have been exerted in a context of growing social inequality and income polarization, with privilege on one side and increased misery and marginality on the other. These are the ramifications of a crisis that affects both genders, though in unequal ways.

In Latin America, the past two decades of struggle against discrimination have had contradictory results. On the one hand, the demand for equality has gained increasing legitimacy and social visibility, even though the region lacks a social consensus and the political will to change. On the other hand, women are still carrying a disproportionate share of the social costs of economic crisis and adjustment. At the same time, although the current wave of neoliberalism implies a reinforcement of duties and responsibilities on the part of the family, it also erodes the capacity of households to command the resources necessary to meet domestic needs. Traditional solutions to the social tasks of reproduction, whether through demands on the state for services or through the invisible extra work done by women in the domestic realm, are no longer viable. Even community organizations, once seen as alternative ways to cope with these tasks, are limited in terms of the resources and efficiency necessary for survival in a neoliberal environment. It is in this new context that the social tasks of reproduction must be rethought.

Thus far we have discussed some of the most noteworthy "invisibilities," but there are numerous others. Only recently, for instance, have sexuality and reproduction become separated and differentiated, and only now are women beginning to enjoy a voice in these issues. The story is well known: Because life originates in the bodies of women, any attempt to exercise power over reproduction requires the appropriation and manipulation of women's bodies, whether in a private or public manner (Population policy could be considered an example of the latter.) The wishes of women can be taken into account, or not. The history of sexuality reveals a similar arrangement: The pleasure is man's, the woman "serves."

Such a cluster of ideologies and practices is not easily transformed. Culture counts: It encompasses *machismo* in all its forms, the cult of the dedicated and suffering mother, the horror evoked by the sterile woman—and, above all, the taboo against naming, talking about, or mentioning sexuality. Concealed and forbidden in words, sexuality is of course very real in everyday life; rendering it visible and exposing the sexual oppression suffered by most women are among the movement's significant achievements. But public and political recognition of this form of oppression, and of the changes that need promoting, has been slower and more controversial. The Catholic Church and ideological traditionalism, along with practices and ideologies that implicate the victim ("Can it be that she incited the rape?" "If she was careless about her sexual relationships, she must suffer the consequences." "It is irresponsible to have so many children. . . ."), have hindered the implementation of legislation, public health programs, and educational services that might otherwise counter such oppression.

And then there is the other taboo, no less invisible or complex; domestic violence. The victims of violent practices within the family—practices also protected by the mantle of privacy—are almost invariably women. (Increased documentation of such incidents since the 1980s has revealed that children and the elderly are similarly victimized.) Evidently it is harder in our culture to speak about domestic violence than about sexual violence—an outcome to which both victims and culprits have contributed.

The last two decades have witnessed a great deal of tension between feminism—the movement of women oriented toward liberation—and movements of women. (In Maxine Molyneux's [1985] terminology, this difference is conceptualized as the tension and contradiction between women's strategic and tactical interests.) At first glance, women active in the struggle for family survival seem far removed from the women who denounce, for instance, the identification of sexuality and reproduction, and thus demand the right to a free sexuality based on pleasure. Given the strength of traditional culture, feminists have often practiced a kind of self-censorship; they have had to show that their struggle focused on what "really mattered," and not on frivolities. The legitimacy of feminists has also depended on their not seeming to impose bourgeois worries and values on women from the popular sectors (Barroso, 1987). Only when such women started demanding sexual education and family planning (in Brazil, for instance) did the feminist movement explicitly take up this issue.

These are only some of the concerns raised by the feminist movement since the early 1970s.[4] The landmarks highlighted here involve areas that can be conceptualized from the standpoint of rights and citizenship. We will return to this subject following the next historical review.

History II: Women and the Human Rights Movement

Although human rights violations have occurred throughout history (a point made even more salient if violence against women and the curtailment of their freedom are taken into account), the human rights *movement* emerged and got its name in relation to massive violations of rights by dictatorial regimes. From the outset, women were at the forefront of this movement. Their commitment rarely stemmed from democratic ideological convictions or strategic calculations in the struggle against dictatorship. The rationale was not political but practical: Women have been directly touched by repression—as mothers, grandmothers, widows, relatives of victims, some missing or tortured. Having lost their fear, many such women were willing to face any risk to satisfy their personal need to learn their relatives' whereabouts, and to recover the victims. The beginnings of the human rights movement were not heroic. The movement was simply a dramatization, and expansion, of the feminine role of devotedly caring for the family. What came afterward is another chapter of history.

Let it be stated clearly from the outset: The presence of women in the human rights movement does not imply that the rights of women were primarily at stake.

This distinction is important, and a failure to recognize it has led to many misunderstandings and disagreements.[5] Nonelite women entered the public arena with demands related to their social responsibilities. But they were not explicitly asserting gender demands. The widespread expectation among feminists that, since activists of the human rights movement are women, they should spontaneously express the "intrinsic" or "specific" demands of women, turned into a demand—often a dogmatic one—that complicated or blocked dialogue with other participants in the human rights movement.

The women who left their homes in search of information about their children did so as part of their personal family drama. The details of such incidents are well known, yet still devastating: the desperation and bewilderment, the search for help, the effort to set up contacts (i.e., with highly placed government and military officials, but also, at times, with fortune tellers) so as not to lose hope, the encounters and commiserations with other women in the same circumstances, the meetings with activists from the human rights movement. In this way the private search for a son or daughter was gradually transformed into a public and political demand for democracy (see, for example, Schirmer, 1988).

A peculiar historical circumstance marked the relationship between women in the human rights movement and feminism: The dictatorships and human rights violations of the 1970s coincided with the period during which women began to gain international attention. The International Year of Women (1975) opened with a large meeting in Mexico, where the subject of women's subordination gained worldwide attention. In subsequent years, women, particularly nonelite women, began to present social demands to governments—many of which were not prepared to meet them.

These events, in turn, coincided with the first encounters between feminist militants from the north and women from the south. These meetings created very special conditions for a dialogue: Some feminists from the north (especially those from Europe) became aware that their own analyses, needs and demands could not be extrapolated to the different circumstances of other countries throughout the world. They learned that among women there are *others* living in more difficult and oppressive situations than their own: Hence the victims of human rights violations became obvious targets for solidarity and cooperation among women. This historical coincidence between feminists from the north and women active in the denunciation of human rights violations in Latin America explains the parallel that many women draw between the human rights movement and the international women's movement.

Consider the case of the Mothers of the Plaza de Mayo, who in the late 1970s and early 1980s generated enormous concern and solidarity in the developed countries, becoming an international symbol of the struggle for human rights in Argentina. (Other organizations, militants, and activists in the Argentine human rights movement received much less coverage abroad.) The Mothers symbolized women who, emerging from deep pain and suffering, and from their traditional role as mothers, subvert the social and political order, thereby revealing the revolutionary potential of women (Feijoo and Gogna, 1987). From a feminist point of view, there inevitably follows the question of whether public action originating in private grief transformed these mothers into women aware of their gender revindications. And did this grief encourage them to fight for these new demands?

Although there is no systematic research on the matter, scattered evidence shows that, in relation to gender demands, women active in the struggle for human rights display the same variety of positions as do the members of the movement as a whole. Their objectives are equally diverse, as are the strategies and political alliances they pursue. In short, they endorse as much (or as little) of feminist thought as do the others in the milieu in which they act.

Wherever there was repression in Latin America, the female victims were systematically humiliated, raped, and tortured; in many cases, they were among the missing (Bunster, 1991). The differences among the countries of the region surface when we consider the practices of oppression of women who, though they are experiencing a similar state violence, occupy varying social spaces. In Guatemala, for instance, the issues facing indigenous people overlap with those associated with human rights: The "tradition" of raping Indian women takes on political meaning when practiced against activist women, whereas the exploitation of and salary discrimination against political widows in agricultural work constitute a clear case of interaction among class, ethnicity, gender, and politics (Schirmer, 1993). The Argentine case was different. Femininity and maternity were employed as part of a strategy: Beyond their loss of fear, beyond their conviction that they "had nothing to lose," the Mothers felt that their status as mothers and as women protected them from physical violence. In rallies and protests, they were convinced that they were less exposed to danger than were men or the young (Feijoo and Gogna, 1987). In Chile, by contrast, the tradition of political socialization fostered a women's movement that was unique in that the personal experiences of direct or indirect victims of repression were converted rapidly into political demands against the regime (Valdés, 1990).

The human rights situation across Latin America remains quite varied to this day. In most countries of the region, accounts with the past are still not settled, but democracy has replaced the terror-based regimes in which state organizations engaged in massive violations of human rights. In this context, should issues related to the subordination of women be posed in terms of human rights? The transitions to democracy have resulted in considerable social awareness of human rights, although at times such awareness has been expressed in a less than progressive manner.[6] The challenge is to transform that social sensibility into a strategy that averts violations, deters violence, and confronts the diverse forms of subordination and marginalization that beset daily life.

Meanwhile, human rights violations continue to be perpetrated in more or less covert ways in several Latin American countries. The network of women active in the human rights movement plays an important role in denouncing abuses and expressing solidarity. In this regard, acts of international recognition, such as the Nobel Peace Prize awarded to Rigoberta Menchú, are exemplary in that they publicize rights violations and confer legitimacy upon those who resist them.

LATIN AMERICAN WOMEN'S RIGHTS AT THE END OF THE CENTURY

What are Latin American women asking for at present, and to what extent do their demands reflect the logic of human rights? For that matter, is it possible to update and confer substance to the *right to have rights*? The following three sections do not contain an exhaustive list of demands; nor do they represent a normative statement about which themes should take priority. Rather, they address some specific issues in order to highlight the inherent dilemmas and tensions involved in the pursuit of women's rights.[7]

The Right to One's Body: Reproductive Rights

Since the 1950s, the link between population growth and development has been a constant focus of discussion and policy intervention in Latin America. The UN Economic Commission for Latin America (ECLA) has played a leading role in the debate, as expressed in dialogues about pro- and antinatalist ideologies; in academic discussions as to whether an automatic link exists between urbanization and fertility, or between education and fertility; in pressures from the Catholic Church to block implementation of birth-control plans; and in the efforts of some international agencies to carry out such plans against the will of those involved.

The controversy reemerged dramatically in 1992 at the United Nations Conference on Environment and Development (UNCED), where debate revolved around the relationship between population growth and the environment. Broadly speaking, the northern countries argued that environmental degradation is a result of the population explosion, and that measures have to be taken to control population growth (in the south). In response, the countries of the south insisted that northern consumption patterns are the real culprit. Actually, this dispute was but a new twist on a long-standing debate combining political, ideological, economic, and even moral dimensions.[8]

Seen from the perspective of women's issues, this matter has a long and multifaceted history. Central to this history is the fact that, because a woman's body begets life, it has a unique social value. Recall Friedrich Engels argument of more than a century ago: that if private property (of men) is to be transmitted through rules of (biological) inheritance, the woman's body has to be monitored and controlled. Through its capacity to bear children, then, the same "object" that provides sexual pleasure is the key to the transmission of property.

Industrial society and modernity have substantially changed the forms of appropriation of that body, but without eliminating the appropriation: New technological means have been invented to prevent pregnancy and to fight sterility; the new ideal type of family is one with fewer children; and the mass media turns the bodies of (young and pretty) women into objects of consumption. Only recently have women started to insist on their power over and rights to their own bodies, thus challenging the consequences of such changes.

In the past two decades, women's activism regarding issues of sexuality and fertility has gathered strength. It has taken on multiple and complex meanings, which, though never ambiguous, are contradictory at times. Even the phrase *reproductive rights,* raised as a banner of the women's movement, implies an apparent contradiction between the demand for autonomy and the demand for sexual equality: "Reproductive rights are the rights of women to regulate their own sexuality and reproductive capacity, as well as to demand that men take responsibility for the consequences of exercising their own sexuality" (Azeredo and Stolcke, 1991: 16).

Let us examine the first clause of this definition. How are the rights to sexuality and reproduction to be exercised? Who will guarantee them? The regulation of women's own sexuality and reproductive capacity entails, above all, their refusal to suffer violence against their bodies. By extension, they must prevent "others" (men) from seeing themselves as owners of women's bodies, and they must possess the power to resist coercion or imposition. Ultimately, the guarantee that the body of a woman will not be subject to actions without her consent and willful cooperation implies the recognition of basic human rights: the right to life, and to freedom. (In this connection, note that Articles 3, 4, and 5 of the Universal Declaration proscribe slavery, bondage, torture, and cruelty.) In the context of human rights, rape is an extreme form of violent bodily harm. But then, so are the imposition of contraceptive methods (the most dramatic being surgical procedures that are irreversible) and, conversely, the denial of access to health services that guarantee the capacity to regulate sexuality and reproduction.

The gap between these rights and standard practices in the contemporary world is immense. The practice of rape is rarely punished; many countries do not concede the right of a raped woman to interrupt her pregnancy; women's sexuality is seldom practiced as an exercise of freedom. As for reproduction, the women's ideal of freedom and self-decision can materialize only under certain conditions. Here, too, social reality differs considerably from the ideal. Population polices, whether they favor birth or birth control, presuppose the demographic planning of fertility—for which the control of women's bodies is crucial. It is one thing to orient women's reproductive choices on the basis of widespread access to sexual and reproductive information and education, but quite a different thing to impose reproductive strategies with no regard for the wishes, options, and choices of women. The absence of education and the lack of means to plan fertility—which account for a sizable portion of adolescent pregnancies—in combination with semicompulsive birth-control programs (e.g., those involving sterilization or indiscriminate distribution of contraceptives) reinforce the vision of woman as an object, a body to be manipulated and subdued.

The current emphasis on new reproductive technologies and the urgent need to legislate the conditions of their use have focused renewed attention on reproductive rights. This time, it is focused on the opposite side of the issue—namely, on the treatment of sterility and on technological manipulation to achieve "assisted" conception and gestation. The paradox is that, whereas issues of reproductive rights (e.g., contraceptive methods and practices) are relevant mostly in peripheral countries and among popular sectors, those related to conceptive practices (e.g., "assisted" fecundity) are being developed and applied in the central countries and among the upper classes of peripheral countries.

Like programs devoted to population control, those that promote the development and use of new reproductive technologies assume a typically Western idea of the individual and of the family: The latter is viewed as a genetic unit that naturalizes social inequalities. In fact, these new technologies respond to the wish for parenthood, to the obsession with having a child of one's own blood, whereby blood symbolizes the bond that transports the essences of persons from generation to generation. In Stolcke's (1991: 82) words, the wish is "for biological paternity through technological maternity."

Let us return to the issues of autonomy and equality, which emerge (albeit contradictorily) when the subject of reproductive rights is approached. Feminism says, "This body is mine." In fact, the notion of the body as property is intrinsic to an individualistic liberal doctrine. Is there a way of reconciling the demand by women to actively choose, decide on, and control the use of contraceptives with the demand that men take responsibility for the consequences of their own sexuality (i.e., their responsibility in paternity)? Both demands are necessary, and both strive for more equitable relations between genders. But their reconciliation necessarily implies negotiation.

At this juncture, a new set of questions must be asked. First, are reproductive rights to be considered women's rights or rights rooted in gender relations? Second, are they individual rights or rights of the couple? And finally, who is in a position to mediate and try to settle these kinds of conflicts? The recognition that women should not be alienated from control over their own bodies is a basic step that, as noted, can be read in terms of basic human rights. Also necessary is the recognition that relations within the couple are asymmetric, such that men (still) have more power to determine their own and their partners' behavior. Although there is a remote danger of turning women's autonomy into a claim of hegemony in issues of sexuality and reproduction—thus denying the participation of men— current circumstances seem to call for assertive action to combat the sexual subordination of women. In the future, ways must be found to resolve the tension between the right of women-mothers to decide when, how, and with whom to have children, and the right of men to paternity on an equal footing with motherhood. For if the desired end is equality in responsibilities and care among both mothers and fathers, the latter must have a say in the "when and how" of their children's gestation. In short, we have to rethink the relational dimension, both of the couple and of society at large, in order to overcome the perspective of "her against him" in matters of reproductive rights.

Defining reproductive rights as individual rights or even the rights of the couple presents another paradox. Because the decisions made by individuals and couples have long-term social consequences, affecting birth and population growth rates, these decisions are the object of national and even international policy interventions. Ideally, of course, the decision to have more or fewer children should be made by the couple in light of the costs and benefits that parenthood entails. State intervention can modify this cost-benefit ratio through population policy, but what priorities should be established, and how? When social expenditures are at stake, class, gender, professional, and business interests come into play. However, the complexity of the phenomenon must not be permitted to hamper the critical analysis as to which resources should be used in order to guarantee which reproductive rights. Issues of this type implicitly bring into question the conventional ways of deciding social policies. They also introduce notions of citizenship and participation into public debates about public policy, thus signaling the need for new kinds of relationships between civil society and the state.

The achievement of reproductive rights is neither easy nor guaranteed. First, there is a cultural barrier to be overcome: Gender socialization and the identity of women remain strongly associated with maternity, as well as with outside control of their sexuality and reproductive capacity. Second, there is a material and instrumental barrier: A woman's right to make her own decisions about her sexuality and reproduction is possible only under certain conditions, such as access to basic welfare and quality of life.

The Fight for Equality: Toward the Elimination of All Forms of Discrimination

The fight for equality takes place on more familiar ground and generates less controversy, even among governments. Many countries have ratified the United Nations Convention; but this formal act does not ensure that all the signatory countries have finished adjusting their legislation in all fields, much less that they have implemented all policies capable of undoing actual discrimination.

The language of equal rights is, as we have seen, the discourse of nondiscrimination. In labor law and in the operation of labor markets, occupational discrimination and segregation—as well as the effects of existing legislation—have been revealed and even quantified. That men and women enter the labor market under very different conditions is undeniable. Also quite clear is the fact that equal opportunity—the conceptual ground for the formulation of economic and social rights—is a fiction. Some tasks are socially defined as "feminine" and others as "masculine," thus generating occupational segregation. In turn, occupational segregation leads to the devaluation (in terms of money, prestige, labor stability, and career potential) of "feminine" jobs. Women also suffer discrimination on the basis of an (attributed) incompatibility between their productive and reproductive roles (García, Gogna, and Jelin, 1990).

Women's reproductive roles have been a central consideration in labor legislation. Ever since the early 1900s, when labor law appeared in Latin America, legislators have worried about "protecting" the laboring woman. This protection has had many dimensions: physical force, morality, enforcement of the family role. Women (as the "weaker sex") were not to perform heavy work, or work night shifts (to protect their morality), or perform unhealthy tasks (because of their weakness and to safeguard their reproductive capacity). But motherhood has also been "protected"—through contract and license conditions. Historically, such measures have had a boomerang effect: Given the added costs of protection, hiring women became more expensive to employers, thus increasing the incentive to practice discrimination. Inevitably, women wound up in precarious jobs with no social benefits, were segregated in "feminine" occupations, had fewer possibilities for promotion, and suffered salary discrimination.

How does one secure opportunities in such a context? What is equality under unequal conditions? For equality to exist, a considerable portion of the supposedly "protective" legislation has to be eliminated and replaced with principles that consider technological change (e.g., "heavy jobs" are not the same today as they were at the turn of the century) and new demands for equity rooted in reproductive rights. Toward this end, however, the relation between the spheres of production and reproduction must be deeply revised—above all, so as to redefine men's and women's responsibilities and tasks in domestic chores and family roles.

Of course, changes in domestic life and family responsibility are inevitably slow and difficult, given the weight of cultural tradition. Especially with respect to those changes that entail the de-feminization and de-masculinization of occupations, commitment to equal opportunity principles in the labor market may require counterbalancing policies that acknowledge gender differences and promote equality. Otherwise, the call for antidiscriminatory policies based on a presumed equality could be counterproductive. For instance, the effort and responsibility of the first woman to reach a position of leadership in an organization—given that she is constantly scrutinized and evaluated in terms of her personal capacity and as a representative of the feminine gender—is much greater than that of her male colleagues, placing her in highly unequal circumstances. Therefore, the recognition that equality is lacking implies the need to implement distinctive affirmative action policies that can eventually generate more equal conditions.

Specific patterns of workplace behavior also call for strong and immediate denunciation. I refer to those situations in which basic human rights, physical integrity, and freedom of movement (predominantly of women) are at stake. Examples include the semi-servile labor conditions and forced migration besetting prostitutes, which are receiving increasing international attention, and the problem of sexual harassment in the workplace, which is gradually being acknowledged as a violation of human rights in the developed countries.

In the region as a whole, these are incipient issues. Sexual harassment in the workplace is a very common experience, although its magnitude cannot be gauged with accuracy—particularly given the persistent reign of silence on the subject as well as the widespread tendency to blame the victims. As with domestic violence and rape, social recognition of sexual harassment and the provision of support and help services for victims are important. But until women get access to legitimate institutional channels through which to press charges, and until harassment itself is understood as a violation of human rights, it will remain a private act, reproved by some, tolerated and even applauded by others. In short, it is only when the state guarantees the human rights of citizens of both genders that their "equal opportunity" can be guaranteed in the world of labor, premised on an explicit recognition of the differences between men and women in gender relations.

Global Rights: Peace, Development, Environment

The paradigm of human rights has faced important challenges in recent decades. The current emphasis on third- and fourth-generation rights, related to global rights and the rights of peoples, respectively, leaves behind the individualistic paradigm; such rights require action in public spaces that go beyond the nation-state. Indeed, the institutional importance of the international scene has increased, as Kathryn Sikkink details in Chapter 4 of this volume. In relation to women's demands, the international network was and remains a key element in the recognition of the widespread incidence of gender subordination, in the development of an awareness of women's past isolation and invisibility, and in the promotion of solidarity.

Of course, we are also living in a period of transnational globalization, in which the territorial dimensions and spatial limits of phenomena are fast losing relevance. Ours is an era of instantaneous globalized communications, globalized economy, and globalized perspectives on environmental issues. Three concepts encapsulate this global dimension: peace, development, and environment. In the 1992 UNCED declaration, they are described as "interdependent and inseparable."

Two questions arise in this connection. First, are peace, development, and environment components of human rights—and if not, should they be? Second, do women play a role in this issue—and if so, what is to be gained by taking a gender approach?

At first glance, the global-individual dichotomy seems a difficult one to reconcile in the context of human rights. For instance, what demand for positive rights—that is, for rights *to* something rather than for the freedom *from* something associated with the negative rights of Western liberalism—can be deduced from acknowledgment of the greenhouse effect? Or from recognition of the future depletion of traditional energy sources? Such issues force us to go beyond the limits of a narrow conception of rights into the wider framework of global systems of sociopolitical relations. At present, international proposals call for the incorporation of this global dimension—in terms of peace, development, and environmental protection—into international treaties and legal instruments that regulate the protection of human rights. Indeed, this step follows logically from acceptance of the "right to have rights," even though it will eventually lead to a radical transformation of the (liberal) paradigm in which the subject of human rights was originally framed.

In this regard, note that the vitality of the women's movement was quite evident in the response to the 1992 UNCED declaration. That response consisted of a long and multifaceted list of women's demands, reflecting positions ranging from critical analyses of transnational political economy and the relationship among population, poverty, and pollution, to more romantic visions of women as the main allies of nature (DAWN, 1992; Oliveira and Corral, 1992). The documents presented at UNCED, as well as eco-feminism's more lyrical and expressive texts, reflect the agenda of revindications put forth by women—especially those of the south. That this agenda serves to denounce situations requiring attention and change is undeniable, although a lot more reflection and elaboration will be necessary if it is to become a substantial contribution to solutions and concrete strategies for action.

CONCLUSIONS

Obviously, there is no unique way to approach the subject of human rights and women other than to recognize that demands evolve historically. Nor can one devise an "Agenda for Women" that presents each demand in terms of basic human rights. Rather, a dynamic process of debate, dialogue, and contestation is called for.

Meanwhile, we can find at least some general points of reference. Above all, acceptance of the historicity of demands implies abandoning the idea that there are natural, transcendental, universal standards, free of the constraints of time and space. Recognition of the contingent nature of struggles and demands should not, however, imply abandoning ideals and utopias. It only means that a more humble approach must be taken—one that acknowledges the absence of absolute truths and that, in the quest for partial, dialogued, contingent truths, seeks the realization of ideals such as the elimination of suffering and oppression or the promotion of solidarity and concern for others (Rorty, 1991).

True, there is no single way of resolving the basic contradictions that permeate the relationship between women and human rights—but these contradictions *can* be made visible, such that their implications for a gender perspective on human rights become recognized. The most critical contradictions are those between

- individual rights and collective rights;
- the principle of equality and the right to be different;

- the perspective rooted in universal rights and that rooted in systems of social relationships;
- public responsibilities and respect for privacy and intimacy.
- the development of desires and subjectivities (historically and culturally formed) and the occasional tendency of these desires and subjectivities to impede democratization and equity.

What, then, is the connection between women and human rights? Insofar as the word *and* denotes two preexisting objects that now come into contact, however bereft of action and transformation that contact may be, the phrase is sterile. As it lacks a "project," it must be replaced by a combination of several other words that highlight the potential linkages involved: (1) "Women *without* rights" clarifies the struggle to obtain human rights *for* women. (2) "Women *for* human rights" and "women *in* (the movements for) human rights" clarify the role of women as participants in a democratizing struggle that can permanently expand recognition of the universal right to have rights. And finally (3) "women *in relation* to human rights" clarifies women's active participation in the constant redefinition of the very notion of human rights—a redefinition capable of overcoming the masculine-Western framework that originally defined human rights, but without abandoning the ideals of freedom and equality that inspired it.

Notes

This chapter is a revised and excerpted version of Elizabeth Jelin's, *About Women, About Human Rights* (Lima: Red Entre Mujeres, 1993).

1. A listing of all discriminatory laws in the countries of the region would be very useful, since it would permit collective action to push for change. Such legislation currently includes differing definitions of adultery for men and women and, as well as references to "[feminine] offenses against [masculine] honor."

2. This legitimacy is not universal, however. As Teresa P.R. Caldeira argues in Chapter 11, the identification of the human rights movement with the rights of marginalized and victimized groups is generating a paradoxical reaction in Brazil: Large sectors of the public reject the cause of human rights because they identify the movement with the defense of criminals and other transgressors. This interpretation is also expressed (though probably to a lesser degree) elsewhere in Latin America.

3. Domestic violence is a widespread phenomenon, kept silent until very recently. In countries where rates of domestic aggression against women are registered, they range from 40 to 80 percent (Matus, 1992).

4. Other issues addressed by the movement include the presence of women in public and political life, the development of feminist perspectives in the arts and in science, and the manifestation of women's creativity.

5. Schirmer (1988: 68) quotes a woman from Chile's *Agrupación* (consisting of relatives of missing persons) as saying, "We are *mothers,* not women."

6. As noted earlier, in Brazil extension of the discourse of human rights to the defense of unpopular social groups (e.g., prisoners and sexual minorities) has had a paradoxical effect on the broader political culture: As the sense of insecurity and fear of criminality increase among the public, the human rights movement becomes identified with the defense of "criminals," thus generating strong social opposition to the movement and its demands.

7. One major issue, violence against women, was discussed earlier in the context of the defense of human rights; therefore, it will not be brought up here.

8. The Cairo Conference on Population and the Beijing Conference on Women are new instances of the same international debate.

References

Azeredo, Sandra, and Verena Stolcke. (1991). "Introduction." In Sandra Azeredo and Verena Stolcke (eds.), *Direitos reproductivos.* São Paulo: Fundaçao Carlos Chagas.

Barroso, Carmen. (1987). "Sexo y crisis." In *Mujeres, crisis y movimento: América Latina y el Caribe,* vol. 9. Santiago: Isis International-MUDAR, Ediciones de las Mujeres.

Bunch, Charlotte. (1991). "Hacia una revisión de los derechos humanos." In Ximena Bunster and Regina Rodriguez (eds.), *La mujer ausente: Derechos humanos en el mundo,* vol. 15. Santiago: Isis International, Ediciones de las Mujeres.

Bunster, Ximena. (1991). "Sobreviviendo más allá del miedo." In Ximena Bunster and Regina Rodriguez (eds.), *La mujer ausunte: Derechos humanos en el mundo,* vol. 15. Santiago: Isis International, Ediciones de las Mujeres.

DAWN. (1992). "Environment and Development: Grassroots Women's Perspectives." Document presented to UNCED, Rio de Janeiro.

Donzelet, Jacques. (1979). *The Policing of Families.* New York: Pantheon Books.

Facio, Alda. (1991). "El principio de la igualdad ante la ley." *El Otro Derecho* 8.

Feijoo, Maria del Carmen and Mónica Gogna. (1987). "Las mujeres en la transición a la democracia." In Elizabeth Jelin (ed.), *Cuidadanía e identidad: Las mujeres en los movimentos sociales Latino-Americanos.* Ginebra: UNRISD.

Garcia de Fanelli, Ana, Monica Gogna, and Elizabeth Jelin. (1990). *El empleo de "Cuello Rosa" en La Argentina: El caso de banco estatal.* Buenos Aires: CEDES, Documento de Trabajo, vol. 24.

Jelin, Elizabeth. (1993). *About Women, About Human Rights.* Lima: Red Entre Mujeres.

Matus, Verónica. (1992). "Derechos humanos, Derechos de las mujeres." In José Aylwin (ed.), *Derechos humanos: Desafios para un nuevo contexto.* Santiago: Chilean Human Rights Commission.

Minow, Martha. (1990). *Making All the Difference: Inclusion, Exclusion and American Law.* New York: Cornell University Press.

Molyneux, Maxine. (1985). "Mobilization Without Emancipation: Women's Interests, the State, and Revolution in Nicaragua," *Feminist Studies* 11, no. 2 (Summer).

Oliveira, Luciano de. (1989). "Derechos humanos y Marxismo: Breve ensayo para un nuevo pardigma." *El Otro Derecho* 4.

Oliveira, Rosiska Darcy de, and Thais Corral (eds.). (1992). *Terra Femina.* Rio de Janeiro: IDAC/REDEH.

Romany, Celina. (1991). "Ain't I a Feminist?" *Yale Journal of Law and Feminism* 4, no. 1.

Rorty, Richard. (1991). *Contingencia, ironía y solidaridad.* Barcelona: Paidós.

Santos, Wanderley Guilherme dos. (1979). *Cidadania e justica.* Rio de Janerio: Editora Campus.

Schirmer, Jennifer. (1988). "Those Who Dies for a Life Be Called Dead: Women and Human Rights Protest in Latin America." *Harvard Human Rights Yearbook,* vol. 1 (Cambridge, Mass.:? Harvard University Press).

―――. (1993). "The Seeking of Truth and the Gendering of Consciousness: The Co-madres of El Salvador and the CONAVIGUA Widows of Guatemala." In Sarah A. Radcliffe and Sallie Westwood (eds.), *"VIVA" Women and Popular Protest in Latin America.* London: Routledge.

Stolcke, Verena. (1991). "Derechos reproductivos." In Sandra Azeredo and Verena Stolcke (eds.), *Direitos reproductivos.* São Paulo: Fundacao Carlos Chagas.

Valdés, Teresa. (1990). *Mujeres y derechos humanos: "Menos tu vientre."* Santiago: FLACSO Work Document, Social Studies Series No. 8.

◀ 11 ▶

Crime and Individual Rights: Reframing the Question of Violence in Latin America

TERESA P.R. CALDEIRA

In 1992, during the last week of September and the first of October, Brazilian society witnessed two impressive spectacles of opposite meaning. On September 29, the country came to an abrupt halt and citizens flowed into the streets to watch on large television screens installed in public squares as the National Congress voted the impeachment of a corrupt President Collor. In the weeks preceding this moment, vast networks of corruption involving the president were exposed and denounced, the facts were investigated and communicated to the public, and hundreds of thousands of people, mainly youth, gathered in street demonstrations, demanding justice and morality. The military remained behind the scenes. The impeachment was celebrated universally as a victory for democracy and as testimony not only to the importance of ethics in public affairs but also to the strength of democratic institutions in Brazil.

A few days later, on October 2, on the eve of municipal elections, the scenario was radically different. The military police, in an action apparently aimed at controlling a fight between gangs inside São Paulo's largest prison, killed 111 prisoners. Not a single police officer died. Machine guns were used inside a closed space. The massacre had Dantesque overtones, as prisoners were fired upon randomly, beaten, attacked by dogs trained to bite the genitals, and stabbed with knives. Some were forced to carry their dead colleagues and to clean up the blood, because the policemen were terrified of being contaminated with AIDS. (One reason given by the police to justify their action was that the prisoners had attacked them with darts dipped in AIDS-contaminated blood.)

The mass killing was not an isolated act: For many years the state administration of São Paulo had enforced a "tough policy" to "fight crime," a policy that supported not only killings by the police but also public attacks against defenders of human rights.[1] In 1991, 1,171 people died in São Paulo during "confrontations with the police," compared to 27 in New York City; the following year, 1,470 people were killed, including the 111 prisoners of the Casa de Detencão (Detention House).[2] Although the police usually make public the statistics on deaths (because they think the numbers indicate their efficiency), the events at the Casa de Detencão were initially kept secret owing to the impending elections. Two days later, however, pictures were distributed widely throughout the print and broadcast media, revealing naked and mutilated bodies with big black numbers written on the legs, arranged side by side in open coffins in the corridors of the Institute of Legal Medicine—a vision reminiscent of the Holocaust.

According to a television survey conducted by the newspaper *Folha de São Paulo,* one-third of the population of Sao Paulo endorsed the police action. Another daily, *O Estado de São Paulo,* reported that 44 percent of the population supported it.[3] Many people took to the streets to demonstrate in favor of the police and against human rights advocates who had critized the prison massacre.

It is difficult to believe that democracy could have been celebrated in the same society and at the same historical moment, as these prisoners were being massacred. The incongruence is all the greater when one realizes that these events occurred in São Paulo, the most modern city of the country, where social movements and trade unions are strong and have transformed conceptions of political participation since the 1970s and 1980s, and where the mayor at the time of the prison massacre was a member of the leftist Party of the Workers (PT). Nor are the two events exceptional.

Over the past two decades in Brazil, various social movements have been organized, trade unions have gained independence from the state, new institutions have been established, and new opportunities for the exercise of citizenship have been created. Yet at the same time, the country has witnessed a proliferation of prejudice and violence against accused criminals—violence committed not only by the police but also by private guards and vigilante groups known as *justiceiros* (literally "justice makers"). This trend has been reflected in the violent attacks perpetrated by neo-Nazi groups against organizations devoted to defending the rights and identities of minority groups—organizations such as S.O.S. Racismo (in behalf of blacks), numerous Jewish associations, and Rádio Atual (a radio station that transmits programs for northeast migrants in São Paulo). Thus, on the one hand, we observe many events that attest to the expansion and consolidation of political rights and democratic institutions; on the other, we witness disrespect for individual, civil, and human rights as well as increased violence.

What, then, do those disparate events reveal? In short, they highlight important transformations in both the exercise of state violence and the manifestation of segregation and discrimination in a highly segmented country such as Brazil. They may also indicate changes in the way in which citizenship rights are being expanded and contested in the post–cold war era.

In this new context, as we shall see, the main focus of state violence and of conflict over the extension of citizenship is moving out of the political arena and into the sphere of civil and individual rights; yet the latter themselves are also undergoing new forms of politicization. Democratic political systems and procedures have become a reality in such Latin American countries as Brazil, Argentina, Chile, and Uruguay, which until the 1980s were ruled by dictatorships. Indeed, democracy is now actually valued, official barriers to political participation have been lifted, and political rights are formally protected. Yet the democratic transition does not guarantee either the full exercise of individual rights or their protection: Despite the consolidation of political rights, certain forms of both civilian and state violence have proliferated over the past decade. Now the most visible forms of violence stem not from ideological conflicts over the nature of the political system but from delinquency and crime. This new scenario raises questions about respect for individual and human rights, about the role of the judicial system, and about the democratization of everyday life.

During periods of dictatorship, the suspension of citizenship rights certainly affected everyday life, but the suppression of rights reflected the contestation over competing political options. At present, by contrast, political rights are largely assured, but that contestation is articulated in the idiom of crime, and struggles for the expansion of citizenship are not so much about the right to express one's political opinion as about civil rights, the right to justice, and the "right to difference." It is in this context that reactions to the expansion of claims of equality and incorporation are being articulated, and that abuses have been perpetrated with support from large segments of the population. Instead of military violence against leftist political opponents, police violence is aimed at common prisoners; the "hunt for communists" of the cold war era has ended, but we now witness the spread of racist theories as well as neo-Nazi attacks on immigrants, blacks, homosexuals, and AIDS victims and, in Brazil, on accused criminals and defenders of human rights. In short, the constraints that limit the democratization of Brazil, as well as that of other countries in Latin America, are to be found in the areas of justice and individual rights, and in the popular conceptions of both, rather than in conflicts over the political regime among political actors and parties.

The Brazilian case makes especially clear the tortuous and often unpredictable paths that may or may not lead to the expansion of citizenship rights and democratization. There is a tendency in the social sciences to think of such expansion in sequential terms, taking European experience as a model. No theorist influenced this tendency more than T. H. Marshall (1949), whose classic historical essay on citizenship presents an optimistic view of the expansion of citizenship in Western countries. Analyzing the British case, Marshall argued that citizenship evolves not as a unit but, rather, through a sequence of rights: First come civil rights, then political rights, and finally social rights. From this perspective, the disjuncture between political and civil rights seems characteristic of the history of democratic citizenship wherever it emerges. However, recent criticism of Marshall's analysis has cast serious doubts not only on his evolutionary framework but also on his optimistic view of the development of rights, which implies that citizenship is always expanding (Hirschman, 1991). Questions have also been raised about the empirical accuracy of Marshall's model, even as it applies to the restricted realm of Western nations. For instance, Byron Turner (1992: 40) argues that "the character of citizenship varies systematically between different societies," and that Marshall failed to recognize that the expansion of citizenship rights can occur in at least one of two ways: from above or from below. Many accounts of citizenship seem to consider only the former, thus disregarding the role of social movements that have been crucial to the expansion of citizenship rights throughout the world.

The experience of Brazil and many other Third World countries reflects the variety of processes through which citizenship rights historically have expanded and contracted. The development of citizenship rights in these countries has differed considerably from that described in Marshall's British example. Social rights—which are associated primarily with labor rights—expanded in Brazil and other Latin American countries before other rights, even under dictatorships that had suspended political rights. Moreover, in populist dictatorships such as those of Getulio Vargas in Brazil and Juan Domingo Perón in Argentina, social rights were presented as a "gift" from above, given to those below, rather than as a result of working-class struggles (as was the case in Europe). In Latin America, political rights have had a convoluted history, going back and forth from being guaranteed to being taken away; at present, they are largely legitimated and exercised. Individual and civil rights, however, have remained underdeveloped—as has the justice system, which, in principle, is the institution responsible for ensuring these rights. In contemporary Brazil, as in other countries of Latin America, individual rights are extremely weak compared to social rights—hence the lack of respect for individuals—and the feebleness of a justice system designed to serve elites and adapted repeatedly to uphold dictatorships. Criminals are far from being the only victims of this system of discrimination and disrespect for individual rights. Yet it is their situation in particular—the violation of their bodies by state violence and the total lack of respect for their elementary rights—that dramatically highlights the dilemmas produced by the expansion of individual rights and the rise of democracy in countries such as Brazil.

More substance is given to these ideas by the following analysis of recent events in São Paulo. As we shall see, the construction of the image of the criminal, as well as the centrality it acquires in everyday life, problematizes the whole issue of individual rights and justice in a country that, in the past decade, has respected political rights and considerably expanded social rights. Although the scope of citizenship has been deeply transformed in Brazil, individual rights are precarious—as evidenced by the power (both public and private) still exerted over the bodies of the dominated. At stake in the stigmatization and killing of common criminals are justice itself, social equality, and individual and civil rights. It is in these areas especially that the expansion of democracy in Brazil encounters most resistance.

BUILDING THE IMAGE OF THE CRIMINAL

To investigate this hypothesis about the issues at stake in contemporary Brazil, we must take a closer look at the dark side of the events described earlier—that is, at the underworld of crime and police violence in which disrespect for rights is paramount.

Crime and fear have increased considerably in São Paulo over the past decade, as a result of several factors: (1) economic crisis, increasing levels of poverty, and processes of downward mobility affecting members of all social classes; (2) social discrimination and spatial segregation in the city of São Paulo; (3) the transition to democracy and the election of new governors and presidents; (4) increased police violence and decreased confidence in the judicial system, and the consequent tendency to resolve problems privately, even in situations involving crime; and (5) commonsense beliefs about the nature of evil and the role of authority.

Owing to space limitations, this chapter concentrates on the last two factors only. Though commonly overlooked in debates about violence, both are crucial to an understanding of recent transformations and the challenges they pose for the consolidation of democracy in Brazil. Toward this end I offer an elaboration of the image of the criminal as well as a theory about the nature of evil and of authority. My analysis is based on an interpretation of what I call the "talk of crime"—that is, the narratives and everyday commentaries in which cases of crime are repeated, thus both counteracting and magnifying violence and the fear of violence. The conversations on which this analyis is based were recorded in individual and group interviews conducted with members of all social classes in the city of São Paulo from 1989 to 1991.[4]

In the "talk of crime," the image of the criminal is constructed through a combination of various complex elements. At the most general level, people of all classes stereotypically associate criminals with the poor, with black people, with migrants from the northeast of Brazil, with sons of single mothers, with consumers of drugs, with promiscuity, and with *cortiços* and *favelas*.[5]

As with most stereotypes, these descriptions are not specific but contextual: They represent simplistic and synthetic ways of making sense of a given situation. When details are necessary, or when the discourse is more specific, these generic categories become insufficient. People start to use more ambiguous and less clear-cut categories when they feel it is necessary to establish differentiations among the categories: The poor are not all the same, not even the *favelados* are all the same, and certainly not all poor people or all migrants are criminals. To look for differences and to provide more accurate descriptions of crime is to change the reference of the discourse. Understanding the specificity of crime, then, is a process that goes from the level of society to that of the individual.

Paradoxically, however, it is also a process that implies a shift away from displaying sympathy toward those suffering the consequences of poverty and unemployment, and from making the government responsible for the situation, to blaming the poorest individually. This shift occurs as a result of prejudice against the poor, who in turn become associated with criminals. Even people conscious of the extremely unequal distribution of wealth find a way of blaming the poor themselves for their situation; they claim that poor people are not rational, do not plan their lives, have too many children, and so on. Yet this process of stigmatization is repeated by poor people themselves: The prejudices attributed to them shape their own explanations of their plight. In order to preserve their self-esteem and identity, however, they must eventually direct the stigmas to another place, a worse place, usually represented by the *favela.* In so doing, poor people reinforce the prejudice directed against even poorer people, distancing themselves from their neighbors who live in quite similar conditions. Hence their discourses about the criminal are the most elaborated, although in general these discourses are not much different from those of people from other social classes.

As noted earlier, explanations of crime are not limited to socioeconomically based references. Crime is also a matter of authority and of cultural constructions intended to tame the forces of evil. It is important to investigate these conceptions because they relate to a particular view of the justice system and are used, among other things, to justify the defense of the death penalty—often in the form of the summary execution of those accused of being criminals, as occurred in the Casa de Detenção.

THE FAILURE OF AUTHORITY AND THE SPREAD OF EVIL

Many residents of São Paulo emphasize that crime is always associated with authority. They see the increase in crime as a sign of weak authority—whether of the school, the family, the mother, the church, the government, the police, or the justice system. These forms of authority are blamed because people generally think of crime as provoked by the spread of evil, something authority is supposed to control. In the "talk of crime," evil is conceived of as powerful, but also easily dispersed. Once it touches someone in a weak position—for example, a resident of a *favela,* who may lack the "proper" social attributes—it is likely to dominate this person. And if evil achieves such control, it is very difficult to get rid of. Widespread among the residents of São Paulo is the feeling that the authorities and institutions are failing to fulfill their responsibility for controlling people's behavior—and thus are leaving open spaces in which evil can spread (to infiltrate and to infest, as the people say). Indeed, since evil is contagious, the danger that it will spread rapidly is immense. One significant consequence of this belief in contagion and the perceived failure of the appropriate authorities to control evil is that people have intensified their efforts to enclose and control the spaces in which they live—specifically, by building barriers, both symbolic (through prejudice and the stigmatization of some groups as the embodiment of evil) and material (by means of walls, fences, and the electronic paraphernalia of security).

Anthropological data suggest that Brazilians of all classes conceive of evil as something that exists in nature and can be controlled only by the labors of culture and reason. The model that many São Paulo residents seem to have adopted is very similar to Hobbes' conception of the state of nature, a source of evil that creates a need for the social contract. In the absence of a common social contract that ties people to restrictive rules, and in the absence of authorities able to enforce that contract, there is a "war of all against all." When the social contract fails, people return to the violence of the state of nature. Order and peace are difficult to maintain, requiring a great deal of work and control.

Brazilians also conceive of evil as being in opposition to reason. It is that which does not make sense, but also that which takes advantage of people whose rationality can be considered precarious. Children, women, teenagers, the poor, and people in a state of disturbed consciousness, such as drug users, are most vulnerable to the spread of evil and should be controlled in a closer way. Moreover, because small children and females are considered to be easier to control, the group most in danger of being affected by evil consists of young males. Being young, they are not yet fully formed and thus lack some of the attributes needed to defend themselves; and because they are not yet totally rational, they still need to be controlled. Being male, however, they resist control and are drawn to environments, particularly the streets, in which evil abounds. In those environments they may encounter drugs that disturb consciousness and are therefore directly connected to crime. And as people on drugs do not know what they are doing, they are easy targets for the forces of evil.

Evil is associated with human nature; it is something to which everyone is vulnerable. Nevertheless, as I have just argued, poor people are considered to be closer to nature and farther away from reason than are other people. In addition, they are physically closer to the sites where crimes actually occur. Consequently, they are also believed to be more at risk of being caught by evil.

In what amounts to a very pervasive conception of social order in Brazil, authority, institutions, work, reason, and control are viewed as the weapons to combat the spread of evil: Power and the proper authorities, both private and public, are required to keep evil under control. When the existing public institutions fail, however, people perceive a need to extend private controls and to take matters into their own hands, thus refashioning power. When the environment is considered to have become too dangerous, the risk of "contagion" becomes excessive and the best solution is to build barriers everywhere, both symbolic and material, and to intensify all types of private control. As prejudice mounts, people hire private guards, build walls, adopt electronic means of security, and support *justiceiros* as well as the private illegal acts of vengeance committed by police.

It takes more than economic and political conditions to produce a criminal, but sometimes only very little more. Minor attributes associated with a lack of education, unemployment, or frustration with one's family may be sufficient. People can resist such dangers, but doing so requires a strong mind. (Many of my interviewees stated that people who are confronted with very stressful conditions or who have grown up in troubled environments—beset by family problems or by poverty—need a strong mind in order not to despair and to resist the perils of bad influences. But if they lose their heads—that is, their reason and good judgment—they are lost. People from all social classes in Brazil believe that a strong mind is developed inside a strong family, which can provide the proper control of children and sufficient barriers to repel bad companions and influences. Such opinions regarding the need to control children and women and to avoid contact with unknown people are indeed quite widespread. They constitute strong arguments against living in apartment buildings, and especially in *favelas* and *cortiços*: Given the proximity to others that is inherent in these settings, people have more trouble controlling their children and keeping them apart from anyone who can be deemed "inappropriate." In this context, Brazilian people of all social classes tend to use exactly the same phrases and to favor similar types of control.

One could argue that evil is one of the most democratic elements in the realm of crime. Evil comes from everywhere and can affect everyone (although the weak are most vulnerable)—so, by implication, everybody should be controlled. However, the consequences of this concern with constant surveillance extend beyond crime. People highly preoccupied with control have a hard time accepting limits to the surveillance they exercise, and they rarely acknowledge the individual rights of people they perceive as potential threats. They do not believe that children may have some rights of privacy and choice, such as selecting playmates: Rather, children should do what their parents want them to do and they should play only with those other children their parents select for them. In Brazil, lessons in separation and prejudice start early in life. One can only guess the point at which this worldview would grant rights to choice, privacy, and individuality, especially for those "in need of" closer control, such as young people and women. The denial of individuality, and consequently of the recognition of individual rights, is rooted in this conception of evil, its spread, and its prevention. The denial of individuality to people considered to be in need of control has had widespread repercussions in Brazilian society, affecting the rights of all minority groups in various ways. An example drawn from the realm of crime illustrates this point for the case of women.

Two juridical constructs in Brazilian law severely limit women's individual rights and legitimate the violence exercised against their bodies. The first is the legal classification of rape. According to Title IV of the Penal Code, rape is a crime against custom and not a crime against persons. Thus it is included in the category of "unusual sexual acts," akin to seduction, prostitution, oral sex and so on—a categorization that reveals a great deal about Brazilian conceptions of sexual roles, sexuality, and individual rights. The Penal Code also specifies that, in the case of rape, the judicial object to be protected is custom, not the women's body. The aggregation of crimes in this category of "custom" is one more indication of the degree to which Brazilians conceive of women's sexuality as something under control, and of how far they are from recognizing women's integrity and rights.[6] The second juridical construct is the "legitimate defense of honor," a legal argument used to acquit men who kill their wives. In those cases, women's behavior is presumed to justify their death. This rationale, whereby the spread of evil justifies the elimination of the bodies of those who dare to behave "inappropriately," has been transferred from popular belief to law.[7]

Another element in the context of controlling bad influences is the necessity of occupying people's minds and time. An old working-class man told me once that "an empty mind is the devil's workshop."[8] And in popular culture, it is work that constitutes the best protection from the devil's influence. Unemployment is thus perceived as dangerous because it leaves people not only under stress but also faced with empty time. If people are not working, they must at least be occupied with something. Unoccupied time is a risk for everybody. Men can "lose their heads" when unemployed, and women who do nothing are said to leave their minds open to bad influences. Another common belief is that prisoners are hard to resocialize, in part because of the difficulty involved in extirpating evil once it catches someone, but also because of the idleness associated with imprisonment. For this reason, many Brazilians think that the only way out of the world of crime is to force prisoners to acquire job skills while still in jail.

In sum, the popular theory about the spread of evil has a counterpart in the perceived role of authorities. Recall, however, that many residents of São Paulo believe that the authorities in charge of public order have completely failed to protect the population. They accuse the police of being corrupt, of releasing dangerous criminals who are able to pay for their freedom, and of arresting primarily the very poor as they cannot buy their way out of custody. They also accuse the police of being too mild in cases of real crime and too harsh in unimportant matters. Moreover, the military police, the principal agency called on to patrol the streets, have committed countless killings, are subjected not to the system of civil justice but to that of military justice, in which they are usually acquitted. Although this practice is a holdover from the period of military dictatorship, it is now used even more widely than before. Thus, the system of justice is widely conceived as being *un*just. "Justice is a joke" and "impunity is widespread"— these are among the most common phrases I've encountered during my interviews. In addition to being biased and serving the interest of elites against the poor, the justice system is perceived as corrupt, excessively bureaucratic, and too slow. In short, it is perceived to be ineffective in its task of distributing justice.

As noted, both the theory about the contagious character of evil and the perceived weakness of the public authorities in charge of controlling the spread of evil have prompted the use of private protection, along with attempts to isolate groups considered to be dangerous and to clamp down on individuals deemed to be weak. But they are also linked to conceptions about appropriate forms of punishment for criminals. Because people think that evil is contagious as well as difficult to get rid of once it is installed in someone's body, the death penalty is widely considered to be not only an adequate form of punishment but a necessary one. Only death is sufficient to stop evil at its root, thus preventing its spread; only death can solve the problem irreversibly. At the same time, very few people believe that criminals can be rehabilitated, even when the best methods of making them work and produce are used. Hence the perceived necessity of the death penalty, especially given that the public authorities in charge of rehabilitation and punishment are themselves seen to be weak.

According to a January 1993 survey carried out by *O Estado de São Paulo,* 70 percent of those interviewed favored changing the constitution in order to introduce the death penalty. This opinion varied little according to gender, education, or socioeconomic status. Religion, however, proved to be relevant. Only 37 percent of evangelic fundamentalists supported capital punishment, compared to 74 percent of Catholics and 68 percent of *umbandistas* (followers of the Afro-Brazilian religion).

At this point we should ask, If Brazilians see the judicial system as weak, biased, and unable to control violence, why would they choose to augment its power by granting it the prerogative of executing people? In other words, if this system does not work in general, why would it succeed in deciding matters of life and death? In fact, there is no paradox here, because Brazilians refer to the death penalty not in terms of a legal sentence but in terms of summary execution. They distrust the justice system and think that evil should be eliminated without any mediation, by killing those who have been contaminated. (The majority of my interviewees stated that someone caught committing a crime should be killed right away, especially if the crime involved violence. Similarly, many of them supported the use of death squads and vigilante groups, arguing that, unlike the police, they are not corrupt and that they do a good job "because they only kill.") In sum, Brazilians have legitimated both private actions and violence in what they perceive to be an urgent fight against the spread of evil.

The power of these conceptions of evil and its contagion can be demonstrated in many ways. It is present not only in the silence of the citizens as they hear public announcements of the number of people killed by the police but also in their open support of the "police who kill" and of the *justiceiros.* In fact, its presence is underscored by the fact that at least one-third of São Paulo's population was in favor of the massacre of the prisoners of the *Casa de Detenção* and in opposition to those who defend human rights in Brazil.

CYCLES OF VIOLENCE

Several conclusions can be drawn regarding these conceptions of the criminal and of the nature of evil and its control. First, the image of the criminal and the discourses that support it are part of a social process of exclusion and demarcation of limits. Individuals associated with crime should not merely be kept away; they are to be eliminated. Second, the symbolic construction of evil and of crime is a process of naturalization. Evil is conceived as a force of nature, something against which society is largely powerless. As a consequence, death—the elimination of the bodies that carry evil—is thought to be a stronger solution than social measures such as recuperation. Third, conceptions about controlling the spread of evil preclude individuality as well as the struggle for individual rights and for the "right to difference"—especially among those groups "in need of" control, such as women and children. Fourth, the institution responsible for guaranteeing individual rights, the justice system, is considered not only ineffective but also incapable of remedying the damage caused by the spread of evil.

These conceptions about evil and its diffusion have long been held in Brazilian society. What calls attention to them at this particular time is the fact that they have acquired an important political role and are thus central to everyday life concerns. During the years of the cold war, military dictatorship, and the "Dirty Wars" in Latin America, the construction of evil took on political implications: Evil was embodied in the image of the communist guerrilla. Today, this characterization provokes fear throughout Latin America. In many big cities of the region, however, violence, drugs, and crime have become symbolically empowered to provoke cultural and political reactions. In Brazil, at least, those transformations are many: They have generated a new urban structure as well as a new pattern of spatial segregation built upon the dissemination of technologies of security. Even the image of the communist is imbued with a post–cold war symbolism. In contemporary Brazilian politics, those who dare to defend the rights of prisoners, of people accused of being criminals, or of people being tortured or killed without a trial are identified by a single expression: "the human rights." And to refer to "the human rights" (meaning the defenders of human rights and not the rights per se) is to evoke the image of a kind of witch. In short, the defenders of human rights, who bring to the political arena the issue of individual, civil, and human rights of the dominated, are stigmatized today just as the communists were in the past.

Although in theory human rights represent a universal ideal, in fact they are culturally and politically interpreted and modified.[9] The form that this interpretation takes cannot be predicted. In São Paulo, for instances, the defense of human rights has helped both to enlarge the recognition of rights (during the military regime) and to contest them (under democratic rule). The meaning of human rights thus depends on the way in which they are politically articulated at specific moments. At present, as we have seen, they have been reinterpreted by a right-wing discourse that skillfully articulates popular conceptions about evil and the failure of the judicial system and the police.

The stigmatization of defenders of human rights was not widely evident in the middle to late 1970s, when the people for whom those rights were being demanded were middle-class political prisoners and when the process of political transition was only beginning. At that time, respect for the human rights of political prisoners was an important demand of the same political movement that was calling for the end of the military regime. The stigmatization of human rights defenders began soon after the end of military rule, when the first elected governors approached the defense of these rights as a goal of public policy in many states, and when poor common prisoners became the group whose rights were to be guaranteed. Following ratification of the 1979 Amnesty Bill and the release of political prisoners, at a time when political parties were beginning to organize and elections for governors were being held (in 1982), groups defending human rights changed the focus of their actions. Rather than disappearing after redemocratization, human rights organizations turned their efforts to securing rights for groups other than political prisoners—a trend that is evident in many countries today. In Brazil, these organizations focused on poor common prisoners, who were being tortured and lived in degraded conditions, and on mental patients who also lived in subhuman conditions in public hospitals.[10] This change, however, proved unacceptable to the majority of the population, who still thought of criminals in the terms discussed earlier.

The stigmatization of human rights defenders instead of communists, as well as the change in popular perceptions of the human rights issue, supports my hypothesis that both state violence and the scope of citizenship struggles are shifting from the political to the civil arena in countries such as Brazil. An examination of the growing distrust of the justice system and of the increased racism and anti-immigrant sentiment in Europe and the United States would reveal a similar focus on the question of civil rights. But there is a crucial difference between these societies and Brazil. I refer here to the scope of state violence. In no other Western country do the police kill as frequently as in Brazil, and with such a degree of impunity.

In this context, it becomes clear that the areas of justice, expansion of individual rights, and control of police actions are those in which the democratization process in Brazil faces its greatest challenges. Democratization will mean little if it does not affect both the justice system and the degree of respect for people's rights, individualities, and lives.

Of course, changes in the political system do not necessarily transform everyday public relationships, which continue to be marked by a low level of respect and a high level of surveillance, and to be maintained by a very unequal social system. Nor do changes in the political system necessarily transform the practice of the police. Indeed, as the case of São Paulo demonstrates, it was under democratic rule that the "get tough" policy of public security was implemented. The crucial objective today, then, is not the achievement of a democratic political system but the implementation of justice. Justice, in turn, entails reform of the police and the transformation of cultural conceptions about the poor, the need to control the weak, and the use of force to prevent the spread of evil. Fundamental changes are called for in the very system of justice—a system that was institutionalized to serve the elites and their privileges, and that continues to do so by ignoring crimes committed by the police and by vigilante groups.

Crime and violence in contemporary São Paulo are increasingly being dealt with through private and illegal measures. The two trends reflected in these measures—from legal to illegal and from public to private—have led to a very dangerous situation in which the judicial system is no longer capable of conflict mediation. What has resulted are cycles of private revenge in which violence is answered with more violence, but with no legitimate authority to stop it. Under such conditions, violence can only proliferate.

As René Girard (1977) has argued, violence always generates a response: It must be appeased by some form of vengeance. Feuds are one method interrupting cycles of violent revenge; justice systems are another. The latter are more effective, of course, because they transform vengeance from a private into a public matter. The crucial difference, and one that has enormous social consequences, is that "under the public system, an act of vengeance is no longer avenged; the process is terminated, the danger of escalation averted" (Girard 1977: 16).

If a judiciary is to effectively interrupt a cycle of vengeance, it must maintain its authority and legitimacy. But that is precisely what has not occurred in contemporary São Paulo. The failure of the justice system (and thus of the public process of vengeance) has opened the way not only for the proliferation of private acts of revenge, among people who choose "to take justice into their own hands," but also for the reproduction of a cycle of violence that has resulted from the privatization of vengeance. The chances that a rule of law and democratic rule can be established in countries such as Brazil will remain slim if the legitimacy and authority of the judicial system are not restored. Indeed, people will continue to take justice into their own hands and to support private and illegal forms of vengeance.

The case of Argentina provides an interesting contrast.[11] Despite some similarities, increased violence and police abuse have had very different effects on the populations of both countries. Whereas in Brazil private responses to violence have inaugurated cycles of private revenge, in Argentina such cases have been rare. For instance, the members of COFAVI stress a legal strategy of demanding retribution for damages; in fact, legal action against abuses of authority is a gradually spreading practice. Judicial recognition of violations committed by public officials is relevant precisely because it reestablishes a sense of belonging to a community of rights. Yet it is in the area of "criminals' rights" that Argentineans express the greatest resistance against democratization and justice.

The main question is whether the elites in these countries will be willing to give up their power to act privately and with impunity in order to accept the rule of external public authorities—in other words, whether they will be willing to put in the hands of public authorities those processes of vengeance that they have thus far been able to practice and control privately. If not, the cycle of violence will continue and democratic rule for all inhabitants will remain elusive. Advocates of human rights have an important role to play in underscoring the need for public institutions that can effectively confront problems of crime. In doing so, they will diminish the climate of fear that the weakness of those institutions has fostered, thereby promoting the extension of citizenship rights to all social groups, in Brazil and elsewhere in Latin America.

Notes

1. Documentation of human rights abuses in Brazilian prisons is provided by the Americas Watch Committee (1987, 1989), Amnesty International (1990), and Comissão Teotônio Vilela (1986).

2. Folha de São Paulo, October 10, 1992.

3. Ibid; O Estado de São Paulo, October 8, 1992.

4. The following analysis is based on a study of everyday life, urban transformations, and conceptions about violence and crime in three areas of the city of São Paulo: poor neighborhoods in the periphery, a lower-middle-class neighborhood, and two upper-class neighborhoods. The results of this study are reported in Caldeira (1992). Research funds were provided by the Social Science Research Council (SSRC), the Inter-American Foundation, and the Ford Foundation.

5. A *favela* is a set of shacks build on land occupied by squatters. Although people own their shacks and may transport them, they do not own the land, which is occupied illegally. A *cortico* is a type of tenement housing, consisting either of an old structure whose rooms have been rented to several families or of a series of rooms, usually in a row, that are rented individually. In each room a whole family sleeps, cooks, and entertains. Residents of multiple rooms share external or corridor bathrooms and water sources.

6. Disrespect for individual rights is especially clear in the case of women, but other examples can also be cited. For instance, the Penal Code specifies that a death that occurs during a robbery is considered a crime against property, not a crime against persons.

7. For an analysis of trials concerning rape and battery of women, see Ardaillon and Debert (1988); for documentation of violence against women in Brazil, see Americas Watch Committee Women's Rights Group (1991).

8. Another version is the popular saying "Idleness is the root of all evil."

9. Analyzing the question of human rights in the Middle East, Dwyer (1991: 3) argues that broad disagreement exists over the meaning of human rights, an inherently complex notion that needs to be placed "in the context of the local, national, and regional history and culture."

10. Disrespect for human rights in Brazilian prisons is documented in Americas Watch Committee (1987, 1989), Amnesty International (1990), and Comissao Teotônio Vilela (1986).

11. Commenting on an earlier version of this chapter, Laura Gingold pointed out that in Argentina, the feeling of insecurity based on the perception of an increase in delinquency is leading to a search for individual solutions to personal security. According to a survey conducted by the *Centro de Estudios Legales y Sociales* (CELS) in 1991, 39 percent of the people interviewed in the city and suburbs of Buenos Aires indicated that they had bought a device designed to increase private security in their homes, and 9 percent had bought a weapon of some kind. However, except for some notorious cases involving *justicieros,* what prevails in Argentina is a demand for institutional justice. Unlike Brazil, Argentina has witnessed no lynchings or other forms of private retaliation; rather, legal action against

police abuse and against delinquency, including demands for redress of the damage inflicted, is the norm. Even with the escalation of violence on both sides of the law—committed by those in charge of controlling and preventing crime (the police) and by those who violate the law (criminals)—the degree of responsibility of both sides is not seen as comparable. Indeed, the impunity of public officials who break the law generates a sense of vulnerability among citizens. In 1992, a group of citizens, all relatives of victims of police violence, formed the *Comisión de Victimas y Familiares de Victimas de la Violencia Institucional* (COFAVI) to articulate their grievances in this regard. It is interesting to note that, within this movement, criticism of police violence is limited to those cases in which the victims are perceived as "innocent."

References

Americas Watch Committee. (1987). *Police Abuse in Brazil: Summary Executions in Rio de Janeiro.* New York: Americas Watch Committee.

————. (1989). *Prison Conditions in Brazil.* New York: Americas Watch Committee.

Americas Watch Committee Women's Rights Group. (1991). *Criminal Injustice: Violence Against Women in Brazil.* New York: Americas Watch Committee.

Amnesty International. (1990). *Brasil: Tortura e execuções extra-judiciais nas cidades Brasileiras.* London: Amnesty International.

Ardaillon, Danielle, and Guita Debert. (1988). *Quando a vítima é mulher.* Brasília: Conselho Nacional da Condição Feminina.

Caldeira, Teresa P.R. (1992). *City of Walls: Crime, Segregation, and Citizenship in São Paulo.* Ph.D. dissertation, Department of Anthropology, University of California–Berkeley.

Commissão Teotônio Vilela. (1986). *Democracia x violência.* Rio de Janeiro: Paz e Terra.

Dwyer, Kevin. (1991). *Arab Voices: The Human Rights Debate in the Middle East.* Berkeley: University of California Press.

Girard, René. (1977). *Violence and the Sacred.* Baltimore: Johns Hopkins University Press.

Hirschman, Albert O. (1991). *The Rhetoric of Reaction: Perversity, Futility, Jeopardy.* Cambridge, Mass.: Belknap Press of the Harvard University Press.

Marshall, T. H. (1949). "Citizenship and Social Class." In T. H. Marshall (ed.), *Class, Citizenship and Social Development.* New York: Doubleday. (Reprinted in 1965.)

Turner, Byron. (1992). "Outline of a Theory of Citizenship." In Chantal Mouffe (ed.), *Dimensions of Radical Democracy: Pluralism, Citizenship, Community.* London: Verso.

PART FIVE

Conclusion

◄ 12 ►

Convergence and Diversity: Reflections on Human Rights

ELIZABETH JELIN AND ERIC HERSHBERG

What lies ahead? What events and circumstances will determine the content of rights and the extent of citizenship in Latin America at the end of the century? Several convergent themes running through this book suggest some preliminary answers to these theoretical and practical queries. The various approaches adopted in the preceding chapters reflect attempts to grapple with emerging controversies that are likely to become more prominent under the specific conditions prevailing in Latin America, and elsewhere, at this writing. This brief concluding chapter highlights three clusters of analytical issues that we believe merit attention from scholars and practitioners committed to the construction of democracies in which human rights are protected, and in which the rights and responsibilities associated with democratic citizenship become central to everyday life for an ever wider range of individual and collective actors.

The three sets of issues we explore here are as follows: (1) relationships among different types of rights, and the sequential expansion of these rights in Latin America; (2) questions of economic rights, equity, and marginalization in the context of market-oriented economic restructuring; and (3) implications for human rights of the tension between universalist and pluralist norms and institutions in an era characterized both by increasing globalization and by the accentuation of local specificities.

GENERATIONS OF RIGHTS AND THEIR SEQUENCE

One overarching theme of this book concerns the relationships among types of rights or, in United Nations parlance, among generations of rights. The conventional linear model—which describes civil, political, socioeconomic, global, and collective rights as cumulative—bears little resemblance to the historical experience of Latin America. Nor has the expansion of rights followed the sequence assumed in the classic Marshallian framework, inasmuch as reversals and curtailments of rights have been strikingly frequent. Although a review of Latin American history over the past century would validate this point, the experiences of the past decade provide an even deeper insight into the challenges to democratization in the region.

As several chapters in this volume make clear, the transition to political democracy may entail the formal recognition and guarantee of political rights (such as the right to vote), but it does not imply that individual civil rights can suddenly be taken for granted. This is so even when the threat of a return to military dictatorship no longer weighs heavily on the perceptions of key actors. Nor are political and civil entitlements suddenly distributed equally among different sectors of the population. On the contrary, discrimination and inequities persist, often to a pervasive degree, across all dimensions of civil and political rights. Promising expansions of rights in one domain often coincide with disturbing steps backward in others.

Furthermore, as Rodolfo Stavenhagen discusses in Chapter 8 with respect to the rights of indigenous peoples, the contemporary preoccupation with collective and global rights implies the need to reexamine the linkages between individual and collective rights. This preoccupation has created profound theoretical and practical challenges, given the continuing hegemony in the Western world of an individualistic liberal paradigm for conceptualizing human rights. One insight to be gleaned from the tension between the dominant paradigm and contemporary preoccupations is that the very notion of rights has multiple and shifting meanings, underscoring the need for analyses that are historical, culturally specific, and comparative.

Yet recognition of historical contingency and variation does not mean that the relationships among rights are purely random. Indeed, patterns of uniformity have become apparent with the emergence of particular issues as the focus of debate and controversy in various contexts during the process of democratization. The tensions and contradictions among various types of rights, as well as among the meanings and contents that various social groups attach to their claims for rights, have been a constant feature of social struggles throughout the world. As new claims are put forth, debate inevitably follows as to whether they qualify as basic human rights. As Manuel Antonio Garretón (1992) has argued elsewhere, it is often difficult to say whether a particular claim seeks recognition of basic human rights or represents instead the reformulation, in a new discourse, of a long-standing complaint against discrimination. Today, the framing of demands in the language of human rights may be a wise strategy, albeit an opportunistic one, given the international commitment to the promotion of human rights. This phraseology partly explains why the debate about whether human rights should be defined broadly or narrowly has become such a central theme of ideological and ethical dispute. Of course, as Jennifer Schirmer points out in Chapter 5 of this volume, it also helps to account for the cynical manipulation of the language of democracy and rights by powerful actors determined to preserve their dominant status. But even these instances, which present significant challenges to the human rights movement, attest to the existence of unprecedented concern in the international community regarding violations of various sorts of rights. Moreover, sensitivity to abstract notions of rights often is matched by a heightened commitment to creating mechanisms that ensure the realization of rights-related objectives. This trend by no means guarantees that Latin American societies will manage to construct democracies that ensure respect for human rights of all citizens and that extend rights of citizenship to all social groups. It does, however, give grounds for optimism.

DEMOCRACY AND INEQUALITY: HUMAN RIGHTS AMID SOCIAL POLARIZATION, FRAGMENTATION AND MARGINALITY

The debate is a classic one: Can political democracy exist without a guarantee of a minimum level of economic well-being for all citizens? Are basic economic rights an element of basic human rights? What is the "right to development"? Can people enjoy civil and political rights if they lack access to the basic conditions (i.e., not only to measures that alleviate hunger and pain but also to relevant information) that ensure the possibility of exercising such rights? This theme goes far beyond questions regarding the relationship between political democracy and economic outcomes along such dimensions as equity or growth; indeed, it encompasses an essential condition for the emergence of individual and collective rights themselves.

The theoretical and ideological debate about the nature of rights—in fact, the very definition of human rights—tends to obscure a central question: Is there a material "threshold of humanity," such that we can specify the minimum conditions necessary for human beings, as a biological species, to qualify as "human" social subjects? Obviously, mere physical survival is one such condition. In cases of extreme victimization, hunger, physical pain, injury, and torture transform the human subject into nothing more than a body, annihilating its cultural dimension.

At another level, as Hannah Arendt (1949) argued compellingly, the human condition involves a sense of belonging to a political community. This sense of belonging and the possibility of interaction lie at the core of humanity. In other words, human society exists when "the other" comes into being within a public sphere of interaction. But how can we be sure that those facing extreme poverty are still within the realm of humanity? Is extreme poverty not a sign of dehumanization? Exclusion and indigence are fundamentally at odds with the logic of democracy, for they imply the denial of fundamental rights. They constitute the antithesis of social actors and scenarios. Those excluded are located outside the boundaries of society, or are simply defined as nonexistent.

A difficult puzzle arises in this context. Though defined as outsiders by the powerful, subordinate peoples (even slaves) have always been part of the political and social community. Historically, their struggles have been directed toward gaining access to public social and political spaces. Yet social struggles involve collective actors and resources, who by definition are absent in the most extreme cases of poverty and exclusion. No social movement of the oppressed can grow without first having gained a minimum of access and a minimum of humanity (in the sense of belonging to a community, and of having the self-reflexive capacity necessary for the construction of a collective identity).

One approach to this issue is provided by historians and anthropologists who have documented everyday forms of protest, boycott, and resistance. When power relations are extremely hierarchical and asymmetric, these scholars suggest, subordinate people develop hidden forms of action, alternative social spaces in which they can express their dissent with the discourse of domination. In such spaces, in the backyards and alleys, in the invisible shapes and shadows, in what James Scott (1992) calls "hidden transcripts," a sense of dignity and autonomy vis-à-vis domination and power is constructed and sheltered. These hidden transcripts are the proto-forms of politics, the "infrapolitics of the powerless," through which dignity and a sense of community are constructed (Scott: 183). In order for such processes to take place, however, physical survival and some minimal resource endowment must be secured.

Under conditions of dictatorship, activities of political opposition have often assumed the character of hidden transcripts. Insofar as political opposition was multiclass, economic survival was not an issue, at least for a large segment of the opposition. Resistance to dictatorship easily turned into political acts—indeed, resistance of even the most passive kind was inherently political. Under authoritarianism, the logic of domination was clear; the lines between "us" and "them" could be drawn neatly. Yet the unifying logic of political opposition obscured the continuing importance of the other face of domination—namely, poverty and economic violations of rights, which motivated some political opposition and remained endemic in Latin America long after the formal transitions to democracy came to a close.

Such transitions carry with them confusion and bewilderment. New spaces open up for democratic discourse—for elections and participation. But whereas democratic discourse becomes hegemonic, the reality of economic relations lies in stark contradiction with it. What emerges is a double discourse: a discourse of participation and a nondiscourse of economic exclusion. Under such conditions, the historically constructed "threshold of humanity" is threatened. Since those who are marginalized and excluded do not become individual and/or collective subjects in the newly emerging public and political sphere, they may refuse to accept the rules of the democratic game or accept them only partially. They may resist and protest, and/or they may retreat into a universe of violence, acting out instead of participating.

Violence is often understood as a last resort, deployed when words and dialogue become impossible. It can also be conceived of as a kind of discourse, as an extreme way of speaking, as a language for expressing social conflicts, or as a desperate attempt to participate in the defining of the political arena. In such cases (the Zapatistas in Chiapas are a recent and noteworthy example), violence gives voice to a collective actor with a strong sense of identity, resorting to a political discourse that will resist being ignored by the powerful.

Of course, other forms of violence are also relevant to discussions of human rights in Latin America. In addition to the anomic violence of the excluded and the violence used as sociopolitical discourse, there is the violence of groups that reject the democratic rules of the game, out of pecuniary interest (as in cases of drug traffic or other corruption) or refusal to recognize the right of "others" to participate in the public sphere—a stance that in practice readily leads to state terrorism, violent racism, and so on.

But even when state terrorism appears to be relegated to the past, the most extreme degrees of impoverishment and exclusion obstruct the formation of social movements. In so doing, they impede the articulation of conflict in terms that reflect societal tensions and social relations. Thus created are fertile conditions for the emergence and spread of racist and xenophobic attitudes among broad sectors of the population. When the members of downwardly mobile social sectors live in fear of those below them in the social hierarchy (immigrants, minorities, etc.), elites come to define social problems in racial terms (i.e., they blame "foreigners" for creating problems), thus providing a convenient distraction from discussions of domination and class exclusion (Wievorka, 1992).

This line of reasoning has significant implications for the construction of democracy in Latin America. Civil society, popular participation, and a culture of citizenship and social responsibility are never automatic by-products of formal political democratization. On the contrary, these achievements are highly uncertain, because they are contingent on developments within a number of separate spheres, particularly that of the economy. In this regard, considerations of the significance of growing marginalization are of more than academic interest, as governments throughout Latin America have implemented ambitious programs of market-oriented economic restructuring, abandoning the state-centered approaches to development that prevailed until the debt crisis of the 1980s. Although an assessment of these policies is beyond the scope of this chapter, we can conclude on the basis of broad consensus that their implications for equity may be extremely negative, at least over the short term. Not only has income grown more concentrated in almost every Latin American country over the past decade, but the resulting hardships have been magnified by the erosion of state services that, at least in some instances, once provided mechanisms for supplementing the meager incomes of the poor. And although market-oriented models have begun to stimulate economic growth in a few countries, the benefits of renewed expansion continue to elude vast segments of the population.

The simultaneity of democratic transitions and economic transformations in contemporary Latin America adds an additional layer of complexity to efforts to broaden citizenship rights in societies long plagued by extreme levels of poverty and social exclusion. To be sure, growing sensitivity to issues of human rights, along with increased activism around demands for the extension of both collective and individual rights, offers grounds for a degree of optimism about the prospects for constructing more robust democracies in Latin America at the close of the twentieth century. As we have seen in various contributions to this volume, however, significant economic obstacles continue to limit the capacity of important segments of the population to realize citizenship rights in practice.

GLOBALIZATION, LOCALITY AND SOVEREIGNTY

Ours is an era characterized by powerful trends toward globalization and transnationalization, but these pressures combined with others to bring about a revitalization of locality. On the one hand, we are witnessing a proliferation of supranational institutions and an increasing globalization of communications, economic interests, population flows, environmental hazards, and arms races. On the other hand, we are experiencing renewed sensitivity to local roots and identities, revealed sometimes violently in rivalries among ethnic and cultural groups. The tension between the two phenomena is unmistakable, yet globalization and intensified concern with the local are closely related. In this context, it becomes essential to reconsider the relationships among international, national, community, and interpersonal levels of social identity and interaction.

Changes taking place in recent decades have disrupted traditional units of analysis. No transformation is more noteworthy than that involving the notion of the nation-state. The nation-state was construed during the past two centuries as the "natural" focus of loyalty—as the locus of citizenship and solidarity, political power, and sovereignty. Today, this centrality is strongly questioned: National boundaries seen at times to be irrelevant in the face of the globalization of production, trade, culture, and financial flows. Governments have lost much of the control they once exercised over events within their boundaries, and sovereignty is further curtailed by changes in regional and supranational alliances and institutions. Meanwhile, states (partly as a result of their weakening) are being challenged at a subnational level by the rebirth of solidarity groups grounded in a variety of collective identities—regional, linguistic, religious, and ethnic—as well as by innumerable social movements that generate solidarities of their own. These groups contend with the states for loyalty of the population, at times even supplanting them.[1]

The erosion of traditionally fixed boundaries, along with the proliferation of new units of analysis and identity, implies a diversification of the sites in which public action takes place. To analyze this phenomenon, Boaventura de Sousa Santos (1991) resorts to a cartographic model, which recognizes that in contemporary societies different sets of normative standards operate simultaneously, varying in terms of the groups they regulate, the duration and degree of their institutionalization, and the way in which they are practiced and enforced. This model was designed to clarify the plurality of juridical arrangements, but it can also be usefully applied to social norms in general. As in cartography, what counts is the definition of scale:

> The modern state is founded on the assumption that law operates according to a single scale, the scale of the state. . . . Research on juridical pluralism calls attention to the existence of local rights, . . . [to] forms of infra-state law, [which are] informal, unofficial, [and] relatively customary, and [to] . . . an international juridical space where different types of agents, whose behavior is regulated by new international rules, operate. In general, this level of law is highly informal. . . . What sets these forms of law apart from each other is the size of the scale in which they regulate social action. (Santos, 1991: 222–223).

In addition to differences in scale, we must consider the effects of interactions among the various levels. The implication is that any concrete historical circumstance entails a mixture of codes—namely, complex patterns of symbolization whose meanings are seldom transparent. More than ever before, expressions of collective demands at the local level (whether they are labor demands voiced by a union, neighborhood demands for public services, or protests against pollution or environmental hazards) embody the multiplicity of meanings resulting from the articulation and overlap of different levels. Conversely, the human message of the grand international conferences and events that garner worldwide attention are revealed fully only when the global themes are interwoven with specific local conditions. The personalized, intimate story of the suffering and pain of an experience of rape in Bosnia, transmitted via television to a universal audience, has the potential to influence attitudes and behaviors not only in Bosnia but throughout the world.

The tension between recognition of universal rights and respect for diversity and plurality is another reminder of the links between the local and the global and of their consequences for sovereignty. The Universal Declaration of Human Rights, adopted by the United Nations in 1948, provides the basic framework for a universalist perspective. The principles it upholds have sustained constant struggles and actions aimed at expanding the social base of citizenship (as when voting rights are granted to women or to the illiterate) and at extending rights to minorities, victims of discrimination, and dispossessed social groups who, as citizens, can finally demand equality before the law.

Yet, to which (whose) laws are demands for equality directed? It was interpretation of the past two centuries of modern history, emphasizing its colonialism and racism, that provided the ideological background for the Universal Declaration. Meanwhile, some intellectual groups (consisting of well-meaning anthropologists and humanists) saw an urgent need to embark upon an era of cultural relativism, which has entailed the scientifically demonstrated refutation of white racial superiority and the discovery of the complexity of "primitive" cultures.

Recognition of plurality was to be the antidote to the recurrence of massive crimes, genocide, and cultural annihilation, committed in the past on the basis of ideologies and interests that implicitly or explicitly denied victims the status of "human beings with rights." The ideology of universal human rights would thus serve to protect potential or actual victims. Paradoxically, the flag of universalism was raised in defense of the rights of the "different," in a struggle against those who wanted to impose uniformity and the idea of universal progress.

Can cultural relativism be combined with the defense of universal human rights? And can the alleged objectivity of science be combined with an ethically committed defense of principles? The Universal Declaration was widely criticized for adopting an underlying notion of human rights that was individualistic and Western. Even the will to extend it worldwide was criticized as imperialist, discriminatory, and ethnocentrically arrogant. This anti-Western argument would in turn be used politically to justify gross violations of rights, while the offending governments shielded themselves with a discourse of cultural relativism, national sovereignty, and self-determination—all invoked to justify the rejection of humanitarian intervention, international monitoring, and controls.

After years of debate and dialogue, issues of cultural diversity can now be approached somewhat differently. If the original idea of universal human rights reflected an individualistic view of rights, today it hinges on groups and communities. To speak of cultural rights, then, is to speak of the rights of societies and cultures (who define themselves as such) to live according to their own lifestyles, communicate in their own languages, use their own clothes, pursue their own objectives, and receive fair treatment from the laws of the nation-state in which they happen to be living (almost invariably as "minorities").

Yet the prevalence of universal human rights does not guarantee the prevalence of people's collective rights. Conversely, the right of a people to live according to their own lifestyle may imply not only cruelty toward certain categories of individuals within that culture but also the denial of their basic human rights. Is it possible to escape this dilemma? If so, what criteria can be used for evaluation of claims to rights and denunciation of violations of rights?

In Chapter 8 of this volume, Rodolfo Stavenhagen confronts this issue directly. Claims that indigenous peoples are entitled to rights based on ethnicity compel a profound revision of the original notion of human rights, given its bias toward universality and individual subjects. To claim that indigenous peoples and minorities have rights is to imply that the very notion of "human rights" can acquire meaning only in specific cultural circumstances, which thus become prerequisites for, and constitutive of, human rights. In this framework, reference to the human rights of indigenous peoples, or to those of traditionally oppressed or marginalized groups of the population (categories to which women obviously belong), implies the recognition of a history of discrimination and oppression, as well as an active commitment to reverse this situation. Indeed, it entails acknowledging the inevitable tension between individual and collective rights.

Yet there are obvious dangers in doing so: Recognition of the rights of peoples can foster fundamentalisms of various sorts, as well as the proliferation of exclusionary and racist communitarian identities. The latter may be defensive, rooted in a determined "search for scapegoats," or aggressively expansionist (Wievorka, 1992). Fundamentalisms of either kind can be interpreted in terms of the opposition between social movements and communitarian action, between the weakening of the former and the reinforcement of those racist forms of communitarianism that one witnesses in much of the world today. This opposition is not absolute, however, and its potential resolution lies in recognition of the fundamentally social roots and expressions of tensions that often are articulated as communal or racial conflicts rather than as social ones (Wievorka, 1992: 265). The point is not to destroy communitarian identities in the name of modernity but, rather, to "uphold sympathetically the efforts of those actors who resist disassociation and who endeavor to invent formulae for integration in which reference to a collective agent in no way impedes appeals to progress or participation in modernity (Wievorka, 1992: 266–267).

POLITICS, CULTURE, AND SOCIETY IN TRANSITION

The chapters in this volume emphasize the degree to which transitions to democracy are seen differently when the full range of human rights violations and the enhancements of citizenship rights are taken into explicit consideration. Competing pressures from military actors and from civilian victims of past violations pose a significant challenge for the process of legitimation of democratic governments—and, indeed, there is no single recipe for resolving these antagonisms. This is especially true in an era of profound economic crisis and restructuring, during which the tension between political forces and economic constraints is compounded: The contents of the democratic agenda in Latin America, and the characteristics of democratic regimes in the region, will partly depend on the way in which these challenges are met.

Many of the persistent obstacles to societal democratization in Latin America will need to be addressed through institutional innovation. As just one particularly important example, consider the several chapters in this volume that imply the need for more systematic discussion of the role of the Judiciary and of legal institutions. Yet in this context as in others, social scientific analyses of institutional reform have to incorporate not only a normative and instrumental perspective but also a cultural one, such that we must ask: What is the role of legal institutions in shaping "subjects of law"? By what means can their legitimacy as ultimate authority to mediate in conflicts be established? Stated differently, how is "legitimate legality" constructed?

The introduction of the cultural dimensions of rights and citizenship implies the need to reconsider not only distinctions and linkages between micro and macro levels of analysis but also the nature of relationships between individuals and social processes. Patterns of repression, violence, and subservience; acceptance of the rules of the game and of duties; legitimation of authority to regulate conflict; solidarities and responsibilities—all of these factors are culturally constructed and take on specific meanings in different settings. This book suggests that they can be studied at the global, national, community, and interpersonal levels, and that their meanings may vary across these spatial categories, as well as across historical periods. No linear extrapolation is possible; yet the levels of meaning are not totally independent of one another.

Notes

1. The growth of the global economy, however, does not entail the disappearance of the state. As Calhoun (1993: 30) argues, "States remain the organisations of power through which democratic movements have the greatest capacity to affect economic organisation. . . . States remain the highest level of institutional structure at which programmes of democratisation themselves can consistently be advanced. And states remain the most crucial objects and vehicles of efforts to achieve 'self-determination' or autonomy as a political community."

References

Arendt, Hannah. (1949). "The Rights of Man: What Are They?" *Modern Review* 3, no. 1 (Summer).

Calhoun, Craig. (1993). "Nationalism and Civil Society: Democracy, Diversity and Self-determination." *International Sociology* 8, no. 4 (December).

Garretón, Manuel Antonio. (1992). "Nuevos derechos o viejas discriminaciones?" In José O. de Aylwin (ed.), *Derechos humanos: Desafíos para un nuevo contexto*. Santiago: Comisión Chilena de Derechos Humanos.

Santos, Boaventura de Sousa. (1991). "Una cartografía simbólica de las representaciones sociales: Prolegómenos a una concepción posmoderna del derecho." In *Estado, derecho y luchas sociales*. Bogotá: Instituto Latinoamericano de Servicios Legales Alternativos (ILSA).

Scott, James C. (1992). *Domination and the Arts of Resistance: Hidden Transcripts*. New Haven: Yale University Press.

Wievorka, Michel. (1992). *El espacio del racismo*. Barcelona: Paidós.

About the Book and Editors

In this pathbreaking contribution to debates about human rights, democracy, and society, distinguished social scientists from Latin America and the United States move beyond questions of state terror, violence, and similar abuses to embrace broader concepts of human rights: citizenship, identity, civil society, racism, gender discrimination, and poverty.

Following an introduction that sets forth the conceptual framework, the first section of the book analyzes the impact of past human rights violations on the consolidation of new democracies, highlighting unresolved issues of civil-military relations and the need to maximize accountability for past violations. Contributors then consider the international context for contemporary debates about human rights, focusing on the emergence of an international network of human rights organizations and on the strategic responses of Latin American militaries to international pressures to respect human rights. A third section examines notions of citizenship and links them to debates about definitions of rights and about the relationship between democracy and capitalism. Finally, the book features case studies of rights-related concerns in light of enduring patterns of discrimination against a variety of groups, including indigenous peoples, women, and racial minorities. This section concludes with an essay on a new kind of state-sanctioned rights violation—the assault on the human rights of common criminals, which has followed in the wake of public outcry for a more vigorous response to growing crime rates in urban areas.

Elizabeth Jelin is a researcher with CONICYT, Buenos Aires. **Eric Hershberg** is director of the Program on Latin America at the Social Science Research Council, New York.

Index

227